g

Hermeneutic
Phenomenological
Research

SAGE was founded in 1965 by Sara Miller McCune to support the dissemination of usable knowledge by publishing innovative and high-quality research and teaching content. Today, we publish over 900 journals, including those of more than 400 learned societies, more than 800 new books per year, and a growing range of library products including archives, data, case studies, reports, and video. SAGE remains majority-owned by our founder, and after Sara's lifetime will become owned by a charitable trust that secures our continued independence.

Los Angeles | London | New Delhi | Singapore | Washington DC | Melbourne

Doing Hermeneutic Phenomenological Research

A Practical Guide

Lesley Dibley

Suzanne Dickerson

Mel Duffy

Roxanne Vandermause

Los Angeles | London | New Delhi
Singapore | Washington DC | Melbourne

Los Angeles | London | New Delhi
Singapore | Washington DC | Melbourne

SAGE Publications Ltd
1 Oliver's Yard
55 City Road
London EC1Y 1SP

SAGE Publications Inc.
2455 Teller Road
Thousand Oaks, California 91320

SAGE Publications India Pvt Ltd
B 1/I 1 Mohan Cooperative Industrial Area
Mathura Road
New Delhi 110 044

SAGE Publications Asia-Pacific Pte Ltd
3 Church Street
#10-04 Samsung Hub
Singapore 049483

Editor: Jai Seaman
Assistant editor: Charlotte Bush
Production editor: Manmeet Kaur Tura
Copyeditor: Sharon Cawood
Indexer: Cathryn Pritchard
Marketing manager: Susheel Gokarakonda
Cover design: Shaun Mercier
Typeset by: Cenveo Publisher Services
Printed in the UK

© Lesley Dibley, Suzanne Dickerson, Mel Duffy and Roxanne Vandermause, 2020

Foreword © Sharon L. Sims and Elizabeth Smythe, 2020

Apart from any fair dealing for the purposes of research or private study, or criticism or review, as permitted under the Copyright, Designs and Patents Act, 1988, this publication may be reproduced, stored or transmitted in any form, or by any means, only with the prior permission in writing of the publishers, or in the case of reprographic reproduction, in accordance with the terms of licences issued by the Copyright Licensing Agency. Enquiries concerning reproduction outside those terms should be sent to the publishers.

Library of Congress Control Number: 2020934539

British Library Cataloguing in Publication data

A catalogue record for this book is available from the British Library

ISBN 978-1-5264-8573-1
ISBN 978-1-5264-8572-4 (pbk)

At SAGE we take sustainability seriously. Most of our products are printed in the UK using FSC papers and boards. When we print overseas we ensure sustainable papers are used as measured by the PREPS grading system. We undertake an annual audit to monitor our sustainability.

Contents

List of Figures, Tables and Explanatory Boxes

List of Figures

List of Tables

List of Explanatory Boxes

Lesley Dibley is Reader in Nursing Research and Education, who also leads the Centre for Chronic Illness and Ageing in the Institute for Lifecourse Development at the University of Greenwich, London, UK. She was awarded her PhD in 2014 for an interpretive phenomenology study of the experience of stigma in people with inflammatory bowel disease (IBD), has recently completed another funded project on the experience of kinship (family) stigma in IBD, and has other active projects including an exploration of the experiences of young adults living with long fusion for idiopathic scoliosis, the experience of adjustment to intestinal stoma in people with IBD, and the complex care needs of older people with IBD. Lesley teaches qualitative methods to undergraduates, phenomenology theory to postgraduates, and supervises Masters and PhD students. She publishes regularly in high-impact international journals and presents at national and international conferences.

Suzanne Dickerson is a Professor and Department Chair of Bio-behavioural Health and Clinical Science at the University at Buffalo, School of Nursing. Her current research focuses on sleep science with the goal of understanding patients' contextual meaning of sleep–wake disturbances through hermeneutical phenomenology. This insight forms the basis of new knowledge that can be instrumental in translating clinical research to practice that embeds meaningful approaches into care practices to improve sleep. She has developed an online course in the methodology and mentors PhD and visiting faculty in the approach. She is a senior member of the hermeneutic phenomenology institute group and is mentor to other members as well.

Mel Duffy is Assistant Professor in Sociology and Sexuality Studies in the School of Nursing Psychotherapy & Community Health, Dublin City University, Dublin, Ireland. She teaches courses in sociology and sexuality studies at both undergraduate and graduate level. After completing her PhD at DCU in 2008, she has pursued an active research programme in qualitative research, with a particular focus on hermeneutic phenomenology. Her work focuses on lesbian, gay, bisexual, transgender, queer and intersex individuals' experiences of living their lives in the world they find themselves in, writing and presenting on: lesbian health and health care; coming out; relationship and sexuality education; disability; identity; residential care and experiences of health outcomes. She holds a BA and an MA by research from the National University of Ireland, Maynooth and a PhD from Dublin City University.

Roxanne Vandermause is the Interim Dean, Professor and the Donald L. Ross Endowed Chair for Advancing Nursing Practice at the University of Missouri-St. Louis College of Nursing. Her research involves the use of hermeneutic phenomenology and mixed methods to study addictions and racial/ethnic and gender disparities in the care of mental health and other chronic conditions. She has presented across the USA and internationally and published widely in various venues. She teaches all educational levels in nursing and across various graduate-level disciplines, including coursework in ethics, theory and qualitative methodologies. Many of her PhD students use hermeneutic phenomenological methods to study human phenomena in the context of health and well-being and she is sought after for her expertise in these methods.

Foreword

Once upon a time, nurses and others were awoken to the possibility that 'they' could do research. But how? When they read quantitative studies, they yawned. The patients and clients they worked with, the students they taught, were real live people. Their lives were complex, colourful, with rich histories. Reducing a person to a measurable unit that could be analysed in disregard of their own context of possibilities and constraints went against the grain. So began the search for methodologies and methods that would allow them to investigate these rich lives in order to expand their understanding of the human experience. Nancy Diekelmann, Patricia Benner and David Allen, among others, did germinal work in bringing Heideggerian hermeneutic philosophy into the world of nursing research.

Amid this era of emerging scholarship, Professor Nancy Diekelmann and her husband John Diekelmann began the Heideggerian Hermeneutic Institute. They spoke of a way of research in which people living a particular experience of interest could tell their stories. As researchers, we first need to listen, and then listen again and again for the meaning within each story. To attune our hearing/seeing, we were introduced to the philosophical writing of Heidegger and Gadamer. We were so out of our depth! Yet, there began a lifelong journey towards attuning to the meaning within everyday experience. Alongside of that attunement came the development of research methods that fit with hermeneutic phenomenology.

The authors of this wonderful book are a new generation grown out of the original community. We salute them. Like all of us who have walked this road, they know that it is one thing to become passionately enthusiastic about doing hermeneutic phenomenology. It is quite another thing to conduct the research. The challenge is that laying down detailed, prescribed steps may undermine the spirit of the methodology, which is attuned to finding its own way. Yet, it is negligent to send a novice researcher on the unlit way without a lamp as a guide.

This book lights the way into the worlds of human experience, meaning and understanding. The authors have achieved the fine balance between staying true to the philosophical underpinnings, while at the same time offering wise counsel as to 'how' one goes about each phase of the research process. They accomplish this by demonstrating how each 'step' of the process is imbued with hermeneutic phenomenology, and by reminding readers of the constant reflection, thinking and writing needed to enact the research effectively.

Each phase of the research process is presented in such a way that novice researchers will feel more confident as they enter this world for the first time, and experienced researchers and teachers will appreciate the cogent and detailed descriptions in each chapter. Through the liberal use of explanatory boxes and signposting, the reader is pointed toward fuller explanations and additional resources. Each chapter is enriched with examples from the authors' research that serve to illuminate the issues being discussed.

As one small example, the chapter on population and sampling does a wonderful job of situating sampling techniques within the methodology and purposes of a given study, the type of data being collected, and the methods of analysis to be used. This sounds quite pro forma, but it is counterbalanced with the understanding that sample sizes for hermeneutic phenomenological studies can't be calculated in advance. It is refreshing to see a discussion of purposive sampling that doesn't begin with a warning about its relative weakness, usually from a quantitative perspective. Rather, the authors point out that 'any sampling strategy that is wrongly applied is weak'. Thus, purposive sampling is weak when applied to a clinical trial, but strong when used to identify people who have the experience that is being studied hermeneutically. Of course, the chapter is much richer than this brief example can convey, but it serves to illustrate the authors' approach to the methods.

It is refreshing to read a book about research that doesn't feel the need to demonize those who study phenomena from a different paradigm, or for these authors to be apologetic about their chosen paradigm. The authors simply point out where methodologies diverge, and why that difference makes a difference, so to speak, in terms of the processes used in hermeneutic research. As a result, we could envision this work to be useful to those in the quantitative sciences who desire a greater understanding of qualitative, post-positivist research. Thesis and dissertation examiners should also find it very useful.

This is not a book simply to be read. It is akin to the guidebook one takes when one makes the journey into unfamiliar territory. Without it, there is the danger of getting lost, of finding oneself in strife, of missing the experience that the trip was seeking to find. This guidebook to hermeneutic phenomenological research needs to stay by the side of the one who embarks on such a journey. At the end, it will be thumb-marked, coffee-stained; it will fall open to key pages. There will be sections underlined, highlights in different colours, with commentary scrawled in the margin. This is a book that will live the journey to become a faithful companion. It would be foolish to embark on the way without it in one's hand. It is a book that will be cherished. It will become one's own.

Sharon L. Sims and Elizabeth Smythe

Introduction

The philosophy and methodology of hermeneutic phenomenological research is a complex yet engaging pursuit which has taken hold of the four of us in interesting shared and individual ways. As regular attendees at the Institute for Heideggerian Hermeneutics, started by Nancy Diekelmann in 1992, we first began talking about this book when the Institute was under the stewardship of Professor Sara Horton-Deutsch at the University of Denver, Colorado, in 2017. As supervisors of Masters and Doctoral students, we each found ourselves repeatedly trying to convey a robust understanding of the philosophical underpinnings of hermeneutic phenomenological research, without a 'go to' textbook to refer our students to.

Our shared vision was clear: to produce a resource which would enable scholars of hermeneutic phenomenology, and their supervisors, to design and deliver hermeneutic research studies which not only acknowledge, but also actively design and maintain, the links between the philosophy, the methodology and the methods of this approach to research. Our thinking and doing of hermeneutic phenomenological research is grounded in the philosophy of Martin Heidegger, who did not propose his philosophy as a way of doing research, but as a way of understanding the world that we are – as humans – necessarily situated in. The challenge to us and our predecessors has been to develop and articulate the ways of translating the principles of Heidegger's philosophy, into the principles of hermeneutic phenomenological research methodology, and the methods – the tools in the research toolbox – which support our ability to carry out robust phenomenological research. In writing this book, which has itself been a glorious hermeneutic scholarly endeavour, we hope to have shaped a resource which will enable students to create and sustain the golden thread of Heidegger's philosophy throughout the design and delivery of their projects – so that the imprint and influence of that philosophy is evident at every stage of the research process. From thinking about and designing the research question, searching literature, sampling, ethics, data collection and analysis, presentation of findings and discussion, to writing and dissemination – the philosophy should be evident.

In this book, we introduce you to the fundamentals of the philosophy and direct you to other resources that will broaden your perspectives and enhance your understanding, all the while reminding you that, being philosophy, it requires thinking. There are no quick fixes and no absolute answers to anything – understanding takes time and requires an openness to the possibility of what 'is'. Our approach, which reflects the way we learnt to understand hermeneutic phenomenology, is not to set this philosophy in stone, but to introduce you to thinking, reading and exploring, so that understanding will grow over time.

We then take you through the familiar components of the research process, linking frequently back to the philosophy to show you how it informs the thinking about how to do hermeneutic phenomenological research. We use exemplar cases from research alongside examples from everyday life to explicate concepts and illuminate that 'golden thread', and we signpost you to additional resources which will help your thinking.

We would also like to acknowledge the many colleagues and scholars who have, over the years, influenced our own travels with phenomenology: philosophers, including Fred Kersten, Hubert Dreyfuss, Thomas Sheehan, Ken Maly, Karin Dahlberg, Richard Palmer, Gail Wirth, Andrew Mitchell, John Russon, Kirsten Jacobson and Kevin Aho; and nursing and social science scholars, including Nancy Diekelmann, Pam Ironside, Sharon Sims, Liz Smythe, Deb Spence, Melinda Swenson and Patricia Young. Our thanks to you all for teaching us to think deeply and to hold ourselves open to the possibilities of what is and what it means to 'be'.

Part I
Philosophy and Thinking

Introduction

This part will help you to understand the philosophy that grounds hermeneutic phenomenology. It situates hermeneutic phenomenology within a philosophy of science that guides the questioning process. How are we to think about phenomena, the happenings of our concern? In hermeneutic phenomenology, we are interested in questions of meaning. We seek to understand common human experiences about 'being' itself – what it means to live experientially in a given situation. We question 'how' an experience transpires. The 'how' of doing is accompanied by a 'way of thinking' that brings a particular understanding. In this part, we summarise the philosophical history and the thinking perspective or theoretical lens by which the hermeneutic approach to inquiry is guided. We describe an ontological exploration of meaning, conveyed in the works of Heidegger and Gadamer, whose philosophical views challenged dualism and reductionism. We focus on the interpretation of common human experience and seek understanding of that which already lies within our scope but may be hidden or overlooked.

1

Philosophical Perspectives

Chapter Overview

This chapter provides an overview of the phenomenological movement. It relays some of the history of thinking that grounds phenomenological research. The thinking of scholars that instigated this progression of ideas within a philosophy of science, that were responsible for an evolution of thinking in the human sciences, is briefly summarised. Phenomenology includes hermeneutics and is a broad umbrella under which various approaches have emerged. The differences across these approaches may be delineated in various methodological descriptions that are guided by particular philosophers or scholars. Their contributions are exemplified here and provide the foundation of phenomenology as it is generally understood. In this way, we set the stage for a more in-depth look at hermeneutic phenomenology as the form that underpins our methodological work, and as further described in Chapter 2.

The interpretivist paradigm is a philosophical movement known to researchers and scholars in the context of a philosophy of science, but it is often overlooked as a way of thinking that guides research in a particular way. The philosophy that guides the methodology of hermeneutic phenomenology is situated in this interpretive paradigm and can be understood as a historical movement in research. It follows positivist and post-positivist paradigms that have evolved in human thought since the Age of Enlightenment (1600–1800) and the Scientific Revolution of that period, which signals the beginning of Empiricism. The subject–object dualism of Cartesian thought, with its emphasis on reason, cause/effect and calculation, is focused on a different kind of questioning than that found in the interpretivist tradition. The underlying philosophy of hermeneutics, thus, changes the kind of questioning and purpose of research in the interpretivist tradition from the science that came before.

Explanatory Box 1.1

Empiricism

Empiricism generally means what is observed, going back to Aristotelian philosophy. In this context, phenomenological understandings could be conceived as empirical. However, empiricism became associated with scientific concepts and procedures during the period of the Enlightenment, requiring protocols for a 'scientific method' based on rules and measurement (Willis, 2007). Even today, the term 'empirical' is generally used to describe factual understandings that can be verified using a controlled system of quantitatively derived methods. Empirical/analytic research has been reduced to the use of statistical measures in the conduct of research (Baker et al., 1998).

In the interpretive tradition, *situated* knowledge is considered over universal rules and factual discovery; that is, questions related to an understanding of contexts and the inclusion of multiple influencing perspectives are explored. Differences among the various quantitative and qualitative research paradigms are explored by many scholars and explained in research texts. For example, Willis (2007) provides a particularly in-depth discussion about the history and characteristics of research paradigms over the past centuries and differentiates the movements that inform science. The history of philosophies of science includes a trajectory that begins with the origins of what is often called 'quantitative research' and takes us through an evolution of methodologies that includes, most recently, interpretive paradigms. These are methodological approaches that emphasise meaning and understanding in context. They often include interpretation and narration that are an expression of experience. The hermeneutic tradition is one of the interpretive forms that is the focus of this book and guides the research methods we will discuss.

The hermeneutic tradition is situated within the phenomenological movement that is characterised by a search for understanding of naturally occurring phenomena and includes various perspectival views. These are views that arise from the work of specific philosophers who rejected foundational ideas that posit universal truths. The phenomenological movement compels understanding of multiple and alternative views; hermeneutical understandings further require an interpretive or a translational stance.

Phenomenology

There are myriad texts that explore phenomenology as a philosophical tradition. In research, phenomenology seeks to understand a phenomenon as it presents itself to us as conscious human beings. Social experiences, things (inanimate objects) and events have no meaning in and of themselves; they only hold meaning because human beings confer them with meaning (Jones, 2003). This is why phenomenology has been described 'as a human science, the purpose of which is to describe and understand particular phenomena as lived experience' (Cutcliffe, Joyce and Cummins, 2004: 308). Thinking phenomenologically includes interpretation and description, but its beginnings are based on description: 'The phenomenological approach is primarily **descriptive,** seeking to **illuminate** issues in a radical, unprejudiced manner, paying close attention to the evidence that presents itself to our grasp or intuition' (Moran, 2002: 1; emphasis in the original).

In this form of thinking, subjectivity over objectivity is expressed; that is, description is favoured over analysis, interpretation over measurement, and agency over structure. Phenomenology is concerned with people's 'perceptions or meanings;

attitudes and beliefs; feelings and emotions' (Denscombe, 2003: 96). It inquires how individuals experience, describe, interpret and understand a phenomenon under investigation. Thus, the lived experience:

> is the 'originary' way in which we perceive reality. As living persons, we have an awareness of things and ourselves which is immediate, direct, and nonabstractive. We 'live through' (erleben) life with an intimate sense of its concrete, qualitative features and myriad patterns, meanings, values and relations. (Ermarth, as cited in Bergum, 1989: 56)

Bergum (1989) indicates that the lived experience goes beyond the taken-for-granted characteristics of life. Lived experience involves the interpretation and meaning that individuals give to everyday life experiences. We act towards new 'things' based on the interpretations and meanings we have given to previous experiences of similar situations. In this way, individuals create their own reality, which may be similar or different to that of other individuals experiencing the same situation. Benner suggests that to understand the lived experience we need to go beyond the taken-for-granted explanation and 'uncover meanings in everyday practice in such a way that they are not destroyed, distorted, decontextualized, trivialized or sentimentalized' (Benner, as cited in Bergum, 1989: 57).

Thus, there is a particular 'showing' that we seek to uncover as an understanding of meaning is sought. We attempt to go to the heart of the matter, to the essential aspect of the phenomenon we seek to understand. Understanding, in this way, leads us to interpretation that is genuine. We will discuss this further as the chapter goes on, but we start with an effort to describe what we see: the descriptive phenomenological view gives way to the interpretive.

Phenomenological analysis generally is meant to clarify understanding. For example, Giorgi, a contemporary descriptive phenomenologist, suggests that clarity of a lived state can lead to change, as there can be a discrepancy between what we think about life and the reality of the actual experience: 'A discovery of this difference and its correction can lead to more authentic living and interaction with others and thus a better world' (Giorgi, 2005: 77). In other words, a deeper understanding of the lived experience can change a person's reality and what it means to be a human being. A closer look at a phenomenon of concern expands awareness of what is and broadens human perspective. Further, a phenomenological view acknowledges that multiple realities exist, and that groups or communities share in these realities. Therefore, it allows for a number of meanings that may be derived from the same shared experience.

The roots of phenomenology lie in the philosophy of Husserl, which was further developed by his student Heidegger. Phenomenology is seen as a descriptive study of phenomena that presents itself to the consciousness, precisely in whatever way it presents itself (Sokolowski, 2000). That is, what you see is what you get.

The question is, what can we see when we look closely, deeply, around and through the phenomena of interest? The focus on phenomena in particular situations is driven not by a set of doctrines, but by a way of seeing things (Palmer, 1969; Moran, 2000).

Edmund Husserl (1859–1938)

Husserl was concerned with epistemology, that is, the nature and grounds of knowledge (Cohen and Omery, 1994; Ray, 1994; Grbich, 1999). He asserted that the definitive basis for knowledge was experience (Draucker, 1999). Husserl insisted on the superiority of the lived experience as it is experienced over any other form, indicating that all human activities originate and begin with the lived world, and rejecting the claim that empirical science is the only producer of 'truth' (Johnson, 2000; LeVasseur, 2003). He claimed that the empirical sciences, while objective in their research, could not uncover the phenomenological meaning of the lived experience: 'Phenomenology aims to describe in all its complexity the manifold layers of the experience of objectivity as it emerges at the heart of subjectivity' (Moran, 2000: 1). Thus, the phenomena of phenomenology include: 'all forms of appearing, showing, manifesting, making evident or "evidencing", bearing witness, truth-claiming, checking and verifying, including all forms of seeming, dissembling, occluding, obscuring, denying and falsifying' (Moran, 2002: 5).

Phenomena, thus, include all parts of the human lived experience, which in turn contain all that is already recognisable as well as what is hidden from us. We are drawn into a *way of knowing* that includes understanding 'the things themselves'.

Explanatory Box 1.2

Truth

Truth claims differ across paradigmatic perspectives. In the modern era (post-Enlightenment to today), there has been a dominant mode of thought that anchors in the scientific tradition, where neutral and objective understanding based on rational, experimentally tested processes are deemed factual. However, alternative understandings that include dynamic and relational experience that may be subjective and include multiple possible views have become acceptable in the past century, leading to the paradigmatic discussions that undergird philosophical and scientific discussions about 'truth'. The thinking that grounds the research we discuss in this book rejects subject–object dualism and rational, logical and empirical thought as the only way to knowledge. Rather, it embraces multi-perspectival, embodied and experiential ways of knowing. The congruent methods of inquiry are very different avenues to 'truth'. Further resources to explore the concept of truth are provided at the end of this chapter.

Understanding 'the things themselves' means getting to the essence of experience itself. We can unearth that which is hidden through careful and thorough examination that enables us to uncover the meaning of the lived experience. In other words, the initial meaning of the lived experience may be the 'taken-for-granted' but, by unpacking it or stripping away the initial or superficial meaning, we can uncover more of that which is hidden (Sokolowski, 2000). Such analysis gets us closer to the heart of the matter – that which is significant or meaningful. Husserl implies that it is the character of the natural world to be hidden from us because we view it from a *natural attitude* that enables us to live in the world. Our common and familiar understanding of the world and the things in it become our basis of understanding. The *natural attitude* constitutes our normal everyday life and the things in it. Sokolowski (2000) explains that the natural attitude does not give us a complete understanding; if we knew everything, there would be 'no hiddenness, no vagueness, obscurity, error and ignorance' (p. 167). There is more to know and understand. Phenomenology moves us toward that deeper understanding.

In order to approach the lived experience within a philosophical framework, Husserl suggested the use of *phenomenological reduction, epoché* and *bracketing* to attain the phenomenological attitude (Stewart and Mickunas, 1990). Husserl did not use these three terms as three separate entities; rather, they are interchangeable and describe a particular approach to observation and understanding (LeVasseur, 2003). Husserl uses these terms to refer to the reflective process whereby we put aside our understanding, opinion and prejudice of a phenomenon and go back directly to the experience of the phenomenon, finding the meaning of the thing itself. This is bracketing or *phenomenological reduction proper* (Cohen and Omery, 1994). The researcher must set aside their experience or pre-understanding of a phenomenon, so that they will not prejudge or impute pre-conceived ideas about the meaning of a situation or an experience (Ray, 1994; Koch, 1996; Johnson, 2000). Husserl was looking for the essence of phenomena and indicated that, if we were to uncover the true meaning, we had to purge the *natural* attitude and the initially offered assumptions. Bracketing, in this tradition, thus enables meaning to develop and understanding to be genuine.

Husserlian phenomenology, therefore, emphasises a form of bracketing as a means of nullifying historical or pre-conceived theories that could influence explanation of the phenomenon under investigation (Ray, 1994). The meaning of a situation could be gained by a state of *pure consciousness* or *ego* (Grbich, 1999), producing a genuine and not taken-for-granted reality (Cohen and Omery, 1994). Cohen and Omery (1994) suggest we often do not notice the commonplace and take for granted much of our social experiences. They indicated that the research methodology of this approach describes the meanings of experiences as they appear to us, which is called *eidetic description*. The *eidetic* is the belief that *there are essential structures to human experiences*; that is, human experiences have certain objective structures (Draucker, 1999: 361). Caelli (2000) points out that 'eidetic description' is the pre-reflective experience as it has been lived, and this produces the real meaning of the phenomenon. The person experiencing it has not interpreted it; rather it is in its 'raw' state of experience. It is not coloured by tradition or informed by the culture where the experience takes place. In this way, the phenomenon can be studied objectively, even though what is being studied is subjective experience. Researchers bracket their presuppositions and describe the essential structures of the experiences being studied (Cohen and Omery, 1994; Grbich, 1999). The meaning of the eidetic description is 'fundamental and essential to the experience no matter which specific individual has that experience' (Cohen and Omery, 1994: 148). In this description, we bend toward a positivist view of understanding phenomena in the world, and descriptive phenomenologists generally approach inquiry with aspects of this perspectival stance. Phenomenological description is, thus, clear, rich and compelling, and conveys understanding in ways that can expand knowledge, but it is different to the hermeneutic phenomenology we will later describe.

The validity of a Husserlian phenomenological approach has been questioned. Can we negate our understanding of the world and look at situations without any preconceived ideas? (Heap and Roth, 1973; Koch, 1996). LeVasseur (2003) offers a way out of this dilemma by arguing that we bracket things when we come to question them and accept that we do not know or fully understand something that we previously thought we did. In other words, when we re-examine something we are, in fact, suspending our prior understandings to come to new ones. LeVasseur does not indicate what happens if the individual, upon re-examining, comes to the same conclusion or meaning. In other words, how do we know that we have appropriately bracketed our previous views? LeVasseur (2003) asserts that 'our unreflective assumptions mask the thing itself until it falls silent and cannot call out with fresh and vital experience' (p. 418). That is, we may be unaware of our own bias, unable to see the essence of the phenomenon in question. The extent to which we are able to reflect on this dilemma may help break through the problem of human pre-assumption, and be the degree to which we see the essential nature of the phenomena we seek to understand. Edwards and Titchen (2003) emphasise that bracketing is two-fold: that of the researcher and that of the participant, acknowledging that full bracketing of participants' interpretation of their experiences would not be totally possible. In addition, researchers experience themselves as human beings existing in the world. To know that others exist in the world, the researchers must know that they exist both as human beings and researchers (Grbich, 1999). Both parties are called upon for deep reflection. The ability to see essential characteristics without preconception is an argument that has continued in the world of phenomenology and one that often directs the methods chosen within the methodological overview.

The distinction between descriptive and interpretive forms of phenomenological inquiry is commonly found in the literature today.

The researcher cannot exist outside of the social world and, as interpreter of data, inescapably, the researcher 'brings certain background expectations and frames of meaning to bear on the act of understanding. These cannot be bracketed' (Koch, 1996: 176). Koch (1996) argues that a Heideggerian framework allows both the acknowledgement of the researchers' lived experience in the world and that of the participants, which Husserl does not provide. Others argue that the differences around bracketing, *epoché*, are insubstantial (Dahlberg and Dahlberg, 2003). Phenomenological reduction is a term that has been widely explored philosophically and one that we move away from in hermeneutic phenomenology. The following discussion of hermeneutics elaborates on the issue of interpretation and moves our attention toward Heidegger.

Hermeneutics

The hermeneutic tradition, or hermeneutic phenomenology, is also complex and can be traced back to Schleiermacher, an early 19th-century scholar who framed it as a basis for the art of understanding (Palmer, 1969). The interpretation of biblical texts was an early focus. It involved the re-experiencing of the thinking of the author, an examination of the structure of the sentence and the psychology of the author to come to a new insight or understanding. The reconstruction that results is what has been described as the 'hermeneutic circle', a process that is dialectical and negotiates between the whole and the parts of a text to derive new meaning. Philosophers following Schleiermacher contributed further to this notion of a dialectic, a to and fro, a way of understanding that seeks shared or common meaning that includes revealing already known or perhaps previously hidden understandings. Further, uncovering common as well as peculiar or singular concerns makes up the hermeneutical circle of understanding. Variations of Schleiermacher's project evolved over the course of his work, which was taken up by others with their own variations, including Dilthey, Heidegger and Gadamer. In this book, we focus more closely on the influence of Heidegger's hermeneutic thinking, an approach unique to the phenomenology of the time.

Heidegger is one of a number of 'Continental' (European) philosophers of the 20th century who were writing about the nature of understanding as it contrasted with a calculative science. Heidegger's contributions were unique to others in the field and were critiqued for the resistance to reductionism – the form of positivistic assessment common to the science of discovery that opened understanding to extended possibilities not appropriated by a subjective assessment. That is, Heidegger added the interpretive element to textual analysis or analysis of phenomena that manifest, or 'show themselves'. He reclaimed the ancient Greek roots of the word *phainomenon* or *phainesthai* (Palmer, 1969) and went on to explore the meaning of what it means 'to be'. Heidegger's project was to seek the meaning of being itself, an ontological approach to inquiry that stood apart from other philosophical stances. He asked the question of what it means to be human, what it means to be concerned with the meaning of being human.

Explanatory Box 1.3

Heidegger and National Socialism

Biographical writings on Heidegger's life (1889–1976) include discussions of his Catholic upbringing, his rise to notoriety as a philosopher and an educator, his interest in Eastern philosophies and his involvement in National Socialism. One of the fiercest criticisms levied against Heidegger is that he was a member of the Nazi Party in Germany, from 1933 until the end of the Second World War; this affiliation cost him his academic position as Rector of Freiburg University in 1934. He was dismissed altogether after the war and was banned from teaching during the post-war period, until 1951. He never spoke openly of his involvement with National Socialism, except to comment only once that the political engagement was 'the greatest stupidity of my life'. Debate persists about the relevance of his Nazi connections to his philosophy.

Critical opinion is divided on the likely context of his involvement, with notable scholars coming down on both sides of the argument. One view is that he knew exactly what he was doing when he joined the Nazi Party, and that he was a fierce anti-Semitist, evidence for the latter attributed to his Black Notebooks (Escudero, 2015). Notable scholars, including Jürgen Habermas and Pierre Bourdieu, claim that Heidegger's links to National Socialism expose serious flaws in his philosophy. We will never know if Heidegger's comments about the treatment, disposition and social situation of the Jewish population in Germany at the time were philosophical observations (much like Simone de Beauvoir's discourse on attitudes towards older people in France, in the 1970s) or personal opinion. Elden (2003) argues that in Heidegger's work *Beiträge zur Philosophie* (*Contributions to Philosophy*), (Heidegger, 1999) insights can be found in relation to his thoughts on National Socialism. Elden (2003) claims that the central themes shed light on understanding whether Heidegger 'moved into a position of critical distance from the regime, because it is an attempt to comprehend what lies behind these events' (Elden, 2003: 36).

The opposing view is that Heidegger was the victim of attempts to undermine the significant influence his philosophy was having in Europe at the time, that his links to National Socialism were no more or less than those of many others in Germany during that period, and for whom a symbolic gesture of membership was a survival tactic. Those who supported him included Hannah Arendt, Jacques Derrida and Medard Boss – the latter expressing frustration at Heidegger's sustained silence against the many accusations.

Smythe and Spence (2019) briefly describe the controversy that has arisen in Heidegger's association with and fall from Naziism in their article 'Reading Heidegger'. The controversy included those who refuse to acknowledge the work of a scholar associated with Naziism and those who see no inclusion of fascist tendencies in Heidegger's work. Our use of Heidegger's work mirrors that described by Smythe and Spence; we are comfortable with the scholarship we follow and the inclusive thinking generated by the application of Heideggerian philosophy as we understand it.

Hans-Georg Gadamer (1900–2002)

The work of Gadamer, who followed Heidegger and extended his work, is also used to inform the methods we describe in this book. Gadamer was active until 2002 and he offers an extended, though distinct, development of Heidegger's thought. Undergirded by the work of these philosophers, hermeneutic phenomenology, as we use it in our approaches, has also been called *philosophical hermeneutics* (Diekelmann and Ironside, 2011) and is informed by the writings of other existential and critical social philosophers, such as Sartre, de Beauvoir, Butler, Derrida, Merleau Ponty, Arendt and others. Contemporary Heideggerian scholars such as Maly, Stenstadt, Dreyfuss, Sheehan, Mitchell and Aho have contributed to our understanding of Heideggerian interpretive phenomenology, and researchers such as Benner, Diekelmann, Smythe, Ironside, Swenson, Sims and ourselves have developed hermeneutic phenomenology as a methodological approach in very personal ways. Part IV in this book provides an overview of the different routes each of us has taken into hermeneutics.

The approaches we describe in this book are approaches that are interpretive and distinctly hermeneutic. Phenomenology as a descriptive approach (previously described) and interpretations that include critical views (later described) are included in the thinking that we use to understand and disseminate meaning. This unique way of thinking is consciously intended throughout the research enterprise. We often refer to the writings of Heidegger, or go back to reading if not citing Heidegger, as we design, collect and analyse data, and convey the resulting understandings. Each step of the research process involves a way of thinking that resonates, as much as we can invoke, with the thinking that we develop and habituate within ourselves as we approach our topics of inquiry. Ken Maly, a Heideggerian scholar, often talked about 'thinking along with Heidegger' and Gail Stenstad (2006) writes about 'thinking after Heidegger' – both are approaches to thinking that incorporate the distinctive perspectives that guide our way into our research. There are many ways to describe our perspectives but one that may be most relevant relates to thinking that enacts an opening:

> and it is this opening that makes possible the radical and manifold transformations that may arise in thinking with and after Heidegger and that may enable us to free ourselves from dualistic, violent reification of self, others, nature and things (Stenstad, 2006: 9).

The next chapter will explore some of the distinguishing philosophical thought, particularly that of Heidegger and Gadamer, that ground the methods we describe in Parts II and III of this book.

Further Resources

Heidegger and National Socialism

These references will provide access to the breadth of debate and opinion regarding Heidegger's stance, and offer links to wider academic resources.

- Escudero, J. (2015) 'Heidegger's Black Notebooks and the question of anti-Semitism', *Gatherings: The Heidegger Circle Annual*, 5, 21–49.
- The Heidegger Circle: https://heidegger-circle.org
- Richard Brody: www.newyorker.com/culture/richard-brody/why-does-it-matter-if-heidegger-was-anti-semitic
- Jonathan Rée: www.prospectmagazine.co.uk/arts-and-books/in-defence-of-heidegger#.UzMSPyQwwlA
- Elden, S. (2003) 'Taking the measure of the Beiträge', *European Journal of Political Theory*, 2(1), 35–56. doi: 10.1177/1474885103002001278.

Core concepts

These texts help illuminate the influence of contributory philosophers on hermeneutic thinking and related concepts, adding depth to your understanding:

- Derrida, J. (1991) 'Restitutions of truth in pointing', in Kamuf, P. (ed.) *A Derrida Reader: Between the blinds*. New York: Columbia University Press, pp. 277–312.
- Derrida, J. et al. (1975) 'The purveyor of truth', *Yale French Studies*, 52, p. 31. doi: 10.2307/2929747.
- Ironside, P. (ed.) (2005) *Beyond Method: Philosophical conversations in healthcare research and scholarship*. Madison, WI: University of Wisconsin Press.
- Shain, R. (2018) 'Derrida on truth', *The Philosophical Forum*, 49(2), 193–213. doi: 10.1111/phil.12183.
- Stenstad, G. (2006) *Transformations: Thinking after Heidegger*. Madison, WI: University of Wisconsin Press.

The following guidebook describes the backgrounds and methods for applying various descriptive and interpretive phenomenological approaches to research, and provides a useful comparison between philosophies and methodologies:

- Beck, C. T. (2021) *Introduction to Phenomenology: Focus on methodology*. Thousand Oaks, CA: Sage.

2
Coming to Thinking

Chapter Overview

This chapter will help you to understand what it means to think hermeneutically. It underscores the historical philosophical descriptions that are particular to hermeneutic phenomenology. Key Heideggerian and Gadamerian ideas are further explicated, emphasising the interpretive nature of the work that includes an integration of researcher perspectives and the self-showing of research phenomena. Such interpretation of experience as lived is unique to hermeneutic phenomenology. Descriptions, analogies and references to hermeneutic scholars of today are also highlighted in this chapter and major contributions to the literature, including research applications, are reviewed. We hope this will demonstrate how researchers come to the thinking that informs this research. The ways researchers apply philosophical perspectives and some examples of their foci of study are summarised to provide a current view of the work of the past two decades. These summaries lead us into the 'Methods' part of the book.

Martin Heidegger (1889–1976)

Heidegger was interested in ontology, which is concerned with the nature and relations of being (see explanatory box 3.3 in Chapter 3). That is, the study of what it means 'to be', for Heidegger, was a way of thinking that is inclusive of past knowledge and teaching, current everyday experiences and expressions, and recognition of a future of possibilities. He was more concerned with being *in* the world, rejecting Husserl's being *of* the world. Heidegger's concern with 'Dasein' as a Being for which being is a question, positions his thinking uniquely and focuses on what it means to be human. A Being for which being is a question is reflective, aware of their situatedness or place in a world that is ever-changing. Human beings are always involved in experiences, relating in the world and concerned with their own meaningful existence (Johnson, 2000). This state of meaningful existence in the world, or 'being-in-the-world', is a state Heidegger describes as *Dasein* (Heidegger, 1927, 1962: 86). The term has been discussed variously in philosophical literature and is sometimes translated literally, but we have accepted the term to describe a way of looking at meaningful human existence in the context of Heidegger's writings as we understand them through reading his works, along with Heideggerian scholars. *Dasein* is an opening or space by or in which humans experience their world. The world to Heidegger 'is the interconnected context of involvements that gives meaning to everything one encounters within one's individual world' (Johnson, 2000: 137). Dasein involves meaning, a way that humans understand themselves and their relationship to the world.

Explanatory Box 2.1

Publication Dates

Readers may notice that several of the core texts cited in this chapter, and throughout the book, are attributed to more than one date. This is because, although the core text remains the same, there are often several different translations, and, much like finding the most comfortable pair of shoes, the reader must, as we have, find the version that suits them best. Citations may therefore include the original text and a translation, or more than one translation/edition. All are listed in the references at the end of this book.

Human beings do not encounter things in the world in a detached way; rather, there is interconnectedness between the human being and the world around them (Koch, 1996; Johnson, 2000; Lindseth and Norberg, 2004). Human beings make decisions and understand phenomena through their lived experience of the world. However, they interact without necessarily being consciously aware, or thinking through. That is, humans grow into habits of thinking that may be unconscious. They utilise skills for everyday living that they have developed over time and that enable them to live within their community or culture. Humans develop *'everyday skillful coping'* (Draucker, 1999: 361) that becomes part of everyday lived experience. Dreyfus (1991: 85) had earlier stated that 'even in everyday transparent, skillful coping a person is following unconscious rules, and … our everyday background practices are generated by the unconscious or tacit belief system'. Further, these are the skills we take for granted, seldom questioning our use of these behaviours as we become habituated in the lived life.

According to Heidegger, we do not think of things outside of the world in which they take place (LeVasseur, 2003). The human beings understand their own existence but also the existence (being) of other things, such as objects (Gorner, 2002). Certainly, there is an awareness of the world around. Further, humans have a consciousness that there is meaning and mystery in their experience of the world. This awareness is part of Dasein, Heidegger's term for human experience. Dasein may be described as humans 'being in the world' concerned with their own existence, who understands the existence of other things in the world (Johnson, 2000). Humans interact with objects in the world integrally and cannot separate from the experience of the everyday. Heidegger rejects the notion that humans must suspend previous understanding, indicating, rather, that it is through our prior understanding and reflections that we can ask further questions and better understand experience. This interconnectedness of 'all that is' distinguishes Heidegger's thought from that of others, particularly his predecessor, Husserl.

Heidegger's phenomenology is viewed as interpretative (Williams and May, 1996; LeVasseur, 2003; Crotty, 2005), the task of which 'is to interpret everydayness as a pathway (method or way) that attempts neither to deny human agency nor to valorise it' (Darbyshire, Diekelmann and Diekelmann, 1999: 23). Thus, it is the lived experience itself in relation to the world in which that experience occurs that creates a phenomenon or situation that can be understood and interpreted. Heidegger rejects cultural meanings of a given phenomenon as the '*dictatorial voice of* **das Man** *– the "they", the anonymous One*' (Crotty, 2005: 97; emphasis in the original) – because every phenomenon (experience of being-in-the-world) is a happening that is a dynamic unfolding that shows itself uniquely to the individual, influenced and understood by a human's specific knowledge, experiences and cultural background.

Human beings, by choosing possibilities in their lives, are constantly evolving or becoming. In other words, a human being may choose to become a teacher, carpenter, footballer or nurse, but this is not the end of their 'becoming'; it is not indicative of their full potential as each has numerous possibilities regarding what they could become. Johnson (2000: 139) describes three elements to Heidegger's concepts of meaning and human being:

> (1) that prior to and apart from any awareness of this fact or any choice in this fact, humans ultimately are 'already' what they essentially are; (2) that because the essence of human being is finite, it is never complete, finished, or done. It is always in a process of 'becoming'; and (3) that in order to consciously and personally be oneself one must **affirm** one's essence. (emphasis in the original)

This would suggest that a human being must own their essence and become it. Furthermore, in order to be an authentic human being, one moves into one's essence through a way of thinking that is open to what is given or shows itself in the everyday world. From a Heideggerian point of view, a teacher, carpenter, footballer or nurse experiences teaching, carpentry, football or nursing by creating meaning that is neither dictated nor calculated, though it may include frames that are part of the social experience. As Heidegger puts it: 'Dasein is in each case essentially its own possibility; it **can**, in its very Being, "choose" itself and win itself; it can also lose itself and never win itself; or only "seem" to do so' (Heidegger, 1927, 1962: 68; emphasis in the original).

Therefore, I am my own possibility. I can choose openness and thus win myself, but may also become overcome by social frames and lose myself (Heidegger, 1927, 1962). This dynamic interplay between open awareness and covering over is part of the experience of being human. There is an experience of revealing and concealing in all situations and a connectedness to persons and things that is ever-changing.

Hermeneutic Phenomenology

Heideggerian approaches to inquiry not only describe the phenomenon of interest but also find the meaning and deeper understanding of research foci, moving us into a discussion of interpretive phenomenology:

> Heidegger's hermeneutics starts with a phenomenological return to our being, which presents itself to us initially in a nebulous and undeveloped fashion, and then seeks to unfold that pre-understanding, make explicit what is implicit, and grasp the meaning of Being itself. (Crotty, 2005: 97)

Heidegger suggests that hermeneutic phenomenology is based upon the everyday understanding of phenomena. The hermeneutic circle entails a going back and forth in the questioning of our prior knowledge, in the dialectic fashion explicated originally by Schleiermacher (1998) in order to understand the deeper meaning of the lived experience, to think about the parts and the whole. Palmer (1969) suggests that an understanding of the parts and whole must be achieved simultaneously, and this is realised by taking a leap into the hermeneutic circle. In other words, we cannot understand the parts or the whole as separate entities but rather as one, with parts and whole informing one another. This hermeneutic interplay between parts and whole is the core of hermeneutic phenomenological research, influencing methodology and method from design to sampling, through the analytical process and dissemination or revealing of meaning described later in this book.

The objective of a phenomenological study is to uncover the meanings of phenomena that occur in the world, as understood through the interpretation of lived experiences of the phenomena under investigation. Hermeneutic phenomenology does not negate the situation in which the lived experience takes place (Robertson-Malt, 1999), as meaning resides within the context of the experience (Palmer, 1969). In this way, an approach using hermeneutic phenomenological research will uncover experience as it shows itself and is conveyed through careful thinking and openness to see that which may be overlooked or inauthentically represented. The attention to the many perspectives possible in looking at a phenomenon is part of this openness that leads to understanding what might otherwise be hidden.

Overall, the goal of hermeneutic phenomenology is 'to increase understanding of the meaning of human experiences and practices' (Draucker, 1999: 361). Palmer (1969: 68) suggests that:

> A theory of understanding is most relevant to hermeneutics when it takes lived experience, the event of understanding, as its starting point. In this way, thinking is oriented to a fact, an event in all its concreteness, rather than an idea; it becomes a phenomenology of the event of understanding.

That is, the focus on an event becomes a storied account that gives clues to meaning and the self-showing of experience. Such analysis raises understanding and illuminates meaning and significance, pointing to a way to think about a phenomenon in question, allowing meaning to emerge from the situation itself.

Heidegger implies that understanding is the basis for interpretation, and this is projected into the future. In other words, to interpret something, we have to understand it first, and it is this understanding that we take into our future experience(s). 'Interpretation is simply the rendering explicit of understanding' (Palmer, 1969: 134), a way of seeing something. To undertake research from a Heideggerian tradition, the researcher must uncover what it means for the human being 'to be a person in the world' (Draucker, 1999: 361). Johnson (2000: 140) points out that it is in 'the actual **living** of our own stories that individual events acquire significance within the whole to which they belong' (emphasis in the original). Looking across such experiences, such as in the study of similar experiences of persons in a group, we might see understandings and meanings revealed that illuminate mysteries or inform future possibilities about life questions.

Key Heideggerian Ideas

Many scholars have written about key ideas that represent Heidegger's thought, which has spanned decades and resulted in controversial commentary about the man and his scholarship. Common across many texts are ideas such as *Dasein*, *thrownness*, *ready-at-hand/unready-at-hand*, *authenticity*, *technology* and *language*, *time* and *being-toward-death*. Whole essays are written on these topics, and books explicating the ideas by dedicated Heideggerian scholars are available; we suggest that students of hermeneutics read multiple sources and continually revisit some of the basic ideas that guide the thinking we take into our hermeneutic research work. Yet it is helpful to provide a succinct and possibly applicable description of some of the characteristic Heideggerian ideas.

Dasein

The word *Dasein* literally translates into English as 'there-being' and may be explained as 'being there' (being a human in a situated, contextual world), but this concept or idea is complex and not so circumspectly described by Heidegger. The idea has been described as a 'logos' or gathering, an opening, a situatedness and, in Heidegger's major treatise *Being and Time* (1927, 1962), as 'being-in-the-world'. In our work, the idea of *Dasein* is a way of being that relates to the human experience and requires a particular way of thinking. Such thinking requires 'meditative thinking', a way of thinking that is different from 'calculative' thinking, an idea Heidegger explicates thoroughly in his *Memorial Address* (Heidegger, 1966b). He warns, in this essay, that while sometimes necessary, calculative thinking can overtake, be totalising and drive out other ways of revealing or understanding. Thoughtful, contextual engagement in a complex world cannot be fully understood without the meditative thinking that leads to open awareness. Meaningful experiences are the constitutive aspects of Dasein, which is characteristic of human nature.

Thrownness

Heidegger shows us that humans come into the world in particular circumstances that shape their lives and prescribe, to an extent, the way they will carry out their lives. We grow up in educational and societal environments that are already formed and we take for granted our situatedness in our environment. Our 'thrown' behaviour, shaped by those environments, may be automatic. In this way, humans risk becoming appropriated by thinking that is mechanistic and unaware, part of a technology that is unconcerned with meaningful existence. In *Being and Time* (Heidegger, 1927, 1962), the idea of thrownness is laced throughout the text implicitly. Heidegger describes everydayness as 'that Being [Dasein] which is "between" birth and death' (p. 276) a space of possibility despite the risks of living without authenticity. The everyday experience may be without knowing awareness or it may include a broader potentiality. Either way, humans are thrown into a life situation that can shape their existence.

Ready-at-hand/unready-at-hand

We also take for granted the things we use, such as the tools of our lives. In one essay, Heidegger tells a story about a person building a bird house, using a hammer and nails. The tools are *ready-at-hand* – available for the builder to use. The builder may not really notice these tools until the hammer breaks or is mislaid; when the hammer no longer works or becomes unavailable, the builder takes note. The notion can be extended beyond physical objects like hammers and nails, to physiological functioning. For example, women may not think of their fertility (which is unconsciously assumed to 'work', to be 'ready-at-hand') until they find themselves struggling to conceive, when it becomes noticeable as 'unready-at-hand'; in other words, their fertility becomes unavailable to them and stands out in a new way. Such stories exemplify the way humans live in the world without taking notice, which limits potential and interferes with authenticity.

Authenticity

Authenticity is approached by Heidegger in various aspects of his work, and it is a way of thinking about being human that moves beneath or beyond traditional definitions of authenticity. It involves a way of living in the world without the taken-for-granted assumptions that are commonly understood, manifesting in a kind of groundlessness that is entirely experiential. To use an example of identity, can we say then that the teacher, carpenter, footballer or nurse can lose themselves by not consciously choosing their essence? Equally, the question is, can they be other than who they are? A teacher, carpenter, footballer or nurse who rejects or hides their essence, is not being their true self but rather '*only "seems" to do so*'. Heidegger offers the notion of seeing authentically and choosing possibility, but also of being limited by unconscious boundaries:

> But only in so far as it is essentially something which can be **authentic** – that is, something of its own – can it have lost itself and not yet won itself. As modes of Being, **authenticity** and **inauthenticity** are both grounded in the fact that any Dasein whatsoever is characterized by mineness. (Heidegger, 1927, 1962: 68; emphasis in the original)

By 'mineness', Heidegger means 'I am' or 'you are', it is mine or yours; it belongs to me or you and therefore it cannot be given to me or you. It could be suggested from this that a teacher, carpenter, footballer or nurse only can give themselves their authentic self, by choosing their own possibility of being teacher, carpenter, footballer or nurse, by saying 'I am a teacher, carpenter, footballer, nurse'. No other person can do this for them in a Heideggerian sense. However, authenticity is more than subjective identity. It is situational and involves all the relational elements of humans interacting in an integral world.

This sense of authenticity is unconscious at first, and occurs when the prescribed everyday thinking is taken over by experience, 'when busy, when excited, when interested, when ready for enjoyment' (Heidegger, 1927, 1962: 68), suggesting that Dasein does not choose the inauthentic state; rather it happens upon one. Being open to what shows essentially and using meditative thinking to become aware of what is given in the world, are ways humans engage authentically. In Heidegger's *Conversation on a Country Path about Thinking* (Heidegger, 1966a), he alludes to 'releasement', which is a human response to meaningful existence, engagement in an integral, given field of awareness. Understanding this nature of being human is the focus of the interviewing, observing and analysis we engage, using approaches informed by this type of Heideggerian thinking.

Technology

Over several essays and evolving writings, Heidegger warns of the dangers of technology, but not of the devices and tools of the technological world. Rather,

Heidegger warns of a way of thinking and acting that is overtaken by protocol-driven environments where people 'are still not thinking', as described in his *Memorial Address* (Heidegger, 1966b). He cautions that measurement and calculation may be necessary but can insidiously overtake human life, resulting in a commodification of human thinking and acting. This type of commodification is evident in all aspects of life, from finance to health care. For example, internet banking has removed the personal interactions with money handlers and the use of physical money, allowing for potential debt and loss of awareness of a relationship with things (money). Likewise, women in labour may be managed via monitors rather than physical assessment by a midwife, removing an awareness of the essential nature of the labouring experience and the human expression of that experience, and potentially de-skilling the midwife. Hermeneutic phenomenological inquiry allows for investigation of the essential nature of human experience, of humans interacting with one another and with things. This focus on machination and commodification, that is, the replaceable human, laces much of Heidegger's work in his call for thinking that leads to possibility.

Language

Heidegger writes extensively about language, in ways that differ from traditional understandings about the use of speech and words. Language, for Heidegger, is a House of Being, an aspect of human experience that can shape and respond to events in the world. Communication with words is a social event, and is the primary means by which humans interact with each other. It can be a technological, semantic exchange subject to an ordering that is with or without thoughtful awareness. Heidegger often used words in original ways, changing nouns to verbs, using hyphens and coupling words in unique ways to convey new ideas and focus thinking. One cannot read Heidegger quickly and the prose is difficult, as he calls the reader to new ideas that are often conveyed by metaphor or repeated references to words that signal movement, fluidity, relationships. Reading Heidegger is, as Ken Maly, Heideggerian scholar, calls it, 'thinking along with Heidegger'. The language takes the reader into a cadence or way of thinking that brings us into the region of new thinking, jolting readers from the familiar and making space for the essential idea at the heart of inquiry.

Time

The notion of time is also non-traditional. Rather than chronological, Heidegger views time as a salient and significant domain that is meaningful for humans. The unfolding circumstance of being-in-the-world is characterised by the interrelationships of all things registering meaningfully. Time as 'significant', rather than as a series of chronological events, is an idea that permeates Heidegger's work. What is essential to knowing awareness, willingness to be open and releasement to the essential sway of meaningful happenings, matters. What is significant contains historicity, a world of happenings that are a part of what is. This is explained in the first chapter of *Being and Time* (1927, 1962) and is a complex discussion that leads toward human yearning, almost as a calling toward the future. Time is part of a broader issue – temporality. Stenstad (2006: 95) explains:

> Temporality is structured by (1) finding ourselves already in a certain situation (the ongoing unfolding of the things that have shaped us in our world), (2) our being now enmeshed in the midst of beings with their meanings, and (3) understanding and taking possibilities to move toward, with all of this linked through (4) discursive disclosure.

So the basic ideas of being and time make up human life and can be thought about in a way that integrates Heidegger's commentary on thinking, technology, language and other ontological matters.

Heidegger also refers back to the Greek concept of *kairos* – time, the right moment, that which holds essentially in memory and experience. The hermeneutic understanding that is a part of the approach to inquiry of hermeneutic phenomenological research is based in this form of temporality. This is important in the collection and analysis of data. It drives the search for deep, relevant understanding of apparent and covert understandings.

Being-toward-death

The concept of time or temporality is a difficult discussion in Heidegger's work and is integrated with meaningful existence and with *being-toward-death*. Mortality is the human certainty that draws attention and contributes to the groundlessness that is the human condition. In his later work *Contributions* (Heidegger, 1999), first published over 60 years after it was written, Heidegger weaves the discussion of time, language and *being-toward-death* in a way of thinking that characterises thinking in progress. In this way, human life, the progression of life (towards death, the condition of being human) is 'on the way' and always uncertain. We, as humans, are drawn to the issue of mortality and aware of a future ending while living a life that includes all that is past. Thus, time is wrapped up in what it means to be human. All that is ahead, the future, is possibility.

In summary, there are many conversations that can be engaged in considering Heidegger's works. The aforementioned ideas are examples of some of the terms used by readers of Heidegger. There are others. These ideas hint at the thinking that Heidegger developed over the course of his work and ground the view we take as we address the questions of research and inquire into what it means to be human. Heidegger's views are expressed variously across the body of his works, are sometimes cloaked in words and phrases that are unfamiliar and original, and signal ideas that are often contrary to traditional views. Reading and 'thinking along with Heidegger' can open us to new views about what may have been in front of us all along.

Key Gadamerian Ideas

Gadamer extends some of the thinking developed by Heidegger and offers compatible ideas that guide hermeneutic work. Gadamer's project to develop a method for the human sciences did not result in a protocol or framework, and, similar to Heidegger, he developed a way of thinking that is dynamic and relates all aspects of being human in any particular inquiry. Thus, his work often incorporates notions of the Other, and how thinking between oneself and the Other can be done.

Fusion of horizons

Many hermeneutic studies reference Gadamer's comments that relate to ways of thinking and the understanding that results from a *fusion of horizons*. This idea is important because it raises to consciousness the idea that what is true or essential is an integration of one thing and another. In the case of perception, knowledge or belief, an ability to see the thinking of the Other in the context of one's own understanding leads to awareness.

Along with such integration is an appreciation for prejudice (see p. 138 in Chapter 8). The idea of communicating with the Other in a fusion of horizons is brought further into understanding as a discussion of what we commonly call bias. Gadamer's description of prejudice leads us to understand that I and the Other, in a sense, co-create a new situation when ideas come together. Further, the Other's idea *addresses us*. As Gadamer states:

> It is impossible to make ourselves aware of a prejudice while it is constantly operating unnoticed, but only when it is, so to speak, provoked ... For what leads to understanding must be something that has already asserted itself in its own separate validity. Understanding begins when something addresses us. This is the first condition of hermeneutics. We now know what this requires, namely the fundamental suspension of our own prejudices. But all suspension of judgments and hence, a fortiori, of prejudices, has the logical structure of the question. The essence of the question is to open up possibilities and keep them open. If a prejudice becomes questionable in view of what another person or a text says to us, this does not mean that it is simply set aside and the text or the other person accepted as valid in its place. Rather, historical objectivism shows its naiveté in

accepting this disregarding of ourselves as what actually happens. In fact our own prejudice is properly brought into play by being put at risk. Only by being given full play is it able to experience the other's claim to truth and make it possible for him to have full play himself. (Gadamer, 2003: 299)

Gadamer thus moves us forward in the practical application of thinking about communication and brings us further into the thinking that is hermeneutical. The reciprocity between persons or between persons and text is a to and fro that is characteristic of the kind of thinking we employ in hermeneutic work. Reflexivity is an aspect of being open to unexpected ideas. It represents the 'essential sway of being' described in *Contributions to Philosophy* (Heidegger, 1999) and underscores the dynamic aspect of what it means to be human. This idea of prejudice, thus, is Gadamer's contribution to a questioning approach that informs the hermeneutic work we describe in this book.

Art

Finally, like Heidegger, Gadamer is concerned with beauty and the way meaning is represented in art. There is a particular distance and also a familiarity produced by artistic expressions that allow for a more expansive way of perceiving. That is, an image or a sound may be evocative or representative of a whole situation or idea that cannot be conveyed by words alone. Such an interaction with art can convey meaning quickly, in a Gestalt or blink of an eye, creating a grasp of understanding that is whole. The medium of art may include words and poetry, but also visual representations that signify phenomena and their meaning. The ways in which art is created and interpreted are many-fold, as are the interpretations we create; art provides another medium for the expression of meaning that leads to understanding.

Other Interpretive Phenomenological Approaches

Hermeneutic phenomenology is also known as Heideggerian hermeneutics or phenomenology, Gadamerian hermeneutics or phenomenology, philosophical hermeneutics, or interpretive phenomenology. There are various traditions and ways to approach inquiry grounded in the thinking we have described. Some approaches, like van Manen's (1990, 2016) hermeneutic phenomenology, blend some of the philosophical foundations of Heidegger with descriptive phenomenological approaches. Others, like Smith, Flowers and Larkin (2009), use explicit methodological frameworks which are not used in the approaches we will describe in this book.

Interpretive Phenomenological Analysis

Smith, Flowers and Larkins' (2009) Interpretive Phenomenological Analysis (IPA) is a point of confusion for many novice phenomenology researchers. Novice researchers commonly assume that IPA is a method for analysing hermeneutic phenomenological research data, instead of recognising that it stands as a methodology in its own right. Emerging in the post-positivist period when qualitative researchers were building credible theoretical and methodological approaches to enable their work to be accepted in the scholarly community, IPA was designed for, and is used primarily in, psychology. It offers a highly structured approach to exploring lived experience which has been recognised as useful for practical application (Chenail, 2009), but also criticised for having only tenuous links back to the underpinning philosophy, for being too structured and process-driven in direct opposition to the principles of hermeneutic research, and for being reductionist. This last point is a particular concern for researchers who are trying to deliver an authentic hermeneutic study, in which the interaction and relationship between and across data are a core part of hermeneutic phenomenology.

Our origins are based in Heideggerian and Gadamerian philosophy and described by Diekelmann and Ironside (2011) as philosophical hermeneutics. Other informing perspectives that contribute to thinking that is compatible with our work are accepted by hermeneutic scholars as enriching and useful.

Critical approaches

A study in hermeneutic phenomenology takes, as its point of departure, the goal of interpretation. Meaning emerges in the course of data analysis and interpretation and can lead to understandings which may reveal social circumstances and relationships that the researcher must address. The social environment is part of the scope of inquiry when using a hermeneutic approach; historical and cultural situatedness is important to how we understand hermeneutically. Sometimes results point to implications that require critical commentary, including using critical social theories to analyse and develop discussions. Interpretive commentary, study discussion and implications will often include transformative ideas or suggestions for action.

Hermeneutic phenomenologists undertake studies that have as 'their object ... man and what he knows about himself' (Gadamar, 1975: 314). We investigate how we know what we know, more than how we individually create meaning, including how these meanings are structured and constituted by the systems that frame our reality. The logic developed by medicine, the legal system, psychology and other disciplines is part of the experience and interpretation we explicate. The discipline of sociology, beginning in positivism (the idea that truth is objective and waiting to be discovered), has progressed to investigate how what we believe to be objective knowledge is actually a process in which we co-construct reality through shared meanings and collective subjectivities. These collective subjectivities are framed by and emerge as objective reality, further framing how we perceive and make sense of the world around us. Critical theorising provides a lens through which to investigate this process that sheds light on the ways that institutions, logic systems and discourse work to create and perpetuate inequities based on race, class, gender, sexuality and ability. Erman (2017: 301) informs us that the areas of investigation include

> racism, sexism, inequality, marginalization, oppression and domination, and being interested in who has the social and political power to legitimise certain stories about society rather than others.

From a Heideggerian perspective, we are *being-in-the-world*; we have a pre-understanding of our social situation and cannot separate ourselves from that world. Neither do we ask participants in our research to divorce themselves from their realities and everyday experiences. Critical theory invites us to critique the society or culture within which we either reside or research. When we ask students to critique a piece of work, we ask them to move away from the taken-for-granted assumptions regarding their first look at the piece they are reading and interrogate it from different perspectives. In many ways, when we use Heidegger as our underpinning philosophy, we are seeking meaning and understanding of a phenomenon as it presents itself to the person who experiences that phenomenon. Critical theory calls us to critique the situation in which a participant of a study finds themselves. While we are seeking to interpret the meanings and understandings of a phenomenon as is, phenomena do not exist outside the social context. Critical theory adds to the depth and breadth of the analysis. It facilitates a critical reflection on the world in which we find ourselves.

One particular critical theorist, philosopher, historian and social critic, Foucault, acknowledges his debt to Heidegger: 'My entire philosophical development was determined by my reading of Heidegger' (Foucault, cited in Dreyfus, 1991: 9). Foucault's discourse on power, sexuality and gender enabled the transformation of phenomenology into a critical phenomenology. His critique of the human subject is shaped by the view that one's experiences are shaped by society and also by history. As Pariseau-Legault, Holmes and Murray (2019: 5) suggest, 'an experience is therefore contingent on a larger apparatus of discursive power and therefore also on sociohistorical processes of subjectivation and resistance'. Foucault did not see the individual as a passive receiver of their situation in society but as an active self-creating human being. Foucault perceives humans as *being-in-the-world*, situated within an exciting world where others, particularly those in power, create or present a way to navigate that world. There are times when to accept this way can be considered passive, but there are other times when we recreate our own world and actively change our situation. Foucault's work presents an attempt to balance human activity and passivity in the world with agency and structure. This discussion of critical theory, distinct but also a part of the hermeneutic understanding of meaningful existence, is part of a contemporary understanding of lived experience. It is included in this chapter as a distinctive approach to thinking that is part of our interpretive project. It links the shaping of history and contemporary culture with a way of *being-in-the-world* and living mortally toward a future of possibilities.

Further Resources

Core texts

These seminal works present the original thinking on which this book, and any scholar's understanding of hermeneutic phenomenology, is based. Complex and deep, expect to have to revisit these texts several times:

- Gadamer, H. (2003) *Truth and Method* (trans. J. Weinsheimer and D. G. Marshall), 2nd, revised edn. London: Continuum.
- Heidegger, M. (1962) *Being and Time* (trans. J. Macquarrie and E. Robinson). New York: Harper & Row.
- Heidegger, M. (1982) *The Basic Problems of Phenomenology* (trans. A. Hofstadter). Bloomington, IN: Indiana University Press.
- Heidegger, M. (1999a) *Basic Writings from Being and Time (1927) to The Task of Thinking (1964)* (trans. D. Krell). London: Routledge.
- Heidegger, M. (1999b) *Contributions to Philosophy* (trans. P. Eman and K. Maly). Bloomington, IN: Indiana University Press.

Further reading

These additional texts will help extend your thinking and understanding of the complexity of Heidegger's philosophy by exposing you to different explanations and descriptions which together will reinforce your understanding:

- Foucault, M. (1978) *The History of Sexuality: An introduction*. London: Penguin.
- Moran, D. (2000) *Introduction to Phenomenology*. Abingdon, Oxon: Routledge.
- Moules, N. J. (2002) 'Hermeneutic inquiry: Paying heed to history and Hermes – An ancestral, substantive, and methodological tale', *International Journal of Qualitative Methods*, 1(3), 1–21. doi: 10.1177/160940690200100301.
- Stewart, D. and Mickunas, A. (1990) *Exploring Phenomenology: A guide to the field and its literature*, 2nd edn. Athens, OH: Ohio University Press.

Part I Summary

In this first part, we have explored the history of phenomenology and distinguishing characteristics of the thinking that guides the work of hermeneutic phenomenological research based on the philosophical hermeneutics informed by Heidegger and Gadamer. We have introduced other notable scholars who have also informed the thinking of hermeneutic philosophy or have aligned with it in their own work, and addressed the core philosophical concepts that are fundamental to understanding the methodology of hermeneutic phenomenology that we will go on to present. The following chapters provide practical discussions and suggestions for applying the thinking we have begun to explore in these first two chapters.

Part II
Designing the Hermeneutic Phenomenological Study

Introduction

As we have seen in Chapter 2, Heidegger's philosophy is steeped in hermeneutic ways of *being-in-the-world*, so that our experience of life is a constant back and forth between our culture, our background, our past, present and future experiences – all combining to help us make sense of our life world. This deeply connected interrelationship between us (the human being), our *Dasein* (being-in-the-world) and our past, present and future experiences is the 'golden thread' of Heidegger's phenomenology, and one which we need to weave into our ways of doing hermeneutic phenomenological research.

We must therefore reflect Heidegger's philosophy in our research methods at all stages of the research process to ensure consistency and fidelity to the philosophical underpinnings from the outset. Our aim is to weave the thread of the philosophy through the research work we do. Our beginning point must be to identify, explore and define the gap in evidence and so decide what we are going to do about it. These endeavours are not separate processes, but a complex hermeneutic relationship between researcher and existing evidence – the literature review and the research question are inextricably linked together – mutually informative, creative and dynamic, as the researcher goes back and forth between evidence and question until the research focus is refined and determined. In this part, we aim to address the methods – the 'ways of doing' hermeneutic phenomenology research ... and how we weave in that golden thread.

3

Literature Review and Refining the Hermeneutic Question

Chapter Overview

In this chapter, we describe the importance of setting up a study so that the phenomenon of interest is addressed particularly and the gaze is thrust in such a way that an in-depth interpretive analysis is possible. Seeking to gather and understand the breadth of available information associated with the phenomenon of interest allows the researcher to dwell in the impetus driving the study, acquiring an understanding that leads to refinement of the research question. It is important to conduct a literature review that gathers extant scientific data, is an assessment of practical knowledge and an exercise in openness that invites the question that will guide the study. Thus, the research question and hermeneutic stance set the tone and tenor throughout the methods of the study, from inception through dissemination.

The Essential Purpose of the Literature Search and Review

As with any scientific endeavour, hermeneutic phenomenological researchers need to demonstrate that the research they are proposing is necessary. In some disciplines, research may be considered unethical if there is no potential reach and impact beyond the original study, as the project will have gathered unnecessary data and wasted participants' time. However, a research question that interests the researcher comes to the fore for a particular reason which may not be immediately obvious. We often undertake research to cast a light on an area hitherto unspoken, not thought about and unknown. Change can and does come from this, and we do not need to 'know' in advance what influence or impact our researching will have, but we may have to demonstrate the knowledge space or gap that currently exists. Thus, as in any other project, a search and review of the literature is required. We would not expect to approach this process 'cold' – with no idea of topic or methodology – but with an unrefined question or query; we thus usually broadly know what it is we want to explore, and the literature search helps us to see what is already there, while the critique enables us to hone and refine the question.

Developing the Literature Review Question

There are many very good texts to advise on the processes of conducting a literature search (see Further Resources at the end of the chapter) and it is not our purpose to repeat this in detail here but to provide an oversight and address the general advice from the qualitative perspective. First, the researcher needs to identify the preliminary research question, based on their unrefined question or thinking, which will guide the search. Acronyms such as PICO (Richardson, Wilson, Nishikawa and

Hayward, 1995), which structure the question around **P**opulation, **I**ntervention, **C**omparison and **O**utcome, are popular in nursing and healthcare research, but are more suited to developing quantitative questions and locating measurable, factual empirical data. Novice phenomenological researchers may find benefit from frameworks such as SPIDER (Cooke, Smith and Booth, 2012), which helps identify the **S**ample, **P**opulation of **I**nterest, **D**esign, **E**valuation and **R**esearch type to guide a search for qualitative data. The framework assists in devising the question and search terms for the literature search, which will then inform the development of the final research question. The components of SPIDER invite the researcher to specify what they are looking for within the existing evidence. For example, if I (Dibley) wanted to try to understand the meaning young people attach to their involvement in knife crime in high-incidence areas, the SPIDER might look like that seen in Table 3.1.

Table 3.1 SPIDER acronym for developing a search question

	Component	Explanation	Term
S	Sample	The type of participant	Adolescents, teenagers, young adults
P I	Phenomenon of Interest	The particular thing of interest	Inner city, suburbia, suburban, knife crime
D	Design	Specific methods used in previous studies	Interviews, focus groups, surveys
E	Evaluation	Analysis of experience	Experience
R	Research type	Methodology of interest	Qualitative, mixed methods

I would need to keep my search reasonably broad whilst, at the same time, be clear about the type of evidence I am looking for. I would need to accept that my ideas may not be complete, that there may be other ways of exploring this issue, and other ways of representing it that I have not considered. I therefore use a range of search terms related to my topic which increase the likelihood that I will find data that meets my area of interest. My preliminary research question based on the SPIDER acronym becomes: 'What are the experiences of young people who get involved in inner-city knife crime?'

Identifying search terms

Having determined broadly what I am looking for, I now need to identify the key search terms I will use and how these will be refined with truncations, combined with Boolean operators (AND, OR, NOT), thereby creating my search strategy (Table 3.2). Truncation symbols enable me to search for all derivations of a term, by truncating the term to its root structure, hence Adolescen* will retrieve adolescence,

Table 3.2 Developing the search terms and strategy

	Term	Search terms, truncations, derivatives and BOOLEAN operators
S	Adolescents, teenagers, young adults	Adolescen* [adolescence; adolescent; adolescents] OR Teenag* [teenage; teenaged; teenager; teenagers] OR Young adult* [young adult; young adults]
P I	Inner city, suburbia, suburban, knife crime	Inner city OR Suburb* [suburban; suburbs; suburbia] AND Knife crime
D	Interviews, focus groups, surveys	Interview* [interview; interviewer; interviews; interviewing] OR Focus group* [focus group; focus groups] OR Survey* [survey; surveys]
E	Experience	Experience* [experience; experienced; experiences]
R	Qualitative, mixed methods	Qualitative OR mixed methods

adolescent and adolescents. BOOLEAN operators enable me to combine search terms in such a way that it widens or focuses the search. For example, searching for Adolescence AND adolescent AND adolescents would instruct the search engine to find articles which each contain all three of those words; searching for Adolescence OR Adolescent OR Adolescents would instruct the search engine to find articles which contain at least one of those words. The first approach is useful to narrow a search when many 'hits' are retrieved at the first attempt, whilst the latter is useful to keep the search open if the topic is novel or evidence is hard to find.

My search would in fact be made up of several mini searches which could be conducted in a number of ways, for example:

OPTION 1 – conduct each of **S**, **PI**, **D**, **E** and **R** separately, then combine each component using *AND* … **S** *AND* **PI** *AND* **D** *AND* **E** *AND* **R**.

OPTION 2 – conduct **S** and **PI**, and then combine them with *AND* to produce **SPI**; then conduct **D**, **E** and **R** and combine them with *AND* to produce **DER**; then combine **SPI** and **DER** with *AND*.

Limiters

I also would need to think about the 'limiters' I want to set; these allow me to be even more specific in what I ask the database(s) to retrieve. Common limiters are:

Year of publication – depending on the topic, the perceived availability of data and the rate of change within the field and whether or not I wanted an historical perspective, I can set the publication years to suit; the search will then only retrieve publications from within these parameters. History can be particularly useful if there is an interest in exploring how a phenomenon has changed over time.

Location of keywords – I could instruct the search engine to find articles where the keywords appear in the title and/or the abstract; this strategy increases the chances that the retrieved articles are wholly relevant to the topic I am pursuing, because if my search terms do not appear in either of these places, the chances are that the mention of them is a passing comment in the background/introduction, or in the discussion/recommendations.

Full text – this limiter instructs the search engine to avoid abstracts or partial text, and only retrieve full-text articles, which are essential to be able to conduct a thorough critique of the research.

Original articles – by setting this limiter, I instruct the search engine to return original research articles, thereby automatically filtering out non-research papers such as editorials, opinion pieces and letters.

English language – English is the agreed universal language of the scientific/research community; unless I have specific funds to deal with translations, I am likely to avoid foreign-language publications unless these are crucial to my study.

Sample – some search engines/databases, such as OVID, allow the researcher to select some characteristics of the sample, such as age range or gender. For my search on knife crime, I could select the age range which most closely matches the 12–25-year-old window I probably need to inform my research; if the specific age range I want cannot be selected, or I risk filtering papers out when there may not be many to choose from, I would not limit the search in this way, but filter out at a later date.

I would need to decide where within my search I apply these limiters – either with each 'mini search' or at the end when all mini searches have been combined. The first is a good approach if the search is expected to retrieve a lot of hits, but I would need to be consistent and apply all limiters to all mini searches. The latter may be a good option if there is not a lot of available evidence – I can at least then decide whether to limit the search further or change it if it hasn't quite found the relevant information.

Regardless of how the search is conducted, the researcher needs to be focused and systematic in their searching and access the databases that carry the type of evidence relevant to their field – be that health, sociology, education, history, psychology or anthropology, for example. Once the search is complete, the researcher needs to review each article, remove duplicates and then apply inclusion and exclusion criteria. Duplicates occur when the search is conducted across several databases because published evidence is often indexed in more than one database, whilst inclusion and exclusion criteria enable the researcher to further filter out unwanted articles. Table 3.3 gives an example from the imaginary knife-crime literature search.

Table 3.3   Inclusion and exclusion criteria for fictional knife crime study

Inclusion criteria The specific characteristics of an article which would warrant its inclusion in the review	*For example:* Keywords [adolescen*; teenage*; young adult* AND knife crime (or equivalent alternative)] appear in title or abstract Participants are aged between 13 and 25 Original full-text research, qualitative or mixed methods design South American research Knife crime is the main or only focus
Exclusion criteria The specific characteristics of an article which would warrant its exclusion from the review; these should not simply be the opposite of the inclusion criteria – since failure to meet those would result in automatic exclusion. Exclusion criteria are additional limits which are used to further screen articles which do meet the inclusion criteria, but may still not be suitable.	*For example:* Focuses on gang culture rather than on the individual's motivations for getting involved in knife crime Does not have an inner-city focus

Explanatory Box 3.1

Literature Search Advice

For specific advice on literature searching, including access to resources such as databases and electronic journals that are available through their institution, students are advised to access the library services at their place of study. Libraries usually have printed guides and can often offer training sessions for the novice. Alternatively, a plethora of guides, published by universities across the world and freely available in the public domain, can be located online.

Demonstrating thoroughness

The researcher may also need to demonstrate the entire process as a means of evidencing the robustness of the searching. For example, the Preferred Reporting Items for Systematic Reviews and Meta-Analyses (PRISMA) method (Moher, Liberati, Tetzlaff, Altman and PRISMA Group, 2010) serves as a useful model for any study. Alternatively, a simple flowchart can suffice, where 'n' refers to the number of papers identified, removed and remaining (Figure 3.1).

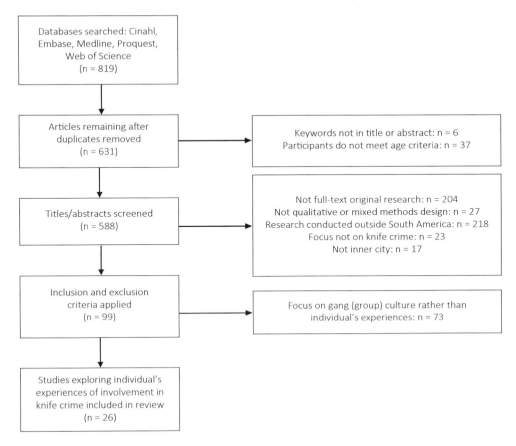

Figure 3.1 Flow chart to demonstrate retrieval, screening, eligibility assessment and inclusion of studies for review

Critiquing the selected literature

Once the searches have been conducted, all retrieved articles have been screened and the final literature for inclusion in the review has been selected, an appropriate critical appraisal tool may be applied to evidence the quality of those selected articles (see Further Resources at the end of the chapter). These tools, specific to the research methodology, guide the reviewer to ask core questions of the type of evidence they are reviewing, in order to make a critical judgement of the quality of that evidence. Critical appraisal tools enable assessment of the quality of the specific evidence being reviewed, rather than assign any form of quality hierarchy as informed, for example, by the Oxford Clinical Evidence-Based Medicine guidelines (OCEBM Working Group, 2011). Using a standardised tool ensures that a rigorous critique can be conducted across all articles. Data extraction tables may be used to draw out the critical aspects of each selected study, identify strengths and weaknesses and highlight key findings, using categories based on the critical appraisal tool. This enables the researcher to present a critical assessment of the extant evidence relating to their proposed topic, demonstrate the need for the study and refine their research question.

Explanatory Box 3.2

Structure Versus Freedom

The degree of structure applied to evidencing the process of literature searching, selection and reviewing varies across disciplines; in health sciences, for example, including nursing, some form of flowchart visualising the identification and selection of articles for review is usually expected. A data extraction table is also common, as this helps the researcher record evidence of their thorough critique of the articles being reviewed. Other disciplines, such as education, anthropology, sociology and history, may require a different approach to literature reviewing, and students are advised to discuss the precise requirements for their project and discipline with their supervisor(s).

How the Literature Search and Review Differ in Hermeneutic Phenomenological Research

Against the background of the general principles outlined above, there are some additional aspects to consider in hermeneutic phenomenological research. Smythe and Spence (2012: 23) explain that:

> Engaging hermeneutically with literature is distinctive. It is not the same as doing a literature review in a quantitative study, or one from another qualitative perspective. The nature of a hermeneutic review is that there are few rules to follow; rather, there is a way to be attuned. While there will be a focus that influences the scope of the literature to be explored, precious insights may be found in unlikely places.

These experienced hermeneutic researchers are encouraging us to think – within the constraints of what we 'should' do when addressing literature – about our relationship with that literature, how it challenges and changes our thinking; our literature review should not be a sanitised process, but should, necessarily, be influenced by us 'as-researcher'.

Exemplar Case

Reflecting back on my doctoral studies, which explored the meaning of stigma in people living with incontinence related to inflammatory bowel disease (Dibley, Norton and Whitehead, 2018), I (Dibley) can acknowledge now that the piece of literature which had the most impact, and greatly influenced my academic thinking about stigma, what it is and what it means to people, was not any of the 12 or so carefully identified, analysed and presented academic papers published within the preceding 10 years which reported studies relating to stigma and incontinence, but a slim, well-worn copy of Goffman's (1963) seminal text entitled *Stigma: Notes on the management of a spoiled identity*. The book featured heavily in my background chapter on stigma, and indeed Goffman's work provided the theoretical framework, alongside Heidegger's philosophy, for my PhD studies. But it also had a profound impact on me, on my understanding that what is stigmatising is not the mark of difference per se, but the way that individuals and collectives in society respond to that mark, and how the person carrying that mark reacts to those responses. I was approaching my scholarship with a seemingly certain assumption that a bowel disease, particularly one that often causes incontinence, MUST be stigmatising and my purpose was to understand that experience – but Goffman's little book changed my thinking, and consequently changed my sampling strategy so that I included people with IBD and incontinence who did not feel stigmatised. As a result, the data revealed new insights that were richer and more rounded, and which showed forth a range of experience and meaning, including transferable findings about how to overcome incontinence-related stigma.

The literature we access and review for the purpose of developing our research question should therefore not just be limited to scientific articles located via core databases, and our purpose should not only be to 'evidence the gap' amongst known facts but also to engage with it meaningfully, bringing our existing knowledge into play, to co-create a new understanding from that literature. Our understanding and interpretation of the literature is over-layered by our thinking about the phenomenon of interest, and we can sometimes reflect this in the review by posing questions regarding potential reach which we pick up later. In other words, we can use signposts in our literature review that point towards what might come.

Hermeneutic phenomenologists do not, like descriptive phenomenologists and grounded theorists, aim to refrain from engaging with literature in an attempt to avoid influencing the study, but to be *'always-already'* connected with and informed by the literature. Spence (2017) explains that engagement with the literature prior to the study adds to and informs our pre-understanding, which we carry with us into our research. Instead of 'bracketing out' our pre-existing knowledge gleaned from experience and literature, hermeneutic phenomenologists recognise and call forth the assumptions and pre-understandings they bring to the work, continually checking their interpretations against the text and among the team. By engaging with the literature in an open, reflexive manner, we bring to the fore our own suppositions, opinions and biases, and adopt an open, accepting attitude toward the possibilities of experience which we seek to explore. This engagement is in itself hermeneutic, as we move back and forth between our existing understanding and the newly identified literature which then informs our approach to and understanding of our topic of interest.

This acknowledgement of and connectedness with existing evidence benefits the research question, enables a co-creation of understanding with participants during data collection (Chapter 6) and informs data analysis (Chapter 7). The practice is rooted in Heidegger's thinking about *'Dasein'* – how *'being there'* (in this case, being there knowledgeably with the participant) enables the hermeneutic development of new insights and understanding.

The search and review can be understood as 'a gathering of that which shows itself', meaning that the researcher engages with and is open to the possibilities of thinking that emerge when their existing understanding meets the literature – such as occurred with Dibley's encounter with Goffman. It requires a flexibility of thinking – a focused search and review, yet, at the same time, an openness of thinking toward the possibilities of other sources of evidence. The literature search and review therefore become a hermeneutic creation between the available and relevant literature and the researcher, whose *Dasein* is fundamental to engagement with the literature and development of the research question. Essential, however, to the overall quality of the study is openness and transparency about the inclusion of other texts and grey literature in the review. Whether a formal PRISMA diagram or a bespoke flowchart is created, it should evidence the inclusion of grey or other sources of literature.

A standard literature review, as described earlier, is a key component of any Masters or doctoral study and it would be a brave soul who abandoned this expectation. Academic papers should be identified, located and reviewed using formal established processes, according to the requirements of their place of study. Additional literature (grey literature, poems, novels and other relevant sources) should be assessed with the focus on our relationship as-researcher with these texts, and how this relationship challenges and changes our thinking.

Once all relevant literature has been identified and critically appraised, and key themes or findings have been identified, the process of developing the research question can begin.

The Researcher as the Source of the Question

Historically, there has been much debate about the apparent weakness introduced into research when the researcher has influence over the research question. The assumption was that any influence the researcher had would be negative, and thus the seemingly disconnected world of the positivistic or quantitative researcher gained ground as the gold standard way of doing unbiased research. This perspective is flawed. Questions for any research do not just come out of nowhere, but are generated by the researcher in some way, who brings their previous experience to the design and delivery of the study, including developing the question. Any researcher – positivist or post-positivist – has an ontological and epistemological view of the world which drives their interest in and connection with the research that they do.

Explanatory Box 3.3

Ontology and Epistemology

Philosophy drapes itself around two core concepts: ontology and epistemology. Each proposes a theory which supports a particular approach to making sense of the world. Aristotle proposed ontology (the nature of being) in terms of physical substances – in his view, 'being' is centred on primary and secondary substances which are the essence of being, and which describe that being. Heidegger's ontology differs considerably, in that he argues that our understanding of Being – of the ways in which humans reveal themselves to themselves and thus understand themselves – is necessarily informed by temporality (non-chronological time) and historicity (past history and experience). Heidegger's ontology, which underpins his phenomenology and informs the ways of doing hermeneutic research as explained in this text, proposes that temporality and historicity are core components in understanding how we experience our world. Our being-in-the-world is an experiential, situated and unique perception informed by the personal understanding and experience of the perceiver and their 'beingness'.

Epistemology (the nature of knowledge and how we know what we know) prompts consideration of whether all knowledge is factual and exists in the world ready to be discovered, or is constructed by individuals, informed by past and present events and an often inexplicable 'knowing' that we bring with us to facilitate new understanding. Each of us, and certainly each researcher, can position themselves ontologically and epistemologically, and has a philosophical view that is a blend of these two philosophical positions.

For example, the positivist or quantitative/scientific researcher would likely hold the epistemological view that reality is factual and measurable, and knowledge is the evidence generated from the interrogation of facts, presented and proven statistically. Their ontological stance may be closer to Aristotle's view of substances, and the naturally occurring similarities and differences between human subjects.

In contrast, the post-positivist or qualitative/naturalistic researcher would hold the epistemological view that reality is a unique, individual perception, and that knowledge is generated from experience. Their ontological stance may be more likely to reflect that of Heidegger, acknowledging that temporality and historicity are fundamental to how humans understand their world. The researcher recognises that each person's experience of their world is unique to them, and that multiple realities are possible amongst different people having the same experience.

As researchers, we need to understand where we sit ontologically and epistemologically, as this necessarily guides the questions we ask and the research we do. All types of research are useful. You cannot interview a cup of coffee/tea regarding its effect on health or blood pressure but you can measure the physiological effects of the caffeine and the changes in alertness and performance, and you can interview someone about the experience of the pleasures of that first morning cup of coffee – or tea.

In hermeneutic phenomenological research, relationships and connections with the research topic, theory or philosophy inform the researcher's *Dasein* and are brought into play throughout the study. Two of Heidegger's philosophical ideas help us here. First, *Dasein* reflects the ontological perspective of what it means 'to be', such that the nature of Dasein is essential to ways of being. In other words, one cannot 'be' without 'being somewhere' – who we 'are' as humans is shaped by the past, present and future influences of our personal and social world. Second, *thrownness* refers to the predetermined way in which we are shaped and being shaped by the specific familial, social and cultural environment into which we are born (in other words, we do not choose the path we take so much as it chooses us). Thus, the role, experience and background of the researcher as the interpretive agent in the reviewing of literature and refinement of the research question are recognised and embraced. Who one is as-researcher in terms of both professional and personal life experience is relevant and indeed important – these are the experiences that make the researcher's *Dasein* a guiding force in the study, the starting point upon which gathered literature will settle and bring forth the research question. The researcher co-constitutes their knowledge of the self and the reviewed literature, to generate a research question which, whilst informed by their own *Dasein* and responding to the predetermined nature of *thrownness*, extends beyond that to reach into a new area of enquiry. The research question is thus not selfish or inward-looking but is the means by which new insight and understanding may be created.

This connectedness between researcher and research, beginning right at the start with the research idea, literature review and generation of the question, is a unique aspect of hermeneutic phenomenology; these 'influences' are not viewed as an undesirable bias but as an essential contextual component of the research, albeit one which requires self-awareness and critical reflection. The starting point of thinking is the start of the hermeneutic circle – as soon as we begin to think in the way of Heidegger, we begin a dialogue among the different aspects of ourselves, the world we live in and the possibilities before us. The ways in which the hermeneutic phenomenological researcher pays attention to the influence of the self throughout the research project is further addressed in Chapter 8: Reflexivity and Rigour.

Developing and Refining the Research Question

By the time the literature search and review are complete, the researcher – who is *always-already* embedded in their thinking about the topic, whilst holding open to the possibilities of thinking (Smythe, Ironside, Sims, Swenson and Spence, 2008) – is tasked with developing the research question. Data extraction and the synthesis and discussion of core themes arising from the identified literature can help inform the question, since these activities focus the researcher's thinking on what is present as well as what is missing from the existing evidence. The process of developing and refining the research question is not linear, nor straightforward; the researcher must move back and forth between their original ideas for the study, the evidence of the literature review, and the necessary philosophical 'thinking' of the hermeneutic phenomenologist to create a question which can be answered, represents the fundamental intention of the study and is philosophically and methodologically sound. This is the point at which the 'golden thread' begins to tie together philosophy (ontology/epistemology) with methodology, and projects forward to inform methods. This connectedness is important, because the same topic, viewed through different philosophical and methodological lenses, will generate a different research question. Figure 3.2 illustrates this, using the example of Dibley's inflammatory bowel disease (IBD) research from the perspective of a selection of methodologies.

In generating the hermeneutic phenomenological research question, we aim to reflect Heidegger's core ontological position of 'being' as experienced within the context of one's world. The example in Figure 3.2 encompasses this by asking what it means *to be* (in this case stigmatised), whilst also *being* a person *living with* IBD, who experiences the illness in the context of their daily lives.

Other Heideggerian concepts may also inform the development and focus of the research question. Ideas about *technology* and *ready-at-hand* (that taken-for-granted attitude that something is available to us, without us thinking consciously about it) might, for example, guide a study exploring the meaning of becoming a parent following an in vitro fertilisation (IVF), i.e. an assisted pregnancy (Gale, 2020). The complexities of enduring IVF treatment and achieving a pregnancy reflect many of Heidegger's thoughts about *technology*, while the failure of the reproductive system to function is a challenge to women's expectations and assumptions about their fertility – that the option of natural parenthood is *ready-at-hand*. Similarly, if we wish to explore notions of what it means to be cared for or be the carer, we could draw on Heidegger's *'leaping in'* (taking over) and *'leaping ahead'* (being an enabler) (Glover, 2017).

Ethnography: *the study of people and cultures.*
Question: How does culture and society influence the experience of stigma in people with inflammatory bowel disease (IBD)?

Grounded theory: *the construction of social science theories arising from data which is gathered and analysed methodically.*
Question: What informs a theory of stigma resistance in people with IBD?

Descriptive phenomenology: *seeks to describe the essence of experience, in its purest form.*
Question: How is stigma experienced by people with IBD?

Interpretive (hermeneutic) phenomenology: *seeks to reveal the meaning of experience, informed by the context in which the experience occurs.*
Question: What is the meaning(s) and understanding(s) that people give to the experience of living with IBD?

Critical social theory: *critiques societies, social structures and systems of power; tends to focus on disadvantaged populations.*
Question: How do power and politics inform the experience of stigma in people with IBD?

Feminist theory: *constructs new knowledge and informs social change; historically embedded in women's oppression but more typically now addresses topics uniquely relevant to women. It embeds feminist ways of thinking in developing theoretical and philosophical discourses. The aim is to understand gender inequality, examining women's and men's social roles, experiences, interests and politics in a variety of disciplines.*
Question: How does society contribute to the stigma experienced by women with IBD?

Post-structuralism: *focuses strongly on language, and argues that to understand language, for example in the form of a text, both the text and the systems of knowledge that produced it, must be studied. In other words, the inquiry is not only into 'what is this thing?' but also 'what informed the creation of this thing?'*
Question: How does social knowledge inform the way IBD is represented in social literary sources such as magazines and websites?

Figure 3.2 Examples of the influence of methodology on the design, structure and purpose of the research question

Or we might take a particular interest in the way that language – considered by Heidegger and Gadamer to be the fundamental means by which humans communicate experience – influences our approach to and understanding of certain human conditions such as mental illness (Fernandez, 2016). For experienced hermeneutic phenomenological researchers, this process is one of being open to the possibilities and skilfully incorporating a wealth of philosophical and methodological 'knowing' alongside the findings from the literature search and review, to create the research question. Novice researchers may find the lack of 'structure' unsettling until they come to understand that such openness of attitude creates exciting possibilities. Structures and frameworks are generally avoided in hermeneutic phenomenological work, because rather than reflecting the hermeneutic complexity of *Dasein* and what it is '*to be*', these tend to force a linear, uni-directional structure onto thinking as a process, rather than a revealing. Frameworks such as SPIDER (Cooke, Smith and Booth, 2012), which we have already seen can guide qualitative literature searches, can also be used to develop the research question in some cases, but can feel cumbersome because all components may not 'fit' with the methodology, may not be included in the question – but be considered in the design – and are unlikely to be used in the original SPIDER order. For example, if, following the literature search and review, I wanted to develop my question for a hermeneutic study of understanding participation in knife crime in South America, the framework might resemble Table 3.4.

Table 3.4 Using SPIDER search terms to develop the final research question

	Component	Item for question
S	Sample	Adolescents, teenagers
P I	Phenomenon of interest	Participation in inner-city knife crime
D	Design	Individual interviews
E	Evaluation	Experience
R	Research type	Hermeneutic phenomenology

The question might then emerge as: *What is the meaning of participating in knife crime for adolescents aged 12–19, living in inner cities in Brazil?* This is a perfectly good hermeneutic question but it does not include mention of method (individual interviews), and the reference to research type (hermeneutic phenomenological research) is only implied through the use of the words '*meaning*' and '*living in*'. To generate an appropriate question, only some components may be used, and this may add to, rather than relieve, the student's confusion.

An alternative option is to avoid the use of a framework, draw on the findings of the literature review and the themes that emerge from the critique, and pay close attention to the structure of research questions reported in published research articles using hermeneutic phenomenology.

Beyond the Research Question

The literature search and review inform more than just the development of the question. 'Rejected' papers – those that contain the relevant search terms but do not meet the inclusion criteria – may still provide evidence to support the development of the rationale for a study, or be utilised during later analysis and discussion to help reveal the relationship between the new findings and existing evidence, enabling the student to demonstrate what their work adds. Such papers may also invite the student to explore philosophical and methodological concepts, providing insights into how previous researchers approached similar topics and the philosophical, methodological and method decisions they made. These possibilities should invite the curious student to explore, so that they build up their own repertoire of understanding of both established and emerging trends which then guide the design of their own work and help them defend their design decisions.

Remaining open to the possibilities encourages uniqueness and creativity in research. For example, students may be advised that a strong argument for them to use a particular methodology is that previous researchers have used the same or a similar approach. This may be taken as evidence that the decision is appropriate. We would encourage supervisors and students to think instead about whether the methodology is right for the question *and* for the student. The first use of interpretive phenomenology to explore a given topic, or the adoption of a new data analysis method aligned to that methodology, can itself be the unique contribution to knowledge that emerges from doctoral studies.

Chapter Summary

The literature search and review create the cornerstone for study design and begin to weave the 'golden thread' which combines philosophy, methodology and methods. Working hermeneutically – moving back and forth between their original research idea, their own understanding and current research evidence – the student interrogates the existing literature and gradually develops and refines the research question which reflects their philosophical position. Exploring philosophical, methodological and method options from included and background articles builds a depth and breadth of understanding which forms the foundation of the project, and enables the student to appreciate, and evidence, where their research sits in the methodological landscape.

Further Resources

These core readings and additional resources will be particularly helpful for extending the reader's understanding of the concepts presented in this chapter:

Core readings

- Hart, C. (2010) *Doing a Literature Review*. London: Sage.
- Killam, L. A. (2013) *Research Terminology Simplified: Paradigms, axiology, ontology, epistemology and methodology*. Sudbury, ON: Author (Kindle edition).

- Methley, A. M., Campbell, S., Chew-Graham, C., McNally, R. and Cheraghi-Sohi, S. (2014) 'PICO, PICOS and SPIDER: A comparison study of specificity and sensitivity in three search tools for qualitative systematic reviews', *BMC Health Services Research*, 14(1), 579. doi: 10.1186/s12913-014-0579-0.
- Moher, D., Liberati, A., Tetzlaff, J., Altman, D. G. and PRISMA Group (2010) 'Preferred reporting items for systematic reviews and meta-analyses: The PRISMA statement', *International Journal of Surgery*, 8(5), 336–341. doi: 10.1016/j.ijsu.2010.02.007.
- Vagle, M. (2018) *Crafting Phenomenological Research*, 2nd edn. Oxford: Routledge.
- Vezina, B. (2007) 'Universals and particulars: Aristotle's ontological theory and criticism of the Platonic forms', *Undergraduate Review*, 3, 101–103. Available at: http://vc.bridgew.edu/undergrad_rev/vol3/iss1/16.
- Wallace, M. and Wray, A. (2016) *Critical Reading and Writing for Postgraduates*, 3rd edn. London: Sage.

Further readings

- Critical Appraisal Skills Programme (CASP): https://casp-uk.net
- Dahlberg, K., Dahlberg, H. and Nystrom, M. (2008) *Reflective Lifeworld Research*. Lund, Sweden: Studentlitteratur.
- Eriksen, M. B. and Frandsen, T. F. (2018) 'The impact of patient, intervention, comparison, outcome (PICO) as a search strategy tool on literature search quality: A systematic review', *Journal of the Medical Library Association (JMLA)*, 106(4), 420–431. doi: 10.5195/jmla.2018.345.

4

Population and Sampling

Chapter Overview

In this chapter, we address the ways in which hermeneutic scholars identify and recruit participants, the role of inclusion and exclusion criteria, and issues of access whilst designing these aspects of the research to reflect Heidegger's key notions of Being and Time. For Heidegger, experience is always 'situated' – it does not exist in isolation from the time and context in which it occurs: 'The self which the Dasein is, is there somehow in and along with all intentional comportments' (Heidegger, 1982: 158) – the person is always within, rather than separate from, their experiences. Hermeneutic researchers are therefore less interested in avoiding confounders and controlling variables which might be assumed to influence perceptions, and more interested in gaining an understanding of the meaning of experience within the life-world of the experiencing person – a life-world in which 'confounders' and 'variables' play a part in the creation of that experience. This philosophical position necessarily influences the methods used to identify a study population and to select, or sample, from that population.

Situatedness

Earlier, we were introduced to the hermeneutic relationship between the researcher and their world. The hermeneutic researcher's *Dasein* is an interplay between self, environment and experience, and is influential in directing their thinking towards certain issues, which often become the focus of their research. This 'being directed towards' something of research interest usually means that the researcher is situated within the very world they seek to research, connected to it on a professional and/ or personal level. Who they are 'as-researcher' becomes meaningful in the context of hermeneutic phenomenological research.

In many methodologies, this situatedness presents problems: it is seen as a negative influence on research which introduces an unwanted bias and is detrimental to the robustness and trustworthiness of the research. This is a reasonable and logical concern in positivistic research where the investigator seeks to present an objective result. Controlling all influences (or variables) which could affect the results becomes essential to the design of a robust study. Yet this is not the case in hermeneutic phenomenological research, where the purpose is to explore, understand and reveal meaning. The researcher is instead part of the research design, and, by their very presence and their interpretive analysis, they generate a result that includes their own experience in its explication. We read in Chapter 3 that this close relationship between the hermeneutic researcher and their research interest informs the literature review and the development of the research question, and that relationship continues when considering the target population and the potential sample for study.

Situatedness and Access to a Study Population

What we term 'situatedness' in hermeneutic phenomenological research informs and reflects the dialogue on 'insider research/insider status' discussed elsewhere (see Chapter 5: p. 73). Both phrases point towards the same issue: on some level, either from professional or personal experience, or perhaps via previous research in the same or similar area which has built a reputation, the researcher has an undeniable connection with the population they intend to study. Much of the early literature on this reflected the controversies over the rights and wrongs of being 'an insider', with intense debate on strategies to counteract the perceived negative consequences of such a connection. For example, Serrant-Green (2002) presented an early and important contribution to the discussion, focusing on the issues of sharing the same or similar ethnic identity with research participants. Perhaps the greatest benefit of *situatedness* is access to a study population, but the challenges must also be addressed. For example, in her study with lesbian parents of sick children, Dibley (2009) was situated as a children's nurse, a lesbian mother and the parent of a sick, premature infant. Her identity as nurse and mother enabled access and recruitment, facilitated data collection due to her professional knowledge as a children's nurse. However, she withheld information about her sick infant to avoid disrupting participants' freedom to tell their own story. Issues of rigour and reflexivity in relation to researcher *situatedness* are addressed in detail in Chapter 8 (p. 138).

Participant Source, Population and Sampling

In any qualitative research approach, it is essential to identify the population and sample most likely to provide data that will address the research question. In research, a *participant source* refers to a place, an organisation or a service that has the potential to provide people for a study; *population* refers to everyone who *could* be included in the study because they meet the inclusion criteria, whilst *sample* refers to a subset of that population. A *sample* is usually needed because including the overall eligible population would be impractical or unnecessary. For example, in a recent study to understand the meaning of kinship stigma in inflammatory bowel disease (IBD) (Dibley, Williams and Young, 2019), the *participant source* was a UK-based charity whose members have IBD. From this, a *population* of those who felt stigmatised by their family members was identified, and a subset of this population who met all inclusion criteria and agreed to take part, formed the *sample*.

Sampling Method

Because the hermeneutic researcher is always exploring an experience, it is essential that participants have had the experience of interest so that they can provide relevant data. Sampling is therefore always purposive – the researcher deliberately seeks out those who can address the research question. Critics can be dismissive of purposive sampling, citing it as weak because it is not free of influence. Any sampling strategy that is wrongly applied is weak – using purposive sampling to select participants for a randomised controlled trial would be a major flaw because it would introduce multiple variables which would confound the results; similarly, using random sampling to select participants for a hermeneutic study would be a major flaw, because of the very low chance of selecting people who will have had the experience of interest. A sampling strategy wrongly applied is a weakness, but correctly applied it is a strength. In the case of hermeneutic phenomenological research, purposive sampling is the method of choice precisely because it selects people who have had the experience of interest, those who are most able to provide insights into the particular phenomenon and therefore most likely to provide data which addresses the research question.

Whilst purposive sampling can overlap with convenience sampling, the two are not precisely the same. Convenience sampling refers to drawing a sample from a readily available population – for instance, if I wanted to understand the experience of ethnic minority youths engaging in team-sport activities, I might recruit from the local sports club because it is conveniently situated. In this case, it is the convenience which drives selection rather than how closely the experiences of the participant source (the local sports club) match the purpose of the study.

Purposive sampling may be as simple as sending out a call for participants to a population source, getting interested participants (*population*) and selecting carefully from there (*sampling*). If the topic is more sensitive or rare, or involves hidden or marginalised groups, snowball (also called chain-referral) sampling may be needed.

Exemplar Case

A hermeneutic study exploring the experiences of lesbian parents when their children required health care collected data in the early 2000s, when the socio-political landscape in the UK was very different from the diverse, inclusive society of today, and revealing a non-heterosexual relationship anywhere, let alone to a public service on which the individual was dependent for care, was risky (Dibley, 2009). Finding participants was challenging, so snowball sampling was employed; confirmed participants suggested others in their networks who met the inclusion criteria, who the researcher might approach.

The advantage of snowball or chain-referral sampling is that hidden populations can be accessed for research, but the concern is that a person's social group tends to reflect their own life view, and the sample can become very similar. However, the hermeneutic researcher recognises participants' *Dasein* as integral to their experience and is not trying to produce generalisable data or a definitive truth, but rather reveal the meaning of experience amongst a given group of participants.

Yet sometimes the hermeneutic researcher does need to try and achieve as diverse a sample as possible; in this case, there will be a call to one or more *population sources* to identify the potential study *population*, but *purposive sampling with maximum variation* is then used. This simply means that, mindful of the inclusion and exclusion criteria for the study, the researcher selects participants to give as diverse a profile to the sample as possible – for instance, seeking equal numbers of men and women, ensuring that ethnic and/or social groups and sub-groups are appropriately represented, and ensuring there are participants from across an age range. This may be particularly relevant if it is a purpose or requirement of the research that the *sample* reflects the demographic profile of the *population source(s)*.

Exemplar Case

A simple example of purposive sampling with maximum variation occurred in a hermeneutic study of the experiences of nurses working across generations. It was particularly necessary to sample nurses from the various generational groups of working nurses; when the number of older nurses volunteering to participate doubled the number of young nurses, the recruitment activities shifted to focus on younger nurses until the population groups corresponded evenly (Vandermause, Sanner-Stiehr and Smith, forthcoming).

Multiple population sources might be required if, for example, there are regional differences in participant profiles. For example, a researcher who wants to understand the meaning of a specific sociological aspect might purposefully recruit from a number of geographical locations to be able to sample people with varied experiences of the same aspect.

Sample Size

According to Baker and Edwards (2012), the answer to the question: 'How many participants are enough?' is 'It depends what you are trying to do.' At first glance, this seems unhelpful, but they make a good point. Although qualitative sample sizes have long fallen foul of positivistic researchers who argue that a small number of participants does not provide sufficient data to answer a question, sample size is inextricably linked to study design, and thus to research question and purpose.

Broadly speaking, if the design is positivistic (quantitative), the purpose is to provide a definitive answer to a precise question; in this situation, sample size is calculated statistically to identify the minimum number required to produce generalisable results. The larger the sample size, the greater the probability that the results are 'accurate'. For example, if 100 people out of an available population of six million test a new product and 60 of them like it, this is hardly convincing enough to endorse the product and urge the remaining 5,999,900 people to use it – because the sample of 100 is unlikely to be representative and the results cannot therefore be generalised across the entire population. But if two million people test the new product and the majority endorse it, the sample is more likely to be representative of the six million population, and so the results can be generalised. The researchers can say with confidence: this is a good product.

However, sample sizes for post-positivistic (qualitative) methodologies, including hermeneutic phenomenology, cannot be calculated. Instead, when determining 'how many participants are enough?', the following criteria must be taken into consideration:

- the overall purpose of the research
- the relationship between rarity of topic and sample size
- the depth and completeness of data being collected
- the method of analysis being used.

The overall purpose of the research

Research endeavour seeks to prove or disprove theory, or reveal understandings, meanings or insights. As we saw in Chapter 3 (p. 45–47), research methodology and design are inextricably linked to the underpinning philosophical perspectives. Understanding the contrasts between different approaches to research is key to selecting the most appropriate methods for the study (Figure 4.1).

Hermeneutic phenomenologists are not trying to prove or disprove anything or provide 'the' definitive answer to a question. We are not trying to claim that an experience 'is' something specific, or that it is more (or less) valid, important or meaningful than another experience. The aim instead is to gain insights into

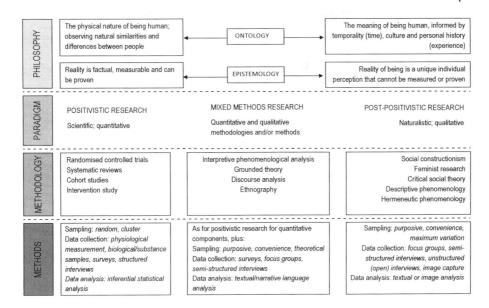

Figure 4.1 The relationship between philosophy, methodology and methods

Note: Methodologies and methods represented are not comprehensive; other options are also available

understanding the meaning of that experience for those people taking part, and to encourage readers to engage with and think about this meaning: 'Our quest is therefore not to prove or disprove, not to provide irrefutable evidence but rather to provoke thinking towards the mystery of what "is"' (Smythe et al., 2008: 1391).

The purpose of hermeneutic research is thus inextricably linked with the philosophy of interpretive phenomenology, and the complex experience of 'being human' in a particular time and place. From these insights, new knowledge may be transferred to other similar or relevant populations but the judgement of the transferability of findings is made by the reader who, invited to thinking, is drawn to the connections between the research findings and their own professional and personal world. Sample size therefore needs to be adequate to provide sufficient data for phenomenologists to work with to 'address' and provide 'an' answer to the research question. There is no such thing as *the* answer in hermeneutic phenomenological research, because, although there may be similarities between experiences, each person's experience and perspective are unique to them.

Sample size becomes a matter of balancing the overall purpose of the research, with the available population from whom the sample can be drawn, and the willingness of members of that population to engage with the research; as a consequence, sample size can vary considerably.

Exemplar Case

In a study on end-of-life care (Duffy and Courtney, 2014), 22 family members participated, while Duffy and Sheridan's (2012) study on the experiences of sexual orientation in the Irish police force had 19 participants. A study on lesbian experiences of health care had seven lesbian nurses and 12 lesbian service users who participated (Duffy, 2008). The sample sizes were reflective of the availability of the relevant populations and their willingness to 'speak out'. In contrast, a current study (Duffy et al., forthcoming), investigating the phenomenon of under 65s living in nursing homes from the perspective of residents (10 participants), families (five participants) and health care professionals (10 participants) had a total of 25 participants. A much larger study (Dibley, Norton and Whitehead, 2018) had 40 participants across four different subsets, because of the intention to explore any differences and similarities in meaning across the experiences of people with IBD who either did or did not experience bowel incontinence, and did or did not feel stigmatised.

Flexibility in the sampling phase, including a willingness to adjust the sample size up or down according to the needs of the study, is always required. All the above are examples of cross-sectional studies – a defined group of participants, all interviewed on one occasion, and their data analysed along with that of other participants. A cross-sectional study is any which collects data at a single point in time. It is a common term in positivistic studies, for example when the intention is to measure responses to a certain factor, or intervention amongst members of the cohort, and demonstrate relationships between different results, and perhaps across different cohorts. A cohort simply means 'a group of people'. In hermeneutic phenomenology, a cohort is the group of participants from whom data is collected.

Study design

Decisions about sample size are also affected by other options for study design; deciding that your study will be hermeneutic is just the start. You also have to decide on the design (or methodology) and the methods for delivering it. Your study might, for example, be cross-sectional, as above, or longitudinal. Or it might be a hermeneutic phenomenological case study with only one participant. Creswell (2007: 244) defines a case study as: 'having boundaries, often … of time and place. It also has interrelated parts that form a whole. It might be an event, a process, a programme or several people.'

By Creswell's definition, a case study involves exploration of an event such as a festival, or a location such as a school or hospital, with detailed explanation of all the 'interrelated parts' that make up that case. Starman (2013: 31) offers a thorough exploration of issues relating to case studies, including the perspective that a case study is 'a comprehensive description of an individual case and its analysis'. This latter definition resonates with education, social science, medicine and health care researchers. For example, Breatnach, Nolke and McMahon (2019) present a medical case study of a very rare combination of two known congenital heart defects in one infant. This focus on the individual is the approach we would recommend for the hermeneutic phenomenological researcher wishing to conduct a case study. Examples include Boden and Eatough's (2014) psychology study exploring one person's experiences of guilt, Hyde's (2010) religious studies' exploration of Godly play, and Roth, Masciotra and Boyd's (1999) education study of a teacher 'becoming' in the classroom.

Another option is to conduct a longitudinal study. This is likely to have fewer participants, because in contrast to the traditional hermeneutic phenomenological approach where each participant is interviewed once, those involved in a longitudinal study are interviewed several times over a defined period. For instance, a researcher might wish to understand the meaning of learning to live with a bodily adaptation, such as a prosthetic limb. They might then collect four interviews from each participant over the course of a year – the first immediately before surgery, and then three further interviews, one each at three, six and 12 months after surgery. The longitudinal approach is necessary to explore the meaning of adjusting to living with the prosthesis and coming to terms with the limb loss over time, since adjustment is a process; the single data-collection point in a cross-sectional study will not demonstrate process. From ten participants, the student will have a maximum of 40 interviews. Even if some participants are lost to follow-up, perhaps because they withdraw from the study, there will still be ample data. For a hermeneutic study, it would produce a lot of data – yet the decision to design it in this way would also be guided by the existing available evidence. The design would be particularly appropriate if there was no available qualitative evidence of the process of adjustment to a new prosthesis.

In contrast, a longitudinal study might have a much smaller sample size, depending on the availability of eligible and willing participants.

Exemplar Case

Gale's study (2020) on the experience of transition to parenting for couples with an IVF pregnancy which is genetically their own, included three couples who each participated in three interviews (before the birth, at six weeks and three months afterwards). The intended sample size was 10 couples, but, despite extensive efforts, the student struggled to locate these elusive participants. The potential limitation of only being able to recruit three couples, was mitigated by having nine interviews in total, amounting to 480 recorded minutes and 187 pages of transcribed data.

As we see later in this chapter (in the method of analysis section: p. 62), there is also a relationship between sample size and complexity of analysis. In the described study, the student conducted a longitudinal analysis across each couple's three interviews, and a cross-sectional analysis across each set of first, second and third interviews. This robust exploration reassures us that the data has been subjected to a thoroughly complex and detailed analysis.

Academic programmes of study

Another issue to consider is why the study is being undertaken. For example, in a taught Masters programme the dissertation may be approximately 12–15,000 words. Here, four to six participants may be considered appropriate as less depth is expected, since research is not the primary focus of the taught programme. In a Masters by research programme, the dissertation may be approximately 20,000 words, so 10–15 participants may be more appropriate. The purpose is to demonstrate a level of competence in research methods, so greater depth is expected. A qualitative PhD may require more participants and the thesis expected to be between 80,000 and 120,000 words in length. A professional doctorate is generally around 80,000 words. However, the final decision about sample size must be driven by the nature of the research, the design (case, cohort or longitudinal) and whether participants are easily accessible.

The relationship between rarity of topic and sample size

The size of the population with the experience of interest does have a bearing on sample size. Hermeneutic phenomenologists do not seek to demonstrate representativeness, since we are not trying to report 'sameness' as evidence of truth and no one person's experience can be 'counted' or 'measured' as being any more valuable than another's. However, there are always similarities and differences in data, so the larger the available population, the larger the sample size might be needed to reveal not just the similarities – what we would call *shared experiences*, but also the differences – the uniqueness of human experiences that add depth and dimension to our understanding of others' worlds. For example, a hermeneutic phenomenologist wanting to explore mothers' experience of caring for a pre-school child with brittle (difficult to control) asthma would need to take into account the available population which is likely to be several hundred thousand. They would have to be very precise then in terms of location and inclusion and exclusion criteria (see below) to narrow down to a more specific population and then sample from that reduced participant pool. In contrast, the hermeneutic phenomenologist wanting to explore the meaning of living with the rare congenital skin condition, harlequin ichthyosis, would have a total global population of about 10 cases to recruit from. In this case, a sample size of two, representing one fifth of that total population, would be appropriate.

The depth and completeness of data being collected

As a general rule, much larger sample sizes enable the collection of vast amounts of shallow data, whilst smaller sample sizes facilitate the collection of a great deal of richer, deeper data. Shallow data leads to descriptive or inferential statistics which tell us something positivistic and measurable about one or more variables. In contrast, richness and depth lead to at least a detailed description of a phenomenon, and in hermeneutic phenomenological research a complex interpretation that addresses the contextual nature of understanding and meaning of experience. Small sample sizes do not necessarily lead to less data than large sample sizes – but to a wealth of situated, experiential data from which insights, meaning and understanding may be discovered.

Alongside depth of data, the notion of completeness must also be addressed. As with the debate about insider status, qualitative methodologists have long deliberated ways of demonstrating that data collection has been thorough. While not used in hermeneutic phenomenological research, a commonly used term that has been adopted by other methodologies is the technique of *data saturation*. Introduced in Grounded Theory by Glaser and Strauss (1967), data saturation suggests that researchers keep collecting until they find nothing new. This is an issue to consider in understanding analysis, but it is also used when discussing recruitment. The key practical challenges with this are that it makes it impossible to determine either sample size or the duration of the study a priori – with obvious implications for proposal writing and funding bids. Although consideration of data saturation has been adopted widely in other methods, qualitative researchers must remain mindful of the philosophical and methodological principles underpinning their study (Saunders et al., 2018). For example, in exploratory qualitative research which has no specific philosophical framework but uses established qualitative research methods to make an initial exploration into an unresearched area (Stebbins, 2001), saturation might be appropriate to attempt to learn all there is to know about that issue. In hermeneutic phenomenological research, however, there is an appreciation that achieving data saturation is fundamentally impossible because:

- study participants may not have experienced everything relevant to the topic being researched
- they may choose not to reveal everything about their experience
- the researcher is not trying to provide a definitive 'this is what this experience is like for everyone' answer, but rather to point readers towards things of interest which, when combined with other available evidence, add up to a whole that is richer than its parts.

It might be more helpful for hermeneutic phenomenologists to consider alternative term(s) besides staturation such as completeness, comprehensiveness and philosophical consistency (Ironside, 2003). In conversation during the 2016 Hermeneutic Institute meeting, Ironside commented that in hermeneutic phenomenology, data saturation is impossible because 'there is always something new which lies beyond the reach of the study'. Recognising this, researchers may instead indicate that recurring patterns/themes observed in the data are sufficient to answer the research question at this time, thus the interpretation is warranted; they acknowledge that, whilst delivering a robustly designed and thorough study, they cannot guarantee to have captured everything. It is useful for researchers to ask themselves: *Have I collected enough data to satisfactorily answer the research question?*

The method of analysis being used

There must be philosophical and methodological fit between how data is collected and how it is analysed. Again, positivistic data is analysed statistically to demonstrate a truth. Larger sample sizes lead to greater statistical power, and greater confidence in the findings. In contrast, post-positivistic data is, essentially, analysed thematically. The range of options available to the hermeneutic phenomenological researcher is considered in detail in Chapter 7: Data Analysis, but the chosen method should reflect not only the specific phenomenology of, for example, Heidegger, Gadamer, van Manen or Ricouer, but also the researcher's skill level. For example, a postgraduate student new to phenomenology may select a generic thematic analysis approach which provides more guidance and structure, whilst a more experienced phenomenologist may adopt one of the bespoke guides which are much less formalised and tend to simply point towards what should be done. As a rough guide, the more advanced/interpretive the analysis method, the smaller the sample size needs to be.

Malterud, Siersma and Guassora (2016) provide a useful model reflecting the relationship between philosophy, methodology and method when determining sample size in any qualitative research (Figure 4.2). A broad aim, limited specificity amongst the sample, an absence of theory or philosophy, weak dialogue between researchers and participants and cross-case analysis are all features of positivistic (quantitative) research, which uses large sample sizes but produces information with less power.

A more focused aim, with a highly specific sample, applied theory, a strong dialogue between researchers and participants and a case approach to analysis are features of qualitative research, which uses smaller sample sizes but produces information with greater power: 'Considerations about study aim, sample specificity, theoretical background, quality of dialogue, and strategy for analysis should determine whether sufficient information power will be obtained with less or more participants included in the sample' (Malterud et al., 2016: 1756).

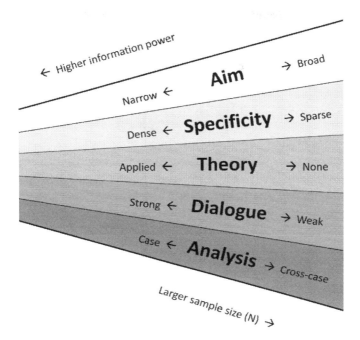

Figure 4.2 The relationship between information power and sample size in qualitative research

Source: Reproduced from Malterud, Siersma and Guassora (2016), with kind permission of the authors and publisher.

Explanatory Box 4.1

Alternative Definitions of 'Power'

It is important to appreciate the difference between the use of the word 'power' in quantitative and in qualitative research. In quantitative (positivistic) research, the term is used interchangeably with sample size calculations, and refers to the ability, having calculated the optimum sample size for the study, to demonstrate difference between participant groups. Jones, Carley and Harrison (2003: 455) explain that:

> The **power** of a **study**, $p\beta$, is the probability that the **study** will detect a predetermined difference in measurement between the two groups, if it truly exists, given a pre-set value of $p\alpha$ and a sample size, N.
>
> If the study has high power, then there is a very high probability that the sample size is sufficient to demonstrate difference between groups.

In qualitative (post-positivistic) research, the term is often used to address 'advantage' in the researcher–participant relationship. For example, Karnieli-Miller, Strier and Pessach (2009: 279) advise that 'Qualitative inquiry ... proposes to reduce power differences and encourages disclosure and authenticity between researchers and participants.' Addressing aspects like where and how data is collected, and who collects it, are necessary to manage the potential negative effect of such power differences. Malterud and colleagues (2016) remind us that 'power' also refers to the impactfulness of the findings. The power of the information arising from the richness of the narratives and from the depth of the dialogue that emerges during exploration of the phenomenon, may also be taken as a measure of quality during analysis.

In hermeneutic phenomenological research, the aim is always narrow (or focused) as the researcher explores the meaning of a very particular experience; specificity, which relates to experience with the phenomenon that is the study's focus, refers to the extent to which participants exhibit precise characteristics and thus belong to a certain target group, whilst still demonstrating some variation of experience. Where there are subsets within the sample – for instance, comparing the experience of becoming a first-time father across six countries in Europe (the different countries being the variation) – a larger sample size would be needed than when there are no subsets (less variation) – for instance, the experience of becoming a first-time father in Poland.

The methodology of hermeneutic phenomenological research is strongly rooted in the philosophy of interpretive (hermeneutic) phenomenology, and thus theory is ever-present and applied; language and the voice of the participant are central to the ways of doing hermeneutic research – the dialogue and communication between researcher and participants is intense and detailed, and analysis is on a case-by-case (transcript-by-transcript) basis in early rounds. These features suggest that in hermeneutic phenomenological research, smaller sample sizes which generate information with greater power (impact) are appropriate. Decisions around sample size should be focused on the narrower end of the model proposed by Malterud and colleagues (2016).

Inclusion and exclusion criteria

Inclusion and exclusion criteria enable researchers to refine participant selection to create a sample which is best able to provide the data that will answer the research question. In positivistic studies, the often very precise criteria are a means of controlling unwanted variables that might otherwise confound the results. In post-positivistic qualitative studies, criteria are likely to be less stringent and, again, dependent on design. By revisiting the inner-city knife crime study from Chapter 3, we can demonstrate what the inclusion and exclusion criteria might look like were the project either an observational study analysing existing data from police databases or a hermeneutic phenomenological exploration of the meaning of involvement in knife crime (Table 4.1).

Table 4.1   Inclusion and exclusion criteria for selecting the sample for two contrasting studies

POSITIVISTIC	POST-POSITIVISTIC
Observational study (retrospective data)	Hermeneutic phenomenology study (prospective data)
Aim: to determine characteristics of young people who get involved in inner-city knife crime	Aim: to explore the meaning young people give to involvement in inner-city knife crime
INCLUSION CRITERIA	INCLUSION CRITERIA
Aged 13–25	Aged 13–25
History of involvement in knife crime, evidenced by criminal conviction or caution	Self-reported history of involvement in knife crime, with or without criminal conviction or caution
Police record of criminal activity	Inner-city location (defined by official city boundary markers)
Inner-city location (defined by official city boundary markers)	
EXCLUSION CRITERIA	EXCLUSION CRITERIA
Involvement in any other form of criminal activity	Inability to give written or verbal (audio-recorded) consent

In Table 4.1, the precise criteria for the retrospective positivistic study would identify all young people on the national police database with a known history of knife crime activity within inner-city locations, but would exclude those also involved in other forms of criminal activity. The sample size has the potential to be large. The researchers would likely be able to build a demographic profile of those involved in knife crime, although it would only reflect the profile of those convicted. The profile may help the police understand who is more likely to be criminally active in this way and may therefore inform crime-prevention strategies. The profile would not illustrate any possible relationship between knife crime and other forms of felony.

The criteria for the prospective hermeneutic phenomenological study would lead to a recruitment of young people within the required age range who may or may not be known to the police, but who would be willing to talk about the 'why' of their involvement in knife crime, rather than the fact that they have been or are involved. The sample size would be small, as participants must self-select/volunteer. The researchers would be able to show forth insights into what it means for young people to be involved in knife crime and where or if this activity is influenced by broader criminal behaviour. The researchers would have a view into the *being-in-the-world* of the participants.

The relationship with Heidegger's philosophy – that '*Being*' (what it is to *be* human) can only be understood in the context of historical (rather than chronological) *Time* – becomes apparent when generating inclusion and exclusion criteria for a hermeneutic phenomenological study. Inclusion criteria are often few and broad to capture the context and *Dasein* of the participant – meeting the minimum age limit for the study, and having had the experience of interest, may be all that are needed. Exclusion criteria may also be minimal and likely to refer to incapacity to consent – or may be absent, to avoid isolating the participant from their *Dasein*. For example, in health research, a study focusing on one particular chronic illness would be unlikely to insist that participants had no other health conditions – since the experience of one illness is understood by participants in the context of any other illnesses they may also have, which adds meaning to the illness that is the focus of the study.

Chapter Summary

In this chapter, we have addressed the philosophical influences on sample size in hermeneutic phenomenology and considered the main factors which guide the selection of sample size. By drawing comparison with positivistic studies, the specific issues relevant to qualitative, and particularly hermeneutic phenomenological research, have been illustrated.

In Chapter 5: Being Ethical, we explore the complexity of ethics, the procedural requirement to secure ethical approvals prior to any data collection in any study involving humans, and the philosophical influences of being ethical as-researcher in a hermeneutic study.

Further Resources

These resources are recommended to help extend the reader's understanding of the influences on sample size that have been introduced in this chapter.

Core readings

- Lee, R. (1993) *Doing Research on Sensitive Topics*. London: Sage.
- Malterud, K., Siersma, V. D. and Guassora, A. D. (2016) 'Sample size in qualitative interview studies: Guided by information power', *Qualitative Health Research*, 26(13), 1753–1760. doi: 10.1177/1049732315617444.
- Saunders, B., Sim, J., Kingstone, T., Baker, S., Waterfield, J., Bartlam, B., Burroughs, H. and Jinks, C. (2018) 'Saturation in qualitative research: Exploring its conceptualization and operationalization', *Quality and Quantity*, 52(4), 1893–1907. doi: 10.1007/s11135-017-0574-8.

Further reading

- Stebbins, R. (2001) *Exploratory Research in the Social Sciences*. Thousand Oaks, CA: Sage.

5

Being Ethical

Chapter Overview

This chapter unpacks the ethical considerations of undertaking hermeneutic phenomenological research. In hermeneutic phenomenology, the aim is to gain insight into and reveal meaning of a given phenomenon, as understood through the account of the experiencing person. To gain this insight, it is necessary to have human participants or a text representing human experience in the world. Once we consider engaging with human participants and participants engage with our studies, there is a requirement to do so ethically. An ethical study is one that encompasses the principles set out in local, national and global policies for human subject research. Local-level ethical principles can be those that reflect, for example, specific University, hospital ethics boards and funders requirements. The UK, USA and Ireland all have national policies which outline the rules and regulations for conducting human research. Globally, human research is governed by core principles of beneficence and non-maleficence which underpin international research codes and policies.

Philosophical Underpinnings

In *Being and Time* (1962: 54), Heidegger informs us that a 'phenomenon, the showing-itself-in-itself, signifies a distinctive way in which something can be encountered'. When we investigate a lived experience, we are seeking participants who have experiences of the phenomenon to show or unfold the distinctive way they have experienced that phenomenon. Heidegger (2001: 217) further claims that 'verbal articulation [Verlautbarung] is given by the fact that existing is bodily existing'. That is, the human experience is a fully embodied and personal happening that individuals can relate to. Through interviewing, researchers are being-present to the story as it is being-articulated by the participant. Further, 'to stand under the claim of presence is the greatest claim made upon the human being. It is "ethics"' (Heidegger, 2001: 217). Within a phenomenological framework, the researcher is being-there. We are open to the Other's story; we are present to the openness of the Other in their story telling. By being with and being open to the story of the participant, we practise from an ethical standpoint by valuing and respecting the experience being shared with us. Gadamer (1975: 314) articulates that human sciences are 'moral sciences' as 'their object is a man and what he knows of himself'.

Being an Ethical Researcher

The *Concise Oxford Dictionary* (Fowler, Fowler and Thompson, 1995: 463) offers two definitions of ethics: (1) 'the science of morals in human conduct' and (2) 'moral principles or rules of conduct'. Every study requires ethical consideration and approval from an ethics committee or Institutional Review Board in the university or organisation (such as the NHS in the UK) in which the study is taking place. Members of the European Union have an obligation to consider the *Ethics in Social Science and Humanities* document (European Commission, 2018) which points to two dimensions of research ethics: 'procedural ethics', pertaining to the aspects of compliance in performing research, and 'ethics in practice', the everyday ethical issues that arise while doing research' (European Commission, 2018: 3).

Procedural ethics begin with questions such as: *why do this study, this way and at this time*? We must ponder on the ethical implications of the research objectives of all projects. *Do the objectives raise ethical issues? How are we going to deal with them?*

From a scientific point of view, every research proposal must address the question of why the planned research needs to be conducted, whether there is any new knowledge to be gained, and whether it is worth spending the time and money to obtain it. Justifying the conduct of any proposed research project means demonstrating that it will offer benefits to scientific understanding, to policy and/or to practice or to social actors in general, thus making the resources spent on research worthwhile (European Commission, 2018: 4).

There is an onus on us as researchers to answer these questions and to seriously consider why we are undertaking this study. Once we are engaging with human participants, we move beyond the idea that this is just an academic exercise to obtain a parchment, qualification or publication. Research, then, must have a purpose: to create new knowledge – such as shedding light on hitherto unknown marginalised groups, or understanding the impact of a specific social or health experience on individuals, and/or contribute to the social good.

The principles of ethical considerations when dealing with human participants are grounded in fundamental human rights. These are:

> articulated in the Charter of Fundamental Rights of the European Union and the European Convention on Human Rights (ECHR) and its Protocols. Other important sources are the UN Declaration of Human Rights and the UN Convention on the Rights of Persons with Disabilities (UN CRPD). Additional central policies and widely accepted declarations that codify principles of research ethics and ethical treatment of research participants include the Nuremberg Code, the Helsinki Declaration, and the Belmont Report. (European Commission, 2018: 5)

History teaches us some salient lessons of what can happen if research is unethical. The Nuremburg Code, formulated in 1947, is considered the most important document for ethical research in medicine (Shuster, 1997). The code has its roots in the trials of Nazi doctors who had conducted unimaginable acts of torture, experimentation and murder on inmates in concentration camps in the name of scientific experimentation and knowledge-seeking. One should remember that these acts were conducted simply because they could be carried out without impunity. The Code underlines today's principles of ethical behaviour towards, and the rights of, participants. While the Nuremburg Code emanated from the trials of Nazi doctors, it applies to all fields or disciplines that undertake research with human subjects. The core components are:

- respecting human dignity and integrity
- ensuring honesty and transparency towards research subjects
- respecting individual autonomy and obtaining free and informed consent (as well as assent, whenever relevant)
- protecting vulnerable individuals
- ensuring privacy and confidentiality
- promoting justice and inclusiveness
- minimising harm and maximising benefit
- sharing the benefits with disadvantaged populations, especially if the research is being carried out in developing countries
- respecting and protecting the environment and future generations.

The Nuremburg Code was a response to the atrocities uncovered in the Nazi concentration camps, where medical experimentation did not consider the individuals who were subjected to medical 'experiments' as human beings. Shuster (1997: 1439) informs us that the Nuremburg Code has not been implemented in law in its entirety though it has had enormous and profound influence 'on global human-rights law and medical ethics'. However, 'its basic requirement of informed consent, for example, has been universally accepted'. For us as researchers, our code of conduct encompasses all of the Nuremburg Code in various ways from beginning to end of the project.

In 1964, the Helsinki Declaration was developed by the World Medical Association (WMA) for the medical community as a set of ethical principles regarding human experimentation. It has been regularly updated, most recently in 2013. Another key document is the 1976 Belmont Report, developed by the US National Commission for the Protection of Human Subjects of Biomedical and Behavioral Research. It is considered one of the leading works concerning ethics and health care research, particularly regarding the protection of human beings who participate in clinical trials or research studies.

Explanatory Box 5.1

Ethical Requirements in Universities

When you are undertaking doctoral studies, there are systemic requirements. All universities and institutions have their own ethics forms. Each section gives guidelines for what is expected and some forms have word counts. It is essential that you utilise the word allocation. Equally, a good ethics form is the backbone of your study as it enables you to think through the process of carrying out a study. The ethics form invites you to think through each step and how you intend to conduct yourself. Most students find these difficult as they require the skill of writing in a different format. Doctoral studies have a particular academic style of writing. An ethics form is required to be written in a format that is accessible to those not initiated in your discipline. A good way of tackling it is to try to write it as if you were explaining it to a friend of yours who is not of your discipline.

Ethical Considerations Throughout a Hermeneutic Study

The ethics of research competency

Researcher competency requires consideration from an ethical perspective. Competency not only reflects the ability to interview but is a requirement from the beginning of the study. A doctoral process takes a novice researcher on a journey to become an expert and a post-doctoral project consolidates that process. However, it can and should be argued that, as students of hermeneutic phenomenology, we are never the 'expert' but always becoming.

It is a requirement to be ethical when we undertake a literature review, making sure that we have exhausted material around the subject of the phenomenon. There is no room for short cuts, and when a dissertation is presented much may – to borrow a phrase from the film industry – be left on the cutting-room floor. This is knowledge that shapes our understanding and thinking about a topic and enables us to think about the data as they emerge. Being steeped in the literature of investigations enables us to move towards a way of undertaking phenomena. Equally, it is important that we read Heidegger and sit with him to gain an understanding of what is being thought about. It is important to recognise that being ethical within the hermeneutic circle begins at the moment we consider writing a research proposal.

Thus, we are *always-already* in places of meaning and interpretation when we engage in a hermeneutic project. We interpret, which is to engage with text (as a conversation, a written exegesis, a gathering of information), in ways that may reduce or sacrifice the integrity of phenomena as a whole. Our interpretations may be good conveyors of meaning or they may be 'off' in a way that hampers meaning. Hermeneutics can be a risky business. Our ethical comportment as researchers is a foundational characteristic.

The ethics of who we are as-researcher

Another aspect of being ethical is being aware of 'our skin in the game'; in other words, knowing who we are as-researcher – professionally, socially and privately. Do we have a conflict of interest which needs to be owned and reported to the supervisors of a doctoral student and an ethics committee? This applies whether we are a novice or a proficient researcher. Conflict of interest does not necessarily mean that we do not undertake the study; rather, it may mean that we resolve the issue and acknowledge this openly in our study. Assessing our pre-understandings prior to project design and implementation is a way of preparing, minimising unconscious biases and refining our attention to the thinking we seek to engage.

Connelly (2014) draws our attention to the roles we hold in society, both professionally and personally. On a professional front, we are required to acknowledge our position and why we are undertaking research that could be construed as a conflict of interest, which might possibly lead to unintended coercion. For example, if you are a nurse, an occupational therapist or a doctor working in the area of oncology, it may not be ethical for you to ask the patients you care for to participate in your study. Patients may feel under an obligation and not want to offend or, worse, may think their treatment will be compromised if they do not participate. Similarly, students who are invited by their teacher to participate in their research may fear detrimental effects on their grades if they do not take part. Under no circumstances should participants feel that they have no choice about taking part, or wonder what the consequences might be if they did not. This is why it is important that a potential participant freely chooses to take part and has the option to withdraw, even after making that choice.

Exemplar Case

When data was being gathered for a study of the experience of being lesbian, gay or bisexual in the Garda Síochána (the Irish police force) project, some participants elected to withdraw a couple of days prior to the publishing of the report (Duffy and Sheridan, 2012). All elements that represented these participants, including quotes and references of their experiences, had to be removed. It meant reworking sections to ensure the ethical right of participants to withdraw at any time, without explanation or consequence, was respected. This is the nature of ethical research whereby participants are protected at all times.

Researchers need to answer the question, '*What do I get from delivering this study?*' That is, what will they gain personally or professionally, and at whose expense? Giorgi's (2005: 77) assertion sheds light on this involvement in the research process: for both the participant and the researcher, the project can lead to a discovery of 'difference leading to more authentic living and interaction with others and thus a better life'. We do have something to gain and it can be rewarding for both researcher and participant. Researchers gain from the enhancement of their research profile and reputation, achieved through publications and other disseminations of their work, while the effects of having opened up and talked about the lived experience may be quite beneficial to participants, even if such benefits, not immediately available, surface later. There is a potential for risk to participants, but also for benefits to researcher and participant alike.

Insider versus outsider research

When undertaking research, a decision has to be made as to how involved to be in the lives of participants. That is, how close to the phenomenon of interest should a researcher be? Insider research indicates your 'skin in the game', whilst, in outsider research, potential participants are not informed if you have any relationship with the topic at hand, or there is no relationship. Byrne explains that being the insider challenges the traditional construct of the research relationship which is presented as 'an objective, expert researcher [with] little in common with research participants and that this is desirable for the production of value-free, neutral, scientific research' (2000: 143). She goes on to identify the potential pitfalls: being an insider 'challenges the supposed objectivity of the researcher and the emphasis on maintaining distance from research subjects' (2000: 145).

Of course, in hermeneutic phenomenological research, perhaps more so than in any other form of qualitative enquiry, subjectivity is the point: the recognition that, as researchers, we are no more isolated and separate from the world we live in, than our participants are. That subjectivity has to be managed, of course, but being 'inside' and connected in some way to the phenomenon of interest, can bring huge benefits in terms of the ability to uncover meaning. Being an insider researcher can allow participants who belong, for example, to a marginalised group, to speak freely, without fear of judgement, or preconceived ideas being made about their experiences, but this is not without potential difficulties for both researcher and participants.

Exemplar Case

When she studied for her PhD on lesbian health care, Duffy (2008) undertook overt (insider) research by stating that she was a lesbian researcher in the advertisement, signalling in this way her insider status to all potential participants. Platzer and James (1997: 627) suggest that researchers who acknowledge their insider status may face the 'threat of stigma contagion ... particularly when taboo subjects are explored which relate to sexuality'. A researcher may experience similar stigma from the group that they are studying. Platzer and James both experienced stigma before, during and after their 1990s research into lesbians' and gay men's experience of health care. It can be argued that the rights of the lesbian, gay, bisexual, transgender, queer and intersex (LGBTQI+) community have progressed significantly since the 1990s, and likely removed, or at least reduced, the possibility of researchers being stigmatised through researching issues relating to themselves. Yet, at the same time, recent repealing of hard-won rights – for example, in the USA – indicates that the positioning of the LGBTQI+ community is not equal to that of their heterosexual sisters and brothers. This socio-political position can constantly be revisited and is given and taken at political will, such that the landscape for insider research with these communities is constantly changing. Insider research is a moral dilemma for any researcher who relies on building trust with participants and enhancing the integrity of the project.

Oakley (2005) and Reinharz (1992) suggest that feminists claim that if a woman's life is to be understood, 'it may be necessary for her to be interviewed by a woman' (Reinharz, 1992: 23). Reinharz (1992: 24) further states: 'A woman listening with care and caution enables another woman to develop ideas, construct meaning, and use words that say what she means.'

At the time, Duffy (2008) argued that, for lesbian women to be understood in a research project, it may be necessary for a lesbian woman to undertake the interviews. This does not negate the fact that other researchers, who are not lesbian, can interview but rather that they may not be privy to the types of revelation(s) that are made available and safely disclosed to an insider researcher. Participants must feel that they can trust that they will not be judged (Claassen, 2005; Clunis, Garner, Freeman, Nystrom and Fredriksen-Goldsen, 2005), or that the researcher will not bring preconceived ideas about their situation to the interview (Reinharz, 1992; McDermott, 2004; Weston, 2004). For instance, Higgins and Glackin (personal communication) found it difficult to obtain a sample in their research on Irish lesbian, gay and bisexual experiences of bereavement. Even though they had advertised in *Gay Community News* for participants, there was little take-up. They were informed by contacts in the gay and lesbian community that the marginalised group they wished to study did not trust that two 'straight' women would be sensitive enough to their experiences. At the time of writing, in 2020, five years after the introduction of marriage equality in Ireland through a constitutional referendum, one might speculate that perceptions amongst the LGBTQI+ community of 'straight' women conducting research on bereavement may have shifted, and this specific community may have since experienced less marginalisation or vulnerability. But the question remains open for consideration: when we investigate the lived experience of specific groups, do we need to be a member of, or connected to, that group to understand the nuances?

Recruiting participants

To undertake any study, a population has to be identified that we expect will enable us to answer the research question (see also Chapter 4: Population and Sampling), but the identification, recruitment and selection of that population must be carried out ethically. The following example demonstrates what we mean.

Duffy, Corby, Corcoran, Clinton and Pierce (forthcoming) undertook an investigation on the lived experience of people under 65 years old living in nursing homes (residential care) in Ireland. They were interested in three cohorts: (1) a cohort of young people with disabilities; (2) their family members; and (3) staff nurses who had experience of caring for people under 65. The phenomenon was to be examined from the following perspectives:

- the understanding young people constructed of their experience of living in nursing homes
- the understanding families constructed of their experience of having a relative living in a nursing home
- the understanding staff nurses constructed of their experience of working with and caring for a young disabled person in a nursing home.

Further, from a Gadamerian point of view, the team was interested in how individuals came to know themselves within the situation they now found themselves in.

Duffy and her colleagues required a sample of individuals who fitted all three categories, but would enable them to find meaning in, and understanding of, the experiences of the members of these three cohorts. Greenfield and Jensen (2010) suggest that what they were seeking would lead to an 'everyday ethic' of how a person aged under 65 lives in a nursing home, and how their family members and their nursing care staff members understand this from their own point of view. Recruiting for this study presented certain ethical challenges, as Duffy explains in the exemplar case on p. 76.

Exemplar Case

To obtain a population reflecting the phenomenon we were investigating, we had to ensure our recruitment strategy was ethical. Each person who participated, regardless of what category they belonged to, needed to self-elect into the study and not feel they were being coerced in any way to participate. People must freely choose and want to tell their story. Initially, the design was to approach nursing homes and invite them to serve as research sites in order to gain access to our research population/sample. We chose this method as we wanted to be ethical, honest and open about the research. The research team consensus was based on the need to be sensitive to the concerns of nursing homes. The image of nursing homes had suffered from the negative press resulting from investigative journalism; shown on national television, it unearthed practices that did not centre on the care needs of residents, leading to mistrust emerging between the public and the nursing home sector. One of the unintended consequences of this was the politicising of nursing homes, resulting in Dáil (House of Parliament) time being devoted to debates about TV programming. As researchers, we had an ethical responsibility to all participants and gatekeepers in our study, particularly in terms of gaining access to nursing homes.

The majority of people aged under 65 in this study had some form of disability which negated their ability to live at home. Traditionally, nursing homes may be considered places where care is provided for older members of a population (65+) who require assistance in their daily living, perhaps also being on an Alzheimer's or other form of dementia journey. It is also a place where people receive end-of-life care. When the norms of expectations are disrupted, the lived experience is transformed.

The participants in this study were not at the end of their life, rather no other suitable residential option was available to them where care could be provided. For the majority of participants, their lives had been disrupted through illness whereby their dreams and aspirations were curtailed. Participants under 65 years old had never envisaged their lives as disabled people, being cared for in nursing homes. Equally, family members had to negotiate their limitations in being able to provide care and revaluate the understanding and meaning they gave to the lives of their loved ones. Staff nurses had to re-imagine and re-interpret what residential care meant. Careful and ethical recruitment enabled the team to reveal meaning in these disruptions.

An enthusiasm for doing research must not override the requirement to conduct ourselves, and our research, ethically. Providing accurate, clear information, written in accessible terms about what the study is for, who is doing the research, what each participant will be asked to do if they take part, how they can withdraw from the study, where they can get more information, and who they should contact if they have any questions or concerns, is a core component of any research study information sheet. These details are embedded in ethical principles and are the main tools that the researcher uses to invite people to participate. Whether they choose to or not is entirely up to them.

We need to be aware of all factors influencing those who choose to participate and those who do not, because these are important realities of the overall research story that may serve as nuanced findings in their own right.

Gatekeeping

Finding your participants requires careful consideration. In the example above, it took two years for Duffy and her colleagues to access participants. However, if you are undertaking a professional doctorate or PhD, you may not have two years to work on gaining access. An obstacle may be gatekeepers who repeatedly/simply refuse access. There may be other gatekeepers who will vouch for you but organisations may feel threatened or fear judgements. We may never know why people refuse us access but we have to accept their response without question. To be ethical is to accept that others have reasons which are not ours to know. If we are seeking access to areas that might have current or historical issues that are problematic, it is advised we have an understanding of that history and/or current socio-political landscape, which may enable us to navigate our access.

Participant recruitment requires consideration. We need a sample that will facilitate answering the research question. In other words, we need a cohort of folk who identify as having the lived experience of the phenomenon under investigation. There are many avenues that can be explored in recruiting participants. Depending on your phenomenon, and the overall population size that has the experience, a letter to the editor of a local, regional or national newspaper about the study may elicit a response. This can be a good way of finding hidden populations, for example if you are seeking to uncover the care needs of older lesbian, gay, bisexual, transgender and intersex (LGBTQI) people. We take it for granted that LGBTQI+ folk are 'out' today but we need to be cognisant of older LGBTQI+ people and how they may have lived the majority of their lives in silence, shame and secrecy. They may not feel 'safe' informing caregivers about who they are, but an advertisement displayed in a local health care centre may prompt a person's interest and then their later participation. Being interested in the lives of people who were never considered 'worthy' by society, can lead to an uncovering of the richness of living and nuanced, diverse life paths. Advertising for hidden populations avoids the researcher making an unethical approach and places the decision to participate firmly in the hands of the individual, who makes the move to respond to the advert. Wherever possible, the potential participant should be able to make the decision to opt in, rather than have to ask to opt out.

Social media provides another opportunity for recruitment. Again, it depends on what your research is but if you are interested in a phenomenon such as how young men cope with testicular cancer, using open chat rooms for recruitment can be a good place to start. Indeed, there may be much information there that could be used by the researcher as long as they obtain ethical approval to use what is publicly available. Most sites have an administrator and it will be necessary to ask permission to put a post on their site seeking participants. Seeking permission from oncology units/centres to place advertisements can also elicit a response. Building relationships with the staff in oncology units/centres may also give you credibility as a researcher, but you must always be careful/mindful to maintain the separation of estates – the researcher and the units/centres. The research must remain independent of the clinic/staff nurse, and potential participants must be informed that the research is not in any way part of their clinical treatment.

Another issue of significance is the age of the young men. Consideration has to be given to the age at which we require the consent of a parent and the assent of young men to participate. This will vary in accordance with where you reside and where the research is being conducted. For example, in the UK, the principle of Gillick competency holds that any child under the legally agreed age of consent (16 years) may give consent for their medical treatment without parental consent or knowledge, if they demonstrate an appropriate level of understanding about the risks, benefits and possible consequences of that treatment. We must take heed of the child protection laws and policies of our own country and indeed of other countries if the research is regional (e.g. across the EU) and will be conducted across multiple jurisdictions. In the USA and the UK, we must submit our recruitment materials and protocol for approval prior to the study. It is helpful to make some aspects more general (e.g, ages, time frame for data collection) so that you don't have to go back for an amendment of the protocol. We will come back to this when we unravel the issues of consent.

If your interest is in how older men talk to each other and how they experience friendship, then the 'Shed' movement (menssheds.ie) may be your source of entry. Aristotle was the first philosopher to write about friendship and the shared life and still, within today's world, friendships are considered one of the great props of wellbeing. If we review the development of society, we see historically how the family was considered the cornerstone of society. As we developed and progressed, friendship became more important and friendships are now considered necessary for our health and wellbeing. As Cooper (1977: 619) informs us:

> Whatever else friendship is, it is, at least typically, a personal relationship freely, even spontaneously, entered into, and ethics, as modern theorists tend to

conceive it, deals rather with the ways in which people are required to regard, and behave toward, one another, than with the organisation of their private affairs.

Hermeneutic phenomenological research uncovers the stories of everyday living such as friendships. In many ways, friendship is the taken-for-grantedness of everyday living until we unravel how social isolation and being lonely can be mitigated through friendship. You may have to decide what category of older men you are seeking, urban or rural, professional or non-professional, blue-collared or white-collared worker, artists, writers, to name but a few.

How you engage with recruiting will be dependent on your research question and, thus, where you are most likely to 'find' potential participants. Consider what may be the most appropriate way to recruit rural participants. For example, if an agricultural event is taking place, having a stand at that event to advertise the study may capture the interest of our potential sample in a meaningful way, or serve to present the study to those who might never have previously considered that they have a story to tell in the first place. We may not simply be able to 'rock up' and pitch our tent, and commence distributing material about our study, but may need permission to do so.

Exemplar Case

Whilst planning a UK study to understand the long-term experiences of having or not having spinal fusion surgery for idiopathic scoliosis, the decision to recruit from social media platforms was driven by the likely location of potential participants. Once scoliosis has been diagnosed, surgery has been offered and accepted or refused by the individual, or has not been offered by the surgeon, treatment may be considered 'complete'. These individuals are not going to be found on hospital clinic lists, and trying to identify possible participants via primary care services (a community doctor/nurse) would be resource-heavy, time-consuming and expensive. However, there is a very active social media site, visited by people who have and have not had surgery, where insights into their lives with scoliosis are openly discussed in the public domain. A request to the site administrator to recruit from the members of the site was met with approval; the study could be advertised on the site, inviting those interested in taking part to contact the research team using the details provided in the advert.

Gatekeeping comes in many forms and being aware of who sanctions our presence, and who literally 'opens the gate' for us, can be half the battle. Equally, for a student, a letter from our university or supervisor vouching for us might enable others to assist us. While the word 'gatekeeper' almost predisposes us to think that they act to keep us out, or give us access grudgingly, we do not wish this to be the take-home message. For most of us, our projects would never happen without the support and active collaboration of gatekeepers.

Gatekeepers can be crucial for another ethical reason and that is that, essentially, they may become part of the study by providing follow-up support. In conversation with a colleague, we reflected on her PhD study which was on the experience of men who engaged in suicidal behaviour. The site for the study was a hospital and, after each interview, she would inform the nursing staff if a man had become upset; they would willingly go to that patient to follow up with his care. The gatekeepers who enabled access also became part of the support strategy for vulnerable participants. This example indicates how, as researchers, we operationalise many complex, multidisciplinary structures to ensure ethical practice and to safeguard our participants' wellbeing, especially in an institutionalised setting like a hospital or a nursing home. It also reminds us of the burden of participation for the research site and its employees/gatekeepers. We essentially make work for them, but their commitment to their patients means they are willing to assume that burden in the interests of learning and understanding and providing more nuanced and meaningful care.

Gatekeepers' trust in us, as people and researchers, is critical from the outset because it passes on from them to the participant. It is the first step towards creating 'safety' in the research space for the participant when one of their caregivers is willing to vouch personally for us as people/researchers, and for the research study. Ultimately, their 'knowing' of their patient and their willingness to share that with us has massive implications for study recruitment, and further validates and supports our ethical research practice. My colleague recalls talking to nurses who would tell her when someone was admitted because of suicidal behaviour, but explain that the person was not quite ready, or perhaps still too distressed, to be told about the study. The nurses would, however, 'keep an eye on him' and get back to her when he was 'better'. My colleague summed up the nursing staff with the words, 'they were amazing'.

Another gatekeeper might be a community leader such as the chief of an indigenous population. Such studies require the permission of clan leaders and negotiations involve understanding the purpose of the study to support the wellbeing of the clan.

Respecting participants' space

Prior to an interview, there may be lively debate engaged on individual bases with potential participants for a study, which may address experiences ancillary to the phenomenon, such as social, legal or political issues. Participating in these debates can lead to easier communication (Oakley, 2005), an appreciation of understanding participants' lives, your credibility as a researcher, and in some cases membership of the community being investigated. McDermott (2004: 177) notes in relation to LGBTQI+ people that 'studies have reported the willingness and eagerness with which participants tell their stories to lesbian and gay researchers', which is not necessarily repeated with other researchers. Consequently, in my role as insider researcher on a study of lesbian women's experience of health care, I (Duffy) was able to facilitate generating and gathering rich data, as well as have unprecedented access to the lives of my participants.

Lee (1993) argues that research on sensitive topics could place threats on the integrity of the individual who participates, or on the researcher. In the data-gathering process, I (Duffy) learned that some lesbian women in Ireland live in constant fear of being 'discovered'. Lesbian women use well-practised 'everyday skilful coping' (Draucker, 1999: 361) in their daily lives; however, the constant anxiety of being exposed is a daily reality for some. They develop well-tested mechanisms of survival, which can be threatened if they feel they will be exposed or revealed (Wojciechowski, 1998).

In some cases, concerns can be so over-powering that it can inhibit people from participation, even when they make initial contact and want to tell their stories. In conversations I (Duffy) had with lesbian women prior to recording their experiences, such concerns were expressed. Some participants spoke about living in the area in which they currently reside, and how they protect their sexual identity by not displaying signs such as the rainbow flag or pink triangle, or overtly alerting their neighbours. Claassen (2005: 20) illustrates this point when she writes that

> lesbian women have built numerous barriers and safeguards around themselves. They know exactly what dangers and pleasures their life story and current lifestyle can bring to them.

I (Duffy) was aware that, by inviting me to their homes, lesbian women were exposing their status and leaving themselves vulnerable, because I knew then where they lived. However, this also points to the level of trust they were willing to place in me, as I would/could not reveal their identity or place of residence. Dibley and colleagues (2014) encountered the same issues amongst participants of a study exploring gay and lesbian people's experience of inflammatory bowel disease. Being aware of one's population is very important; being sensitive to the concerns of others and listening to their fears, needs and desires for their own personal safety emanates from an ethical standpoint. Another example is the study of women leaving abusive partners (McDonald and Dickerson, 2013) who were able to choose the location of their interview. In this study, none of the women had the interview in their home because they perceived their home was an unsafe place, where they would not be able to open up to the researcher. The interviews took place instead in libraries, coffee shops or other, more public places.

Concerns about trust and confidentiality can act as barriers to participation in a study. Issues of trust are not directly related to you as a person but rather to where 'the information might end up' and/or fear about potential exposure. You can reassure participants about your starting point or your ethical consideration, but participants may feel unable to continue out of fear that the material could not be disguised enough to protect their identity. The issue of trust focuses on two important factors – why, and for whom, the research is being undertaken: 'As qualitative social researchers reflexively exploring everyday lives, we must continually confront questions of the nature and assumptions of the knowledge we are producing, and who we are producing it for' (Edwards and Ribbens, 1998: 4).

Edwards and Ribbens (1998) argue against qualitative researchers having to justify their research. However, this argument does raise the issue, for whom do we do research? In other words, why did I or you choose this particular topic and methodology, and how did we expect to contribute to knowledge in meaningful, respectful and ethical ways? We read earlier (in Chapter 3: Literature Review and Refining the Hermeneutic Question) about the origins of research questions and why we as-researchers ask the questions we do. Participants may be less interested in *why* we are asking, and more interested *that* we are asking, but the salient question, 'where does the information end up?', is most important for some participants. Will their voices be lost in the transcribing of their interviews? Or will the material be so insufficiently disguised that their safety will be jeopardised?

Anonymity and confidentiality

The need to protect our participants' identities is always a consideration in human subject research. Often, we cannot guarantee anonymity (particularly when interviews are involved – the participant cannot be anonymous to the interviewer), but we can do our best to protect confidentiality. We identify our participants by pseudonyms (chosen for them or self-chosen) and we take identifying features out of transcripts and publications, but there are always risks of a breach. Sometimes, storied accounts contain context that is identifying – 'I opened the red door of the clinic', and sometimes the story is bound in an identifying racial designation. For example, one of Vandermause and Wood's (2009) participants told a story of discrimination: as the only Native American in the local population sampled, her important story could not be included if they wanted to describe the cohort. The content of the accounts can be identifying and we must take great care to consider that possibility.

Exemplar Case

In a recent small qualitative pilot study to test the ground for a follow-up project, Younge, Sufi and Dibley (2020) explored the experiences of inflammatory bowel disease clinical nurse specialists (IBD-CNSs) who had recently attended a short series of cognitive behavioural therapy (CBT)-based clinical supervision sessions. The aim was to identify the potential of CBT-based clinical supervision as a regular mechanism for supporting staff wellbeing amongst a specialist nurse cohort that is facing high levels of burnout and attrition nationally. Conducted in one hospital, the sample size was four. There was no intention of the study team to reveal identities, but the national network of IBD-CNSs is such that guaranteeing that no other member of the network would be able to recognise participants from their qualitative contributions, even though all data were anonymised, would likely be impossible. The potential problem was put to participants at interview, and because the data was not particularly sensitive and the participants recognised the greater good that could result, all gave permission for the team to publish. A statement confirming their consent to do so was included in the published paper.

From an ethical perspective, this is absolutely fine. Participants, having been alerted to the risk, independently and without coercion, gave permission for their data to be published. Another way of negotiating similar situations is inviting participants to become co-authors on publications, which transforms the study into a co-production of the lived experience.

There are challenges to identification, however. In one study (Sameshima et al., 2009), the primary participant wanted to be identified (sometimes participants will say this prior to the interview) but, after the interpretations were shared, she thought again about what she did and did not want disclosed. In that case, the interpretation could be modified because she was involved in the dissemination, but participants may not have this opportunity. Our interview techniques are evocative and participants don't always anticipate what they will share. We recommend that participants choose a pseudonym, even if they originally feel open to identification, and that researchers use identifiers only after careful thought and discussion.

These examples may carry very little personal risk for participants, but the concerns are issues that every researcher who undertakes research on sensitive topics or marginalised groups confronts (Reinharz, 1992; Lee, 1993). The private and personal social world of participants is presented to an academic audience, thereby bringing into public gaze lives that have been hitherto hidden. Consequently, there are ethical considerations to be taken into account at every juncture of the research process:

Ethics is concerned with the suffering humans cause one another and the related capacity of humans to recognise and address this suffering through empathetic virtues of sympathy, compassion, and caring (Sorrell and Dinkins, 2006: 310).

Researchers are bound by ethics in the way we conduct ourselves while undertaking research, in much the same way that medical doctors are bound by the Hippocratic oath:

I swear by Apollo the Healer, by Asclepius, by Hygieia, by Panacea, and by all the gods and goddesses, making them my witnesses, that I will carry out, according to my ability and judgment, this oath and this indenture (Oxtoby, 2016: 35).

This is the original Hippocratic oath which is a pledge to the gods of healing, to uphold the contemporary medical standards written 2,500 years ago. Today, there are many forms of it and Oxtoby (2016) unpacks what this means for physicians. While there are many versions worldwide, there is still an underlying code of conduct which calls for physicians to be ethical or to have a moral compass. The author points out that the new oath requires physicians to 'respect secrets confided in me', although from another, equally robust, ethical standpoint, the sharing of confided secrets, in medicine and nursing at least, is warranted when the risk of keeping the secret (usually to a greater number of people/the public in general) is greater than the ethical 'right' to have that secret kept. Conducting ourselves ethically calls us to question any and all oaths that we may take.

Explanatory Box 5.2

Keeping of Secrets

It is not possible to facilitate all secrets as it may be inappropriate to do so. We (Duffy and colleagues, forthcoming) carried out a study on stakeholders' experience of the Relationships and Sexuality Education programme in Irish second-level schools. As part of our ethical considerations, we had to develop a child protection policy for those students who chose to participate as they were 12–18 years of age. Under Irish law, sexual abuse is a mandatory reportable offence if a child discloses it. Prior to undertaking the interview, each person, whether at the younger or older end of the age range, was informed that if any divulgence of sexual abuse occurred, the interview would have to stop and the facts reported. All participants, students, teachers, principals and parents/legal guardians agreed with this stance. We included the other stakeholders as there could have been a possibility that if any of them were abused as a child, their abuser may still be alive and perhaps still an active abuser.

Being vulnerable

When undertaking research, you always have to consider the phenomenon under investigation and what population is required to answer your research question, thus enabling the meanings and understandings of the lived experience to emerge. Sometimes, this requires recruiting participants from populations that might be considered 'vulnerable'. What does it mean to be vulnerable? How do I know if someone is vulnerable? Indeed, whose definition of vulnerability are we dealing with? One could argue that there is the potential for any human participant to be considered vulnerable, by some measure or another, at one time or another. Another consideration is whether the research question could be answered another way with a less vulnerable group. However, a real consequence of undertaking research with vulnerable groups is the possibility of stigmatisation, traumatisation or harm of any kind for the participant. These may be the unintended consequences of participating in research. What appears to emerge in the literature is that, no matter what the ethical considerations are with regard to participants, there is ambiguity in relation to what we mean by vulnerability, and who 'the vulnerable' are:

> On one hand, vulnerability refers to a universal shared frailty or susceptibility to harm, giving rise to the idea of universal protections for research participants. On the other hand, vulnerability picks out particular persons or groups who are susceptible to specific kinds of harm or threat. (Lange, Rogers and Dodds, 2013: 333–334)

The European Commission (2018) points out that a person may be considered vulnerable because of their position in society. The list of individuals that fall into this category is not exhaustive – rather a jumping-off point for consideration – but commonly includes:

- children
- refugees
- sex workers
- people with cognitive impairments
- dissidents
- traumatised people at risk of re-traumatisation (e.g. people from conflict areas, victims of crime and/or violence)
- people in dependent relationships with the researcher or the research team (e.g. students doing course work with researchers).

All universities, in their research support units and on their ethics forms, will have documentation that will assist you in deciding whether your particular population is vulnerable, such as:

- older people
- the physically or mentally ill
- people with learning difficulties
- people in care
- bereaved people
- prisoners
- pregnant women
- children

For example, all children are considered vulnerable and policies should be put in place to protect them. If you are undertaking a study on children's experience of a life-limiting condition, a protocol needs to be put in place to protect them but also to provide other, ancillary services should they be required, such as counselling. As an adult, how you feel about the topic may be quite different and you should be aware that there may be unintended outcomes for both the researcher and the child. You will need the consent of parents/legal guardians/foster parents, and children should have the ability to assent. What we have stated previously applies here in relation to consent, in that a participant may withdraw at any time and have aspects of their story removed.

Additionally, the issue of researcher vulnerability merits attention. While I may feel privileged, having been invited into a person's home to conduct an interview, am I confident that it is safe to do so? Is it a safe space and will it be a safe engagement for both participant and researcher? Interestingly, gatekeepers can be very valuable in this regard. The colleague mentioned earlier benefitted from her gatekeepers in this way. Once again, it was the gatekeepers' professional opinion and their knowledge of the person that prevented one particular patient from being recruited to a male suicidal behaviour study. The patient was disturbed and had recently engaged in physically violent behaviour towards a staff member. The gatekeeper's adherence to the ethical script meant that: (1) for his own wellbeing, the patient was not going to be approached about the study while he was considered vulnerable and while his behaviour was presenting as a risk to others; (2) the researcher was protected and kept out of harm's way; and (3) so too was the gatekeeper, whose professional assessment of this patient and his particular needs and risks at that time meant the assessment was undertaken with a significant degree of ethical rigour and prevented any unnecessary harm being caused to the patient, researcher and staff member(s).

Another strategy for addressing safe engagement between researcher and participant is the use of your organisation's lone-worker policy; this provides an assessment of the level of risk, standard reporting procedures to record the whereabouts of a roving researcher, and instructions on when and how to escalate should there be concerns.

Being an ethical hermeneutic researcher

When we set out on our journey to become researchers, we are called upon to be ethical. This too is a voyage as it is through becoming that we learn to be ethical. However, we cannot become ethical or moral human beings by sitting in our room contemplating life. Rather, we need interaction with others. Through opening up and sharing our lives with others, we open up the possibilities of becoming. We not only share our experiences, feelings, emotions, thoughts, loves and hates, but we also listen to others who share on a similar level. This allows us to grow and decide what or who we want to become. Basically, to become moral we need to reflect on and reimagine our norms, values and belief systems. We grow up learning the moral framework of our parents and, if we are lucky, our grandparents copper-fasten what we learn from our parents. As we become adults, we may keep some of this foundational framework, but go on to develop our own moral framework from which we engage with others.

A way of understanding this is for us to do a simple exercise: if you are a woman, draw up a page with your own norms, values and belief systems, then ask your grandmother and mother to participate by adding theirs. In a similar fashion, if you are a man, ask your grandfather and father and write your own. What you are seeking is three or perhaps four generations of norms, values and beliefs. In this way, you will see movement and how ethics or moral codes change over time. In many ways, nothing is cast in stone – rather, with knowledge, we reflect on and revaluate our understanding and meaning of the words.

The European Commission (2018: 3) states that researchers:

> should focus their research for the good of mankind and for expanding the frontiers of scientific knowledge, while enjoying the freedom of thought and expression, and the freedom to identify methods by which problems are solved, according to recognised ethical principles and practices.

This sits with the hermeneutic phenomenological way of undertaking research as we focus on the lived experiences of participants who are *being-in-the-world* with the phenomena we are investigating. This demands of us, as researchers, to be ethical beings and adhere to the rules of conduct in terms of: (1) how we interact with participants; and (2) how we work with the data. However, we can go further and state that, from start to finish, a study requires us to be ethical. We must be moral in our human conduct. Gadamer (1975: 314) tells us that 'human sciences stand closer to moral knowledge than to that kind of "theoretical" knowledge'; in other words, we are not undertaking a scientific study in the sense that physicists do. Our objects of study are human beings and what they know of themselves and the situations they find themselves in. We must be moral in how we interact with participants; we must listen to the stories, without prejudice or judgement, no matter how difficult. We must be open to what is being said and what is to come, for it is upon these principles that trust is built and that the meanings and understanding that participants give to the situations they find themselves in will emerge.

We stated at the beginning of the chapter that Gadamer (1975: 314) articulates that human sciences are 'moral sciences' as 'their object is a man and what he knows of himself'. This is also true for us as researchers: we need to understand what we know of ourselves to be open to understanding what others know of themselves. From a Heideggerian perspective, we are called to be 'concerned with the nature of thinking' (Gray, 1976: ix). Therefore, we must think but 'there is always a struggle to advance a new way of seeing things because customary ways and preconceptions about it stand in the way' (Gray, 1976: x). Thinking then 'is determined by that which is to be thought as well as by him who thinks' (Gray, 1976: xi). For Heidegger, thinking is a way of living. That is why sitting in our room will not get us anywhere. To live is to know, to interact, to be present to others, to see and to hear. We take all of this and give meaning and understanding to what we have encountered, which moves us forward in our becoming. We come face to face with our own humanity through the Other.

As researchers, being comfortable in our own skins enables us to be open to what our participants tell us. More importantly, we are freed up to hear what is being said 'as we can listen best to the pauses and silences of ethics' (Sorrell and Dinkins, 2006: 314). Another important aspect is giving of ourselves; being open with people creates an atmosphere of trust.

Exemplar Case

When I was gathering data for my PhD study (Duffy, 2008), I was out and open with my potential participants. During the initial phone calls of setting up interviews, we had regular discussion about the state of play for lesbians in Ireland. We went from social to political to economic situations. In the true feminist way, we went from the personal to the political. By giving of myself to the participants, we created a dialogue of understanding and they knew where I was coming from. I had chosen the topic because of my experience of having a hysterectomy in my early 30s. It was a salient experience of how to be (not) yourself in a health care setting. My gay male friend was more than once constructed as my husband or, at best, boyfriend. It was possibly the one and only time in my life that I was silent. That was a feat in itself but it was the soul-destroying experience of the reality of my being that catapulted me into the topic. It gave me an empathy with others, and I was honest with potential participants when I was asked why I was interested in the lived experiences of health care among Irish lesbian women. Hermeneutic phenomenology, my embedding in the work of Heidegger, and my love of existentialism through using Sartre enabled me to be present during interviews with participants. We need to be true to ourselves, so we can be true to our participants: how we are with others is fundamentally moral.

Chapter Summary

Ethics is the bedrock upon which all studies are built, regardless of the methodology used. This chapter unpacks the nuances of being an ethical researcher in a hermeneutic phenomenological study. It begins from the moments of thinking about a study when, as Heidegger (1976: 3) suggests, 'We come to know what it means to think when we ourselves try to think. If the attempt is to be successful, we must be ready to learn thinking'. In a similar fashion, the thinking of being ethical is a steep learning curve whereby we must unpack who we are to become a successful researcher. We need to unpack 'our skin in the game' to understand who we are as-researcher and why we come to this particular research at this particular moment in time. We also need to be present and open to those who share their lived experiences with us and, through our writing, bring their voices to the surface to facilitate others' thinking about that which needs to be thought about.

Further Resources

These core readings will add depth to readers' understanding of ethical issues in research:

- Bonhoeffer, D. (1949) 'What is meant by "telling the truth?"', in *Ethics*. New York: Simon & Schuster, pp. 358–367.
- Merkle, J. and Sorrell Dinkins, C. (eds) (2006) *Listening to the Whispers: Re-thinking ethics in healthcare*. Madison, WI: University of Wisconsin Press.
- Mertens, D. and Ginsberg, P. (eds) (2009) *The Handbook of Social Research Ethics*. London: Sage.
- Scambler, G. (2002) *A Sociology of Shame and Blame? Insiders versus outsiders*. London: Palgrave.
- Sieber, J. (2009) 'Planning ethically responsible research', in Bickman, L. and Rog, D. (eds) *The Sage Handbook of Applied Social Research Methods*. London: Sage, pp. 106–142.

Part II Summary

In this part, we have described, explored and demonstrated the core components that are brought together to *design* the hermeneutic phenomenological study. We have explained consistently how developing the research question, performing the literature review, setting up the sampling strategy and determining sample size, and engaging the complexities of personal and research ethics, feed back to, and are led forward by, hermeneutic thinking and the philosophy of Heidegger and Gadamer, as we continue to weave that golden thread. In the next part, we enter the 'engine room' of the hermeneutic study and explore the *design* and *practicalities* of data collection and data analysis. We then address the complexities of demonstrating the credibility and trustworthiness of hermeneutic phenomenological research throughout the project, coming finally to strategies for writing and disseminating the work.

Part III
Conducting Hermeneutic Phenomenology

Introduction

Hermeneutic phenomenology has progressed significantly since its introduction (at least in nursing practice and research) by Patricia Benner in 1994. Academics, scholars and researchers grappled throughout the 1990s and early 2000s with the thorny problem of developing a robust methodology out of Heidegger's dense philosophy. During this period, criticisms of the poor quality of phenomenological research in nursing (for example, Crotty, 1997; Paley, 1998) were countered by the groundbreaking efforts of methodologists such as Koch (Koch, 1995, 1996, 2006), Diekelmann et al. (1989), Caelli (2000), Crist and Tanner (2003), Ironside (2005) and Smythe et al. (2008) to develop methods which were philosophically sound, and led to rigorous, trustworthy research. Nurses, social scientists and other humanities scholars began engaging with philosophy and thinking, enabling them to give more than lip-service to methodology: *I'm exploring lived experience, so I'm 'doing' phenomenology* – without really understanding the deep connections between the two. The movement was juxtaposed alongside the long-running quest in qualitative research across health and social sciences, to break out from the positivistic hierarchy and demonstrate both value and quality in post-positivistic inquiry. These scholars, and many since, have laid down the foundations on which the methods presented in Parts II and III of this book are based.

Having introduced the philosophy of Heidegger and Gadamer in Part I, and demonstrated the methods by which hermeneutic phenomenologists weave the philosophical golden thread into the design of their research study in Part II, we now turn our attention to 'the engine room' of every project, the practical means by which we generate and present new knowledge. In this part of the book, we revisit hermeneutic philosophy and thinking to explain and present examples of techniques for data collection (Chapter 6), data analysis (Chapter 7), managing rigour and the self as-researcher (Chapter 8) and writing up and presenting findings (Chapter 9). We consistently return to the roots of our hermeneutic thinking to encourage the reader/student to maintain their 'thinking along with Heidegger' beyond the completion of their methodology chapter, sustaining and evidencing the philosophical – methodological – method links throughout.

6

Data Collection and Management

This chapter addresses the options for data collection and how these are informed by hermeneutic principles from the key philosophers. In hermeneutic phenomenology, the aim is to gain insight into, and reveal meaning of, a given experience as understood and narrated by the experiencing person. The researcher adopts methods which enable the 'voice' of the participants to be heard by the reader. Heidegger (*On the Way to Language*, 1959) and Gadamer (*Truth and Method*, 1960, 1975) focus on the centrality of language as the means by which humans reveal their experience to others, hence the traditional use of interviews to gather data in hermeneutic studies. However, more recently, other forms of communication, including photography, diaries and poetry, are being used. We discuss the philosophical underpinnings and draw on recent works by hermeneutic researchers across a range of disciplines to exemplify the many ways in which data may be collected in hermeneutic phenomenological research.

Philosophical Underpinnings

In his essay 'On the Way to Language', Heidegger (1959) purports that language is the matter for thinking and saying – in that 'language speaks to us' and points to or shows us matters of concern in our everyday world. In a conversation with others, speaking and listening occur to mediate our understanding of the world. Listening is also an important part of language where silence enables us to listen in a discourse. This dialogue, or listening and speaking, provides the primary means for language used in data collection. The dialogic exchange, according to Heidegger, is a 'pointing' or signal that directs attention toward understanding. Understanding is more than the literal exchange of words. In saying or pointing towards, matters come to focus and are recognised or appropriated and acknowledged by others. An interview is a give-and-take process whereby researcher and participant co-construct the narrative where saying is the means to showing or representing. Understanding is a dialogical experience in which there is an engaged opening for everyday concerns to be disclosed in the narrative telling (Diekelmann and Diekelmann, 2009). Thus, in hermeneutic interviewing, the approach is grounded in the philosophical traditions of Heidegger and Gadamer: iterative exchange between subjects (in this case, researcher and participant) resembles shared conversations in which the language uncovers and expresses meaning. The interviewer seeks to reveal meaning in the language of the story that is interpreted and co-created by researcher and participant (Crist and Tanner, 2003).

In the hermeneutic tradition, early interpretation of historical biblical texts (see Chapter 1) generated a new art of understanding that provided a way of accessing the meaning of literary texts to reveal the nature of the experience, situation or historical event studied. Other scholars and philosophers built on Schleiermacher's work, foregrounding text as the format by which hermeneutic phenomenological analysis of experience is achieved. In hermeneutic phenomenological research, data collection refers to the gathering of narratives exploring experiences of the phenomenon of concern; it also includes transcription of such narratives and the gathering of interpretations and field notes surrounding the accumulation of data. Cohen, Kahn and Steeves (2000) refer to data that includes these varied aspects of language and expression as 'a multi-level text'.

Pre-understanding

As discussed in earlier chapters, the phenomenological approach was first described by Husserl, who proposed the rigorous research of experience to describe the human perspective regarding an issue or a concern. However, he proposed that researchers bracket their preconceptions and beliefs to capture the essence of the lived experience that focuses on pure subjectivity. As a student of Husserl, Heidegger proposed a view of experience as ontological, as living-in-the-world, versus just a subjective view. Heidegger viewed living-in-the-world as an engagement to make meaning through interpretations that involve historical (temporal) and background understandings that provide knowing awareness and anticipation of the possibilities. In this way, researcher and participants are *always-already* engaging in meaning-making though interpretations. Thus, the bracketing of pre-understandings is not part of the hermeneutic phenomenological approach; rather, all orientations of past, present and future provide a hermeneutic circle of interpretation which contributes to understanding (Diekelmann and Ironside, 2011). Gadamer further noted that preconceived understandings are part of the language and openness that shift the focus to an ontological understanding of being-in-the-world, which is expressed in our everyday existence.

Pre-understandings are identified early in the research approach by all researchers as part of the process of rigour that ensures that the preconceptions are not over-valued in the interpretations, and that the voice of the participant remains prominent. This is accomplished by the researchers writing journals in which they acknowledge their own pre-understandings as potential biases and manage these by adopting ongoing reflective practices as the interviews proceed. Another suggestion, in situations where students are being mentored by senior researchers (Smythe, 2011), is for the research supervisor to interview the student on their own experience of the phenomenon. In this way, the novice researchers become more mindful of their preconceived expectations that could influence their interpretations, and they gain an insight into the unique approach to interviewing that is used in hermeneutic phenomenological research. Journalling can help novice and experienced researchers become more mindful of the prejudices (Gadamer) they bring with them into any study. Gadamer (1960, 1975) reminds us that what he calls prejudices – and what other methodologists might call biases – are not always negative. The skill of the researcher is in being aware of their own prejudices, positive and negative, and managing these reflexively (see Chapter 8) to the benefit of the study.

Data Collection

Once the research question has been identified, as outlined previously (see Chapter 3), it is important to choose a congruent method for capturing the textual data for analysis and interpretation of the meaning of the phenomenon. During data collection, the hermeneutic phenomenological researcher often utilises the open or in-depth interview to engage in a conversation with the participant that explicates the experience of the phenomenon. This opening or 'clearing' (Heidegger, 1962; Benner, 1994; Diekelmann and Diekelmann, 2009) provides the space for the participant to narrate their experience. The interview makes sense of the experience by resembling a conversation in which the interviewer's emphasis is deep listening and openness, allowing the participant to recount their life experiences. In this way, the interview is more interpretive, and the researcher and participant, through the conversation, co-create the findings in a fusion of ideas in a narrative text. Thus, the focus of the approach is to elicit the experience of the participants so that the phenomenon can be revealed in the narrative.

As the research question focuses on the experience of a specific phenomenon, the purposive sample engages participants who have experienced the phenomenon. Once recruited, the participants often will choose a location for the interview where they can share their stories, which may be audio-recorded and later transcribed, removing any identifying data. Digital audio-recorders are readily available and affordable, and produce clear recordings which can be easily downloaded and transcribed. It is wise to ensure familiarity with the equipment, to do a short test run when setting up each interview to test recording levels, to carry a spare supply of batteries, and to have a back-up plan in case of equipment failure.

Interview guide

An interview guide is created to prepare for the interview and provide information for the internal review board (IRB) in the USA, university ethics committee in the UK and Europe, and/or health service ethics review panel for approval. Ethical approval from others enhances the study design and is sought within universities and those institutions where the study is taking place, such as hospitals, prisons or venues that have their own ethical committees. Since ethics committees are charged with ensuring participants are protected and not asked to do anything unreasonable, they have traditionally insisted on seeing a full interview schedule, but this does not fit methodologically with hermeneutic phenomenology. Hermeneutic researchers can and do gain approval, by explaining clearly the nature and purpose of the research and why there is no definitive schedule, and providing an indicative schedule which includes the trigger or opening prompt and some examples of possible probes or follow-up questions.

Explanatory Box 6.1

Seeking IRB/Ethics Panel Guidance for a Study

Any research with human participants requires ethical approval, and each country/specialism will have its own structure and processes for review. The student is advised to seek guidance from their supervisor and their institution's ethical approval board, to determine what is needed to cover their study. It is wise to allocate several weeks, or perhaps months, to the process of understanding what is required, preparing the documents and making the submission, and receiving approval to begin the study, especially if external reviews, such as health service ethics permissions, are required. (For a more detailed discussion of the ethical aspects of research, refer to Chapter 5.)

Open-ended questions and possible interrogatives, rather than concrete questions, provide the general direction the hermeneutic conversation will take, but the participant often leads in the telling of the experience in question. The guiding questions can be tested in a pilot fashion with a purposive sample and then refined for the full study. The interview schedule provides a set of guiding questions to facilitate the interaction in a loose agenda. This may, and in many cases does, change once the interview is under way. In a thoughtful interview, the researcher must remain an active listener to allow for deep engagement in the concerns of the participant. At times, this may lead to unexpected turns that provide valuable learning.

Exemplar Case

In the study 'The Journey through Death and Dying: Families' experience of end of life care in private nursing homes' (Duffy and Courtney, 2014), one of the non-directive open-ended questions posed was: 'Can you describe your experience of the end-of-life care provided to your relative in the nursing home?' Duffy and Courtney were commissioned to investigate the practice of end-of-life care with a view to providers improving their care. The commissioning body wanted to know how relatives felt. By using hermeneutic phenomenology as a research approach, they were able to uncover new meanings and understandings of the concept of 'death'. Relatives did not experience death as the last breath of their loved ones but rather as a long process from the moment they needed to intervene in the life of their relative through providing care. Often in a hermeneutic study, the story is situated and contextualised within the life of the participant. It is not divorced from the reality of being-in-the-world. While we were investigating end-of-life care in nursing homes, participants situated this within the life as-lived by their relative.

Explanatory Box 6.2

Seeking Ethics Approval for Hermeneutic Questions

The task of any ethics review panel is to assess the degree of risk to which participants are likely to be exposed, and whether the researchers have, through the way the study is designed, considered the likely risks and strategies to mitigate against these. One way that the ethics panel assesses the degree of risk is by reviewing the interview schedule to ensure that the researcher will ask questions relevant to the overall study, which are likely to address the research question. Rather than simply not providing a schedule, hermeneutic researchers need to explain why a structured or semi-structured schedule is not appropriate, provide examples of the types of questions that may be asked, and explain the prompts that may be used during the interview.

Distinctions of hermeneutic interviewing

The interview's distinguishing characteristics are based in philosophical ways of thinking with the goal of generating meaning and understanding. The goal is to add to extant knowledge in ways that ask new questions of the phenomenon as-lived in the historical context of the experiences. It is in the telling of stories that meaning emerges. Distinctive differences in interviewing for hermeneutic phenomenology are essential to obtaining narratives that explicate the phenomenon. Some distinctive practices include setting the tone of the research, using incomplete sentences, looking for assent and returning the participant to the story (Vandermause and Fleming, 2011).

Setting the tone of the research

Participants who are purposively recruited for a study are often ready to share their stories. However, it is in the telling of the story that meaning emerges from the experiences versus an explanation of opinion or fact. Thus, to set the tone the researcher must ask a question in a conversational and reflective way that places the person in the experience itself to tell the story and think along with the researcher.

Exemplar Case

In a study of the experiences of women who were five-year survivors after leaving abusive relationships that included intimate partner violence, we (McDonald and Dickerson, 2013) began our interviewing process thoughtfully. Rather than focusing on the initial leaving, we wanted to understand the practical wisdom and resources the women developed to meet their current life challenges. The opening questions were:

> You know that I am interested in learning from you about your current living experiences after leaving an abusive relationship five years ago. Can you tell me what comes up for you when you think about your current daily life challenges? Is there a situation that stands out for you that you would like to talk about?

The introduction set the tone for inviting the women to talk about their current life versus focusing on the abuse and initial leaving. The participants chose what they wanted to talk about and what was most meaningful to them, thus revealing the day-to-day experiences and meaningful events in their life. In the telling of the story, meaning emerged versus a historical or journalistic telling. We asked them to describe a typical week, including their challenges and strategies for living. This question focused on their current life; however, they often referred to the challenges of their past and how they managed going forward. The stories told of engendering independence in their lives, revealed a different and deeper understanding than that which might have resulted from a more directed exchange.

An example of an open-ended question (or prompt) is: '*Tell me about your normal day and what happens*' or '*Tell me what a normal day is like for you*'. We need to be sure that our understanding of words such as 'normal' is reflective of the participant's understanding. We might also 'probe' for more detail by asking: '*What was most helpful in meeting that challenge?*' or '*Please fill in the detail about ....?*' or '*What was not helpful?*'

By engaging in active listening, the researcher can take the participant back to something they have already revealed in the search for deeper meaning: '*You mentioned XX, what is it like to have that happen?/How did it feel when that happened?/ What were you thinking about when that happened?*' Guiding the respondent back to issues they have already introduced is often misunderstood by other scholars as leading, or introducing bias. The crucial point is that the researcher, engaged with and dwelling in the moment with the respondent, is not introducing new notions to the conversation but picking up on something of importance that the participant has introduced themselves, because it has meaning for them. The researcher is then inviting the participant to revisit that 'mention' and explore its meaning in greater detail. Similarly, in hermeneutic phenomenology it is perfectly appropriate to bring something into a subsequent interview that participants in previous interviews have addressed. For example, *'Several people I have already interviewed have mentioned X – what does that mean for you?'* By framing the question in this way, you are not giving anything away about what previous participants' thoughts or experiences of X were, but you are following your thinking, arising from engaging with your data, that 'X' itself might be meaningful and you are inviting your current participant to relate this to their own experience. Again, because 'X' is generated by participants and not by you, it is methodologically acceptable to explore it in this way.

Effective opening questions engage the participant in their experience and are helpful in the hermeneutic interview to draw out what is most important to the participant versus directing and leading to an expected answer. One approach used by Benner (1994) is to ask for an example that stands out as being important in the meaning of the phenomenon. For example, when seeking to understand the meaning of sedation for expert nurses working in a post-operative unit where opioids are administered, the nurses were asked: *'Please tell me about a time when you hesitated to give pain medication to a patient'* (Dunwoody, Jungquist, Chang and Dickerson, 2019). In this example, the way in which the question was asked invited a storied response. The nurses described the background situation, the assessment parameters, what the patient looked like and the consequences of the situation, including patient outcomes and workflow issues, even though these questions were not specifically asked. While the nurse could not pinpoint how they judged sedation levels, they could describe experiences where they recognised, because of their expertise, that sedation was extreme and how they responded to the situation. It seemed that they often recalled a disturbing event that was memorable, triggering an emotional response. Thus, otherwise overlooked understandings were revealed through the artful elicitation of experiential accounts.

Clarifying questions and follow-up paraphrasing can help elicit meaning without leading participants. This was helpful when the nurses wanted to give opinions and facts versus stories that reflected the meaning of sedation. The participants and the researcher worked together in the interview to understand the narrative. The participant needs to feel comfortable, trusting that the researcher is hearing their story.

Sometimes a trigger question can be used to place the person in the experience, or an 'ice breaker' is used to show interest in their experience and your willingness to listen, such as *'Please tell me about your experience with the cancer diagnosis'* or *'What do you mean by your statement "I have always had sleep problems"?'* (Dickerson, Sabbah,

Ziegler, Chen, Steinbrenner and Dean, 2012). The researcher aims to encourage the participant to talk at length, inviting them to explore and expand on thoughts and feelings, revealing the experience itself.

Using incomplete sentences

As the interview progresses in the dialogue between researcher and participant, the conversation is guided as a natural flow. Asking a question by beginning a sentence that the participant can complete, helps the participant get started and does not reduce the focus too much. It allows the participant to focus on what is important and opens up the opportunity for them to express themselves fully. In the study 'Cultures of Diversity: Sexual orientation in An Garda Síochaná' (Duffy and Sheridan, 2012), prompts or incomplete sentences were used to facilitate a further understanding and uncovering of what was being said. These included: *Tell me more...*, *it sounds like...*, *what I am hearing is that you really need to be listened to...*, *what is normal for you?*

Looking for assent

During an interview, the participant's story unfolds and an understanding of the phenomenon as meaningful experience emerges. The researcher verifies this by seeking the participant's clarification of the understanding. In their chapter 'Shared Inquiry', Sorrell and Dinkins (2005) explicated that in order to understand interviewing, the interviewer must put themselves in the interview. They further suggest that if *Dasein* is to understand the world, the individual must understand that they are part of the world. Both the interviewer and the interviewed are part of the world. From a Heideggerian standpoint, the interviewer must put themselves in the interview as it is not an ordinary interview, but rather an interview in which the researcher may reveal as much of themselves as the participant does. It allows the researcher to embrace the fact that they are part of the interview. Within this way of thinking, Sorrell and Dinkins propose a Socratic way of interviewing whereby we immerse ourselves in the interview to enable meanings and understandings to emerge. If we practise in this way, we reveal ourselves to those we interview.

Returning the participant to the story

At times, the interview gets off-track and becomes tangential. It is important to assess whether this is relevant and whether the participant should be redirected. In some cases, participants take a path that enables them to get back to the point. It is the interviewer who has the task of refocusing the conversation on the phenomenon being investigated. This can be tricky as the interviewer needs to gently turn the participant back towards the story at hand without negating what may be important to them, if off topic. We need to be mindful as there may be a reason for the participant's 'sidetracked' story, which may only emerge and become obvious in the analysis process.

Pitfalls

Speed

When novices are conducting their first interviews, there is a tendency to set the pace too rapidly. A good way to enable the novice researcher to learn about how to do a hermeneutic interview is by creating the circumstances for the novice to experience the interview as a participant. This works in a number of ways: (1) it enables the novice to participate in an interview and understand how it feels to be a participant; (2) it facilitates the novice to unpack their personal understanding of the phenomenon; (3) through transcribing the interview, they are given an opportunity to reflect on their own perceptions and understanding; (4) it provides an opportunity to reflect on the process of interviewing; (5) finally, the experience allows for a deeper knowing, albeit from their own perspective, of what it is like to speak intimately with another person about things they may not have spoken about in this way before. Thus, the novice becomes familiar with situating themselves within the phenomenon under investigation. By doing some practice interviews and transcribing these, students can evaluate the depth of responses in the interview text and modify their technique accordingly.

Making assumptions

Because we are *always-already* interpreting in our interaction with the participant, as with our interactions with the world around us, it is very easy as-researcher to have an 'aha' moment in which we perceive we have 'found' the nugget of meaning which is the core of a particular experience, or part thereof. This can lead us to blurt out a question which leads the participant to confirm what we think we have just realised, whereas what we aspire to is for the participant to come to this realisation for themselves. In her study exploring stigma in inflammatory bowel disease (Dibley, Norton and Whitehead, 2018), Dibley was interviewing a participant who, having spent some time describing how clean and tidy his childhood was, then repeatedly talked about his embarrassment around having a stoma to manage his Crohn's disease. Mid-question, having perceived that the embarrassment was likely rooted in the participant's inability to live up to the cleanliness standards instilled in him in childhood, Dibley changed her interview question from, 'Right … and was that because (*of the importance of cleanliness in your child-hood?*) to, '*And what is it that makes that so embarrassing for you?*'. The first would have produced a yes or no answer, confirming what the interviewer understood from the situation, but the second prompted the participant to say, '*Because I was brought up to be clean – it's just not nice*' and there, in one lovely moment, the researcher understood the meaning of the stoma for this man, but understood it on his terms, not her own.

Closed-ended questions that reflect expectations/judgements and require a yes or no answer are also problematic in that they lead the respondent to expect that they must give a certain answer. For example, '*Did you have trouble falling asleep because you were afraid of not waking up?*'

Speaking into the silence

Novice researchers often feel awkward if the ebb and flow of conversation stops for a few moments. Knowing how to manage this effectively comes with practice – sometimes, the participant simply needs a little more time to think, especially if they are grappling with a complex concern; sometimes, they genuinely are 'stuck' and do not know how to proceed, and sometimes they are gathering up their courage to reveal something they have never told to anyone ever before. Leaping in too quickly might shut down an absolutely beautiful revelation, whilst waiting too long can mean the momentum of the interview is lost.

Field notes

After the interview, it is good practice to write up private notes. These are the notes on your initial impressions of the interview. As a novice researcher, it allows you to build your confidence by reviewing what went on for you and what you might want to consider doing differently the next time. But, of course, you must always note that interviewing is not an exact science and each person is different. Sometimes what works for one does not work for another; however, if you feel the interview is not transpiring well, previous experiences that you have reflected on enable you to change course or stop the interview appropriately. The kind of questions to ask yourself and note are varied but the following could guide the process:

How did you feel during the interview?

It is important to be at ease with oneself. Depending on the phenomenon under investigation, being comfortable in one's own skin enables us to be present to the participant. There are times when I (Duffy) left a participant, sat in the car, drove away, parked up and cried. The endurance of others never ceases to amaze and affect me, and I must learn to manage such feelings.

Was there anything you would have done differently?

From my perspective, there is not an interview I (Duffy) have done that would not have benefited from being done differently. Imperfection is a gift! Sometimes it is how I responded to the 'you know yourself' comment from the participant. In this comment, we are invited to respond and how we manage that may dictate the remainder of the interview. There are times that I do understand and others I do not as the participant's experience is outside my own. If I do understand I state that, but I indicate that it is the participant's story that I am interested in. Other times it might simply be that I make the typical human response to a situation.

Were you comfortable?

Being comfortable arises in a number of ways. One is the chair you are sitting in. If you become aware of your back, legs or any other part of your body because you are physically uncomfortable, it can have an effect on how you interview. The venue in which the interview is taking place should be a comfortable space for you. Of course, another aspect of being comfortable is the topic you are investigating. For example, if you are undertaking a study on a phenomenon that affects members of the LGBTQI community, it is important to understand how you feel about the topic so that you do not show your surprising feelings during the interview. Being uncomfortable will radiate and may cause issues for you during the interview process. The participant will read your body language and mirror your tension or relaxation, regardless of the phenomenon being investigated.

Did you find any aspect of the interview challenging?

Many things challenge us in life but remembering we are human can assist us when we find situations challenging. If you are wanting to uncover what it is like to be a refugee, how we respond to the stories of becoming, being and finding citizenship will be important to the storyteller. Refugees find themselves in situations and some may experience things that make us question what it is to be human. That questioning needs to be undertaken away from the interview rather than during it. Participants' stories can challenge us and indeed this type of research does change how we view the world and those who inhabit it.

How did you manage your face work?

This follows nicely from the previous question. Again, it is the recognition of being human. If we are a nurse, psychotherapist, clinical psychologist, teacher or anyone working with people, face work becomes second nature to us. We learn how to react without showing it. Indeed, regardless of profession, the best educator of face work is being a parent. So, during interviewing, how did I react, bodily and facially? Did I look surprised? Was it OK to do so? How did my participant react? Did they even notice? Of course, during the most harrowing of human experiences, a participant may reflect on the most hilarious of accounts to enable them to tell their story. Do we laugh? In most cases, yes, we do and it is OK, for there are times when we also want to cry with our participants. Not showing emotion is difficult and may appear cold but you are not there in the professional capacity of nurse, parent or teacher; rather, you are there as a researcher. This is why putting in place access to support services for participants, if they wish to take them up, and for yourself, is important.

So why do we practise this initial note taking? We do it so that we can develop our reflection on the process of interviewing. Most PhDs and professional doctorate dissertations now seek a reflective section in the methodology section. This enables you to reflect on and track your development and growth as a researcher and how you managed stressful situations. It enables you to think and reflect hermeneutically about interviewing. It becomes your story of your experience interviewing others about that particular phenomenon.

Another aspect of field notes is the section on 'what I thought I heard', the emerging areas to be thought about. Heidegger speaks of 'that which needs to be thought about'. Every interview throws up something that sticks in our heads and that we need to think about further. Field note practice enables these ideas to be written down so that we can come back to them. In writing down our initial surface thinking, we may trigger a thought about a particular author whose writing might help us understand what the participant was experiencing. We may begin to make links between the interview and the literature, and between interviews. Write whatever comes to mind and hold nothing in your head, as this becomes invaluable in helping us to develop our analysis later. It is important to understand that in a hermeneutic phenomenological study, the thinking is always there, emerging in the shadows of the day. Note taking may happen immediately after the interview but it is also important on other occasions. Always have a notebook ready to hand. The keeping of such notes can include thoughts that come up during the study, about one's own reflections, assumptions and interpretations, as well as observations about the phenomenon generally. Field notes can include observations during interviews as well as thinking prior to and during the enactment of the study.

Number of interviews

Most students and ethical committee members want to know what number of participants are necessary for a hermeneutic phenomenological study, since this figure is generally used to assess the likelihood of being able to collect enough data to answer the research question. Depending on the phenomenon and the need to obtain participants who have had the experience under investigation, there may not be a precise number that is required. We refer the reader back to Chapter 4: Population and

Sampling, for a detailed consideration on selecting the number of participants, and deciding whether to interview each of them once, or more than once.

The skill of hermeneutic interviewing is quite different to that of other qualitative techniques, and, as indicated earlier in this chapter, takes practice. Novice phenomenologists may be several interviews in before they start to feel comfortable with, and relax into, the technique. Being flexible with the sample size allows for additional recruitment as the student/researcher becomes more skillful.

Other Data Forms

In addition to narratives, oral dialogues may be used for data analysis. Language is the underlying mechanism that provides storied descriptions of experiences that can be analysed, and may include diaries and poetry. Focus group interviews also can be used, although it is sometimes difficult to follow an individual's story line without careful documentation of who was talking. For the purpose of identifying individual voices, it is good to ask demographic details such as age, ethnicity, gender and – depending on the nature of the focus group such as police, LGBTQI, teachers, students, nurses, occupational therapists or doctors, to name but a few – one could ask for length of service. In this way, for transcribing purposes, the identification of voices may be made easier. Another way might be to assign names to each person and ask them to use their name prior to speaking. However, this can be rather awkward and could inhibit free-flowing conversation. Sometimes focus groups can add to additional experiences and identify commonalities and differences in the experience among several participants, although the analysis should pay attention to who might dominate the discussion and facilitators should ensure that all members have a voice. Indeed, there are times when the expectation is a one-to-one interview, but the researcher may find that another person is in the room such as a partner, husband, wife, mother, father or friend. In such situations, the interviewer needs to determine whether the other person is participating or is there as a critical friend. If there as a critical friend, the interviewer needs to be sure of what role they are playing, for example they could be there as a support or as an advocate. It is also necessary to make sure that the participant understands the role of the other person in the room. Depending on the phenomenon being investigated, the interviewer may find the participant wants the other person to engage with the conversation. In such cases, consent must be obtained from both. Always in the process of gathering data, the researcher should be able to deal with the unexpected.

Photo elicitation

The use of photography has developed into a successful method in many forms of qualitative research and may be used as a methodological design itself. It is a form of inquiry that uses photography and visual images to elicit and/or to convey understanding. Approaches such as photo-elicitation, Photo Novella and Photovoice (Hansen-Ketchum and Myrick, 2008; Pain, 2012) are noted in the literature and have been welcomed in the research community. In some cases, participants are asked to find images or photographs of objects, activities and representations of thoughts, feelings or experiences that are the focus of concern, and then communicate with researchers about these representations. In other cases, participants are asked to take pictures following an interview or go forth to identify representations of the phenomenon of concern. The latter often engages participatory research methods (Wang and Burris, 1997) and can offer insights expressed by members of communities that go beyond spoken language. Photographs can be especially helpful in situations where participants have difficulty expressing themselves verbally, such as when they are describing particularly painful experiences (Kantrowitz-Gordon and Vandermause, 2016). Further, images may better convey study findings as artistic renderings or as part of a presentation or publication generating study results. In all of these ways, the use of photography may be incorporated as a data collection, data analysis or dissemination tool, as imagery is a form of communication.

The use of photographs in hermeneutic phenomenological research is compatible with data collection, analysis and dissemination, just as is the use of conversation, spoken or written word. In hermeneutics, the photographs, whether used as part of a conversational interview to explore experience or offered as a representation of findings, should be part of the hermeneutic activity. That is, the use of photography should be compatible with the guiding philosophical stance.

Exemplar Case

In a study of the experience of adolescents who raise livestock (Mott, 2019), participants were asked to bring pictures of their livestock-raising experiences to an interview session. The participant and interviewer then looked at the pictures together and talked about what it was like to raise animals. In this way, a storied account of experience was comfortably conveyed. The controversies, joys and sadness associated with experiences shared in a rural farm culture became part of the understanding of meaning sought in the study. Photographs were NOT used to assess techniques of animal showmanship or to evaluate animal conformation, as might be sought in a different form of qualitative research or for another purpose. *The use of the medium as an instrument of language was the essential element that brought the phenomenon of concern into awareness.* This study, only recently completed, has been published using written language, description and hermeneutic interpretation.

If available, particular photographs could also be used in the dissemination process, appropriately de-identified, and might be visual expressions of meaning. Such expressions have been conveyed as results in hermeneutic work, showing experiences of a person recovering from methamphetamine addiction (Sameshima et al., 2009) and showing metaphors of distress for parents of premature infants (Kantrowitz-Gordon and Vandermause, 2016). In the latter study, discourse analysis was used as a methodological approach but the visual representation of results was an expression of meaning, similar to what is sought in hermeneutic work. Visual representations, thus, can add to the exchange of language and meaning that characterises the hermeneutic project, although ethical approvals and participants' consent to use identifying images must, of course, be secured.

Data Management

Transcription, de-identification and storage

Now that the interview has been recorded, the data file needs to be transcribed, identifying information removed, and saved in a secure location. The researcher can transcribe the interview themselves which provides a beginning to the analysis and allows the researcher to add emotional tone or pauses to the transcript that illuminate more meaning such as when they are laughing or being sarcastic during the interview. Humour and sarcasm do not translate well in a paper narrative unless these tones are added as notations. In addition, this provides an opportunity for the researcher to remove identifying names and places from the transcript. The interview could also be transcribed by an outsourcing company requiring proper confidentiality agreements. It is prudent to use an approved provider; however, there is usually a cost per page or per minute of the transcript. The researcher would still need to re-listen to the recording to confirm the accuracy of the transcription and to de-identify the content.

If the interview is in another language and requires translation for analysis, i.e. if the researcher is required to provide an English translation, there are processes of translation and back translation to follow to ensure the accuracy of translation. In a study of Korean immigrant childbirth experiences in the United States (Seo, Kim and Dickerson, 2014), the interviews were transcribed in Korean to reflect the actual words used by the women. Then the interviews were translated into English by bilingual/bicultural Korean research assistants from a linguistics background to review for cultural accuracy. The Korean bilingual researcher then confirmed that the translation was accurate prior to analysis. This was essential to facilitate analysis when sometimes words were difficult to translate into English. Another approach is to have two analysis teams, one in each language, to compare results that maintain the cultural accuracy of the experience (see further readings at the end of the chapter).

After transcription, at a minimum the file should be saved on a password-protected computer, and if encryption software is available, it would provide an extra layer of protection. For some institutional review boards/ethics committees, the voice data file is considered identifiable, therefore plans should be made to destroy the voice file at the end of the study. During analysis, it is helpful to maintain the file in a secure location if the need arises to verify text and tone that may be confusing, especially if the interview uses humour or sarcasm.

Within a European perspective, there are General Data Protection Regulations (GDPR) that need to be adhered to. Broadly, anyone collecting data from others must notify that the data is being collected, collect what is needed for specific, pre-identified purposes, and explain clearly how the data will be used, how it will be stored and for how long, and how and when it will be disposed of. Alongside these GDPR requirements, each European university has rules and regulations in place and these should be consulted for the effective management of data. These of course will have already been laid out in the ethical approval application process. Adhering to processes and systems that are in place results in an ethically rigorous piece of research.

A laptop or computer should be encrypted for data safety. The ethical application form should clearly state who has access to the data, such as the researcher, the supervisory team if a student, or the research team. If other people will have access to data, then they should be named. If new people are given access to the data after ethical approval, then a notification needs to be sent to the ethics committee.

When transcribing the interviews, all participants should be de-identified and anonymised to protect their privacy and confidentiality. All identifying markers should be removed so that anyone who reads output from the research will not be able to identify participants. At times, the stories or the rarity of a specific phenomenon can be identifiable, necessitating care by the researcher when publishing to specifically use an alternative verbatim quote that reflects the idea but is not identifiable. Approaches to anonymising and de-identifying data include legal and ethical measures, along with the terms of the consent and consideration of what the participant is agreeing to and the relation to their own interests. Reducing the risk of re-identification is a more current issue, especially in biomedical research (Chevrier et al., 2019); however, the basic tenets of protection of the participants' privacy and confidentiality are still valid in qualitative research. In hermeneutic phenomenological research, some researchers give participants pseudonyms rather than a study ID number, as this adds to the reading and richness and emphasises the human situatedness of the research (see Chapter 5: Being Ethical).

Using qualitative data management software

Some researchers use software to organise the transcript data into working themes and patterns. While some researchers prefer to use specialist software to enable the process of unpacking the data, others prefer coloured pens and paper files, or standard word-processing programs which can also be used to organise the data if they are unfamiliar with specialist software.

Most specialist software (i.e. NVivo© or ATLAS©) requires a learning curve to understand how to enter data and the type of files required, as well as how to organise the data under the previously coded and analysed working themes, and link the codes with the verbatim quotes of the transcripts. It is important to understand that the software does not do the interpretations or analysis. The data coding is done by the researcher (and/or their team). To identify the verbatim quotes that reflect the working pattern or theme, the researcher recognises the representativeness of the idea and emerging patterns/themes identified in the interpretations. The verbatim quotes are gathered under the pattern/theme and can be later queried and put into a separate file, giving examples of the pattern/theme along with the participants' identifier (pseudonym or number) and line location in the text. The meanings conveyed in the quotes at times overlap with other patterns/themes and are placed under more than one area. There is an opinion that the use of specialist software to organise data in this way is 'un-phenomenological' because it creates a physical barrier between the researcher and the data, and may disrupt the ability to 'dwell' deeply in the data (Goble, Austin, Larsen, Kreitzer and Brintnell, 2012). (Further readings on the use of software are provided at the end of the chapter.)

All of the interpretive summaries, field notes and texts are collected and filed as components of the text for interpretation that is part of the multi-layered data (Vandermause and Fleming, 2011). The amount of textual data can be very large, especially related to the length and number of interviews included. Therefore, the software can be helpful in organising the files, and provide a mechanism for memoing for textual analysis and show the progression of interpretations in an audit trail. If software is not used, standard word-processing programs with review facilities such as track changes, and/or several dated binders and folders may assist in organising the thinking progress.

Chapter Summary

In this chapter, we have explored data collection and management. We have illustrated how the philosophical way of thinking is embedded in everything we do, from the initial stages of thinking about the project to how we go about interviews and collecting data. We also point out practical consideration when gathering data and the issues a novice researcher should be aware of when undertaking data collection. We introduce ways of collecting data beyond the traditional interview – pointing to a richness in how we may undertake such studies. The following chapter will unpack the carrying out of data analysis.

Further Resources

These resources will help the reader recognise the generic skills and considerations relevant to any qualitative data collection and will provide a sound basis on which to build specific hermeneutic interviewing skills.

Core readings

- Sorrell Dinkins, C. (2005) 'Shared inquiry: Socratic-hermeneutic interpe-viewing', in *Beyond Method: Philosophical conversations in healthcare research and scholarship*. Madison, WI: University of Wisconsin Press, pp. 111–147.
- Vandermause, R. K. and Fleming, S. E. (2011) 'Philosophical hermeneutic interviewing', *International Journal of Qualitative Methods*, 10(4), 367–377. doi: 10.1177/160940691101000405.

Further readings

- Basit, T. N. (2003) 'Manual or electronic? The role of coding in qualitative analysis', *Educational Research*, 45(2), 143–154.
- Cypress, V. B. (2019) 'Data analysis software in qualitative research: Preconceptions, expectations, and adoption', *Dimensions of Critical Care Nursing*, 38(4), 213–220.
- Finch, H. and Lewis, J. (2014) 'Focus groups', in Ritchie, J. et al. (eds) *Qualitative Research Practice: A guide for social science students and researchers*. London: Sage, pp. 221–242.
- Intersoft consulting: General Data Protection Regulation (GDPR). Available at: https://gdpr-info.eu.
- Larkin, P. J., de Casterle, B. D. and Schotsmans, P. (2007) 'Multilingual translation issues in qualitative research reflections on a metaphorical process', *Qualitative Health Research*, 17(4), 468–476.
- Meyer, D. Z. and Avery, L. M. (2008) 'Excel as a qualitative analysis tool', *Field Methods*, 21(1), 91–112.
- Mustafa Al-Amer, R., Rajman, L., Glew, P., Raysir Darwish T., Randall, M. S. and Salamonson, Y. (2018) 'A reflection on the challenges in interviewing Arab participants', *Nursing Research*, 26(1), e-publ. doi:10.7748/nr.2018.e1559.
- Yeo, A. et al. (2014) 'In-depth interviews', in *Qualitative Research Practice: A guide for social science students and researchers*. London: Sage, pp. 177–210.
- Zamawe, F. C. (2015) 'The implication of using NVivo software in qualitative data analysis: Evidenced-based reflections', *Malawi Medical Journal*, 27(1), 13–15.

7

Data Analysis and Interpretation

In this chapter, we describe the various processes of data analysis and interpretation, which are integrally woven activities grounded in philosophical hermeneutics. The data in a hermeneutic study may consist of various representations of experience, including audio-recordings, written text, observational descriptions, or other showings. The representations, therefore, are recognised as hints, or *pointings*, collected to provide a way toward understanding rather than a reducible product. The researcher is an instrument by which the phenomenon may be understood, but the data collected is also instrumental, providing the access to the understandings sought. In this way, data analysis differs from other qualitative forms and must be considered as a dynamic activity that leads somewhere else. The act of interpretation, thus, becomes the rendering that is given as a result of the project.

To begin, we need to consider the iterative nature of our interpretations and that there are no defined steps or stages that must be followed. The guidance is provided by the philosophical tenets that consider the nature of the phenomenon being studied. To aid our thinking around analysis, we will briefly revisit key considerations detailed in the previous chapters.

Philosophical Underpinnings of Heidegger and Gadamer

We follow the thinking of Heidegger and Gadamer, as we understand it, in our interpretive work. The aim of the interpretive process is to gain an understanding of the meaning of everyday experience to offer plausible insights about our interactions with the world we live in. There is no theory or explanation as a result of the analysis. For Heidegger, truth is unconcealment, which is a revealing of that which may otherwise be hidden, through the telling of participants' accounts of their experiences. The whole story can never be told because, as Gadamer relates, the multiplicity of meanings in a story is revealed in plausible understandings that resonate with others.

We humans are self-interpreting beings that make sense of our world through our experiences and interpretations of it. As Gadamer (2003) asserts, all understanding is interpretation in which we come to know through our own perspectives of the world – perspectives that are inclusive of our historical experience and taken-for-granted knowing. The telling of the stories by the participant are an interpretation through language. All have their own horizon of understandings that continually expand through each new experience. A horizon of understanding of each unique individual informs the interpretation of their experiences which is formed by backgrounds and traditions that create the basis of understanding of a person's world from their historical, social interpretations. The researcher also has their own horizon of understanding that informs interpretations which become a fusion of horizons between the interpreter and the participants.

Identifying the Phenomenon of Interest

The goal of an interpretation is to create a research report that engages the reader in the experience of the phenomenon as lived by others, inviting new questions, understanding and possibilities, and to invite new thinking. First, the researcher decides on the phenomenon of interest that is important to them and is experienced in the lives of participants. As outlined in Chapter 4, a literature review provides access to preconceived notions active in the current societal traditions and research narratives. The thinking that occurs as the researcher reviews the literature reflects thinking about what is most important regarding the phenomenon, prior to the interpretive effort. The focus of the research question is then designed to uncover the meaning of a phenomenon to understand the human experience of living it.

Exemplar Case

As I (Dickerson) worked with patients with advanced lung cancer, I recognised that they had profound symptoms to deal with – pain, shortness of breath and weakness/fatigue – yet the one most often ignored was insomnia. Research studies reported that insomnia was present in the majority of patients with lung cancer; however, little was known about the experience of insomnia from the patient's perspective, especially during and after treatment. So, the question became: *What are the common meanings and shared practices of sleep disturbances in people diagnosed with advanced lung cancer undergoing treatment?* We wanted to understand the experience when diagnosed, during and after treatment. A longitudinal interview approach was proposed: at diagnosis, after the second and third chemotherapy sessions, and at six months (Dickerson, Sabbah, Gothard, Ziegler, Chen, Steinbrenner and Dean, 2015).

Uncovering Pre-Understanding

In hermeneutic phenomenology, we consider the researcher as being integral to the analysis, as an instrument of understanding. The researcher is a means to enact the interpretation of meaning of lived experiences. As self-interpreting beings, we have our own horizon of understanding (Gadamer, 2003: 302) that comes from our past experiences, our social, historical and disciplinary perspectives. Alongside that, we need to reflect on our own preconceived thoughts, or what Gadamer calls 'prejudices' (Gadamer, 2003: 299), that reside in our understanding of the phenomenon and brought us to want to study that phenomenon. We must read, think and question our own views to understand our 'horizon of understanding' that emerges from our past experiences, influences future possibilities and is continually enriched and expanded by new reflections and interactions. We prepare for analysis by identifying pre-understanding and journalling thoughts.

Exemplar Case

As a nurse with a background in oncology and chronic illness symptom management, I (Dickerson) believed that patients with a new diagnosis of lung cancer would be thinking about their mortality and the belief that diagnosis was a death sentence. I thought they would be lying awake thinking about the implications of dying, with sleep being elusive in the despair of impending death. I became aware of my expectation to hear that in the stories and kept an ongoing journal to record my thoughts and keep myself open to the participants' experience.

When learning how to uncover preconceptions, as a supervisor, I have students share their own stories and experiences to begin to identify their own pre-understanding of the phenomenon. This practice helps the student to clarify and promote reflective practices, including journalling, to clarify preconceptions. When the student begins interacting with the data, this reflection allows them to be more open to listening to the participants' stories and hear what is important in the telling of the participants' experience. This can be facilitated by reflexive engagement within horizons of understanding (Spence, 2017) by asking students to identify their pre-understanding at the beginning of the process, and considering how it compares to the participants' texts as well as the emotional responses of what matters to them personally. In addition, examining silences or what is not being said, is helpful in lending thinking about what perspectives are privileged over others.

Preparing for the Interpretation with a Hermeneutic Stance

Through the interpretive process, we bring our own openness and engagement to understanding through language, thinking and questioning of the participants' stories, which reflect a situational experience of the phenomenon and our own horizon of understanding. The goal is to interpret the experience by a fusion of horizons that are always expanding through constant, ongoing experience. To think in this way requires a hermeneutic stance/perspective that is different from a calculative scientific view that seeks structure and certainty. It requires meditative thinking (Heidegger, 1966a, 1966b). Humans understand meaning through the context of experience, a context that is often hidden or taken for granted in the everyday, silenced by historical, cultural and/or social perspectives.

We approach the interpretation of the data from the stories given through the participants' telling of their experience. Meditative thinking is required in this activity, which is iterative, ongoing, focused and congruent with an open hermeneutic stance. This stance is open to thinking and questioning and being attuned to listening to the story of ontologic experience. The stance allows listening to the story and reflecting on that which needs to be thought about. This way of being open was exemplified to me (Dickerson) by my ageing, wise mother. Challenged by her visual, hearing and post-anesthesia cognitive trials, she was recuperating from a serious injury and was dealing with being moved from hospital to rehabilitation with all of the change in environment, new caregivers and future potential disabilities. She said to me, as she was falling asleep, 'I wonder as I wander'. Her simple statement was a reflection of how she felt, and it spoke to me of the way in which the hermeneutic stance is enacted. It is an openness to the experience of thinking that arises from all that has come before in one's life, both remembered and taken for granted and in confronting future possibilities.

The goal of hermeneutic phenomenology is to interpret human meaning and experience to give insight into understanding the human experience of being-in-the-world in ways which resonate with others, achieving the 'phenomenological nod'. Human experience occurs while interacting with others within a situation, one that is always changing, yet common meanings and shared experiences reside. Through the interpretations, we provide insights into the understanding of the meaning of the phenomenon – we are picking the lock of the thoughts of our participants.

Explanatory Box 7.1

The 'Phenomenological Nod'

The concept of the 'phenomenological nod' is commonly attributed to van Manen, although it is likely rooted in the work of Otto Bollnow (a German philosopher, 1903–1991), and refers to the way in which humans indicate, through the gesture of the nod, their agreement with something. In phenomenological research, the 'nod' is an affirmation from the reader that the meanings revealed from the lived experience of others in the study have resonance with, or make sense to, them.

Challenges Facing the Novice

Qualitative data analysis is never easy, but, in many methodologies, there are defined, staged frameworks and structures which act as a guide to steer the novice researcher through the process. The challenge with analysis in hermeneutic phenomenological research is that there is no easy way of understanding or visualising the process, because it is not meant to be so formal. We do not, in the world, come to new understanding in formal, linear ways – we move back and forth between our pre-understanding, taken-for-granted knowledge and new evidence, gradually moulding and refining our thinking until the meaning at the core of it all is revealed. Hermeneutic phenomenological data analysis is instead a journey through 'things which need to be thought about' in the spirit of the underpinning philosophy, and, for the novice, learning to think, trusting that thinking, and sitting with the data and trusting that understanding will come, that ideas will 'bubble up' (see below, p. 127), is an act of philosophical and phenomenological faith. We can describe this to students as being similar to Chinese handcuffs or finger traps – these sneaky little devices become tighter and more restrictive the harder the trapped person struggles; as soon as the individual relaxes, and stops trying to resist, the finger trap releases (Figure 7.1).

Figure 7.1   Chinese finger trap

So it is with hermeneutic thinking – trying too hard to force understanding to come, simply obfuscates the view; 'sitting with' and letting the thinking mull and circulate give it room to grow. Suddenly, whilst putting the children to bed, or loading the dishwasher, or doing the ironing, or walking the dog, meaning will show itself.

Enacting Interpretation of Texts

The phases of analysis described below are a compendium of practice of the authors of this book, with some explanatory exemplars. While it is given as a series of phases or steps, it is an ongoing, non-linear, circular and iterative process, going from the parts to the whole and back again in a rigorous, circular process of questioning, writing and thinking, in which data is instrumental to accessing understanding. Table 7.1 summarises the elements that are being enacted in a circular and iterative process.

Table 7.1 Enacting interpretation that is nonlinear, circular thinking

- Uncovering preunderstanding in ongoing reflective ways regarding the phenomenon of study
- Creating and maintaining a hermeneutic stance or attitude toward analysis that is open engagement in thinking and questioning
- Enacting the interpretation in an iterative way:
  - beginning phase of examining first text
  - writing interpretive summaries and identifying emergent themes
  - continuing on with each transcript, distilling themes and coalescing similarities in common themes and shared practices
  - dwelling in the data
  - reading along with the philosophy to aid thinking and questioning
  - thinking/analysing in a hermeneutic circle, examining the parts and whole of each text, back and forth, with the philosophical underpinnings
  - using meditative thinking regarding stories, questioning and thinking to provide a bubbling up of the patterns and themes that interpret the experience
  - rendering of an interpretation or fusion of horizons (participant and researchers).

Starting with transcribing interviews

The interviews must be conducted, recorded and transcribed. Practice guidelines for transcribing include the following: provide date, time and participant identifier on the first page; leave a wide column on the right-hand side for research coding purposes; use a consistent identifier for the interviewer and the respondent, such as the participant ID number; listen carefully and copy the speech word for word, including words such as 'you know' and 'um' to convey the flow of the speech, and using punctuation such as ':' or '...' to indicate pauses or unfinished sentences; include laughter and facial expressions to indicate tone or mood and place in square brackets; mark long pauses to indicate thinking time or interruption; and, finally, edit to remove spelling errors, names and mark areas where the voice is inaudible. These details will give clarity to the interpretation.

Beginning phase of interpretation

Interpretation begins with the very first interview – a story from a participant experiencing the phenomenon in conversation with the researcher who listens carefully during the interview to what is being said. After the recording is transcribed, validated and de-identified, the researcher reads the transcript as a whole from start to finish. The text is re-read, line by line, and the researcher makes notes about what stands out in the text, noting general impressions and the style of responses (emotions). The researcher engages in initial coding of each transcript by reading the transcript and then marking a comment or preliminary code in the right-hand column, using a different colour for each reading (Figures 7.2 and 7.3).

Sleep Apnea study

Date, 5/20/2003 Participant # !5

Interviewer: Can you tell me about your sleep apnea story?

	INITIAL CODING
#15 It was about a year ago when I was feeling extremely bad and I didn't know why. I was dozing off as I drove to work. It shocked me. After a while it started happening not only on the way to work but on the way home from work. One time I was standing in my classroom rewinding a tape on the VCR with my back to the kids, it was a rather high cart with a TV on it, and my hand on the cart, and my head actually went down on my hand. If I hadn't caught myself, I could've fallen right down on the floor, which really scared me. I didn't know what the problem was. And then when I went to see the doctor. He said, "I really think you need a sleep study done." After the sleep study, they reviewed the information and said I qualify for CPAP [continuous positive airway pressure device].	*Falling asleep driving to work in AM* *Worried and shocked* *More frequent* *Happening during class in front of students* *Seminal incident causing her to seek answer* *Went to MD for sleep study* *Severity of sleep apnea needing CPAP treatment*
And then it took a while to get hooked up with the home health care provider. I told him, "You have to get me on something right now. It's got to start immediately because I think I'm dying here."	*Required self advocacy when delay occurred* *Serious issue "dying"*

Interviewer: can you tell me more about how you were feeling extremely bad?

#15 I was, my brain was foggy, it just didn't seem like I could think clearly, and I was very forgetful about certain things, nothing in particular. I'd find things I put in the refrigerator that were really silly that shouldn't have been there. Just like I was old before my time. I felt I was losing it. I was just so tired. I would snore a lot. Almost immediately [after CPAP] I wasn't nodding off, which was a great relief to me. I felt a lot better but it wasn't like oh my, here I am 18 again. It was gradually getting better and better. You have to use it [CPAP] every night and leave it on.	*Memory issues and confusion* *Being old before my time* *So tired* Treatment improved nodding off Gradual improvement with use

Figure 7.2   Initial coding, example 1: Dickerson's sleep apnea (apnoea) study

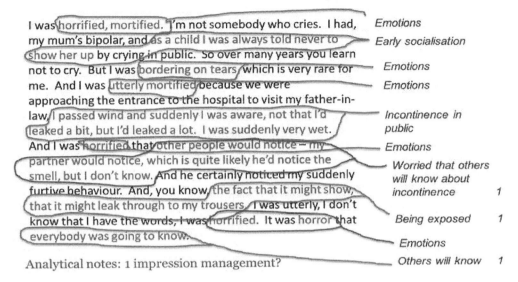

I was horrified, mortified. I'm not somebody who cries. I had, — Emotions
my mum's bipolar, and as a child I was always told never to — Early socialisation
show her up by crying in public. So over many years you learn
not to cry. But I was bordering on tears, which is very rare for — Emotions
me. And I was utterly mortified because we were — Emotions
approaching the entrance to the hospital to visit my father-in-
law, I passed wind and suddenly I was aware, not that I'd — Incontinence in
leaked a bit, but I'd leaked a lot. I was suddenly very wet. — public
And I was horrified that other people would notice – my — Emotions
partner would notice, which is quite likely he'd notice the — Worried that others
smell, but I don't know. And he certainly noticed my suddenly — will know about
furtive behaviour. And, you know, the fact that it might show, — incontinence   1
that it might leak through to my trousers, I was utterly, I don't
know that I have the words, I was horrified. It was horror that — Being exposed   1
everybody was going to know.
— Emotions
Analytical notes: 1 impression management? — Others will know   1

Figure 7.3   Initial coding, example 2: Dibley's stigma in inflammatory bowel disease study

When coding, important and memorable statements can be underlined and a simple explanation noted in the right-hand column. The researcher devises a rudimentary list of emerging themes and patterns. The first read can be somewhat superficial (Smythe et al., 2008) but does show what the interpreter notices first, listening to those ideas that jump out and provoke an emotional response to show what matters to us. If questions arise as to meaning and intent, the section can be highlighted and a note made to return to the audio file. If the question does not seem to evoke a good response, or a valuable comment by the participant is overlooked, a commentary can be noted on the transcript next to that question for further review. As part of the initial text review, the researcher can reflect on the value of the interview questions in evoking the story or suggesting other questions that need exploring.

Explanatory Box 7.2

Sample Early Coding

There is no 'right' or 'wrong' way to carry out initial coding; as long as the process reflects the philosophical tenets upholding the methodology, the researcher is free to deliver this activity in whatever way works best for them, and which facilitates a robust, thorough, reflexive and reflective effort. During analysis, being mindful of the research question acts as a guide to focus thinking, but, at the same time, the researcher must hold themselves open to the possibility of the 'other' – previously unconsidered issues which may show up in the stories of participants. Figures 7.2 and 7.3 show contrasting styles used by two of the authors during an initial analysis of their data.

Writing interpretive summaries

An interpretive summary is written for each interview to summarise the story and the interview's salient points. The interpreter writes out 'working' or 'early' pattern/themes, while staying as close to the text as possible and noting what was interesting or evoked thinking, and identifies verbatim quotes which exemplify this thinking. Emergent themes are not necessarily similar for all participants but rather they represent

> an understanding that we have seen something that matters significantly, something that we wish to turn the reader towards (Smythe et al., 2008: 1392).

An emergent theme is something important that necessitates thinking about and gives an invitation to the reader to think further. Themes can be thought of in another way – they give 'control and order to our research and writing' (van Manen, 1990: 79).

The summary promotes a process of writing, thinking and dialoguing with the text. The summary has as much detail and support as needed to convey a plausible and coherent expression of findings that includes a retelling of the story and/or interpretation of emerging themes and patterns with verbatim support (Vandermause and Fleming, 2011). A summary of working themes is written to be considered, leaving an open space to listen to the insights that emerge with a sense of wonder, questioning and thinking and circling from the parts to the whole. Once a new nuance to the experience emerges in an interpretation, returning to previous interviews occurs to examine if the nuance was overlooked in earlier interviews. Often, the theme is there but was not noticed on the first reading. That is why the hermeneutic circle involves continually returning to the text and examining it for further understanding.

The summaries build with each new transcript and the interpretations will coalesce. Texts, summary and interpretative patterns will arise and theme development will be part of the iterative process (Vandermause and Fleming, 2011). Repeated readings of the parts and the whole of each interview further develop the interpretations. Subsequent interview transcripts are reviewed in a similar fashion, being examined for common themes and patterns. A theme reflects the meaning or understanding that something matters to us, that shows what we see and hear in a text and directs the reader to further thinking. The theme evokes the 'aha' or epiphany (van Manen, 1990) that promotes thinking and rethinking to keep this experience in play. In other words, the theme offers the reader a way to think along with us – letting the text speak. Interviews can be ongoing, inviting new accounts into the interpretations.

Exemplar Case

Interpretive Summary

The stories this nurse shares are meaningful, emotional and heartbreaking. The interview was initially more clinically oriented, with the nurse carrying painful memories which were deeply impactful. The nurse speaks of the focus of care switching to the family more than the patient. She also mentions gratitude from families and patients, and illustrates a very intimate, emotional time after the patient has passed away.

The first story the nurse shared was that of a woman in her late 80s with ovarian cancer. This story is particularly sweet as it demonstrates a special, deep love between a man and woman not commonly seen today. The couple had been married for 60 years. She feared she would die before his next birthday, so she baked him a birthday cake and froze it for him. This was very meaningful to him, and he would always tell the nurse this story. He was very concerned his wife would be comfortable, saying, 'keep my love comfortable tonight, and make sure she's OK'. The nurse felt her care focus changed to comforting the husband more than caring for the wife: 'You had to constantly reassure the family or the loved ones that you were there, it was going to be – you were going to make her as comfortable as possible throughout the night', 'I felt like I was really taking care of him more than her, because I had a protocol for her'. The husband of this woman was also very grateful to the nurse, always thanking her for the care she provided whenever he saw her in the hallway.

In my personal experience, caring for patients is frequently a thankless job. Families are upset, patients are upset and doctors may become upset. The stress associated with this necessitates building a protective wall as a nurse, and care can become very clinical and task oriented. However, as soon as a patient or family member is grateful, that gratitude is enough to chip through the wall and become a real experience. Perhaps this compounded the emotional nature of caring for the patients in these stories. Not only was each case emotionally challenging, but the gratitude from the family caused it to be more real, more emotional and more personal.

The nurse shared a particularly emotional story of a 40-year-old woman who passed away at the end of her shift. This was the second night in a row a patient had died, leaving this nurse feeling very drained: 'I went home, I felt so drained, because it was two nights in a row, two deaths, and, you know, it was just – I started being very overtired and very upset and emotional about it.' The second woman who passed away had a large number of jewellery items that needed to be removed. Removing these was very stressful and emotional for the nurse: 'I'm sweating, and he's crying, and I'm just like, "Oh, my God".' Recalling this memory was difficult for the nurse; she couldn't express herself other than: 'Oh my gosh ... when I see husbands cry over their wives, I'm like, oh my gosh. I remember that night, the second night, when I had the second death, I had to step off the floor for a minute.'

This nurse also spoke of those families not being willing to allow their loved ones to have comfort measures only (removing active treatment and focusing on symptom management, especially pain relief). She spoke of how she prides herself on making patients feel comfortable at the end of life, and how stressful it is when she is prevented from doing this. She shared a story of a man in end-stage renal failure who was alert but confused. His family refused to sign a Do Not Resuscitate (DNR) agreement or put him on comfort measures. As a result, he ended up being resuscitated several times and transferred to the Intensive Care Unit. The family finally decided to sign the DNR, which allowed the treatment team to make the care decisions rather than automatically intubate the patient and keep him on life support. The nurse laments this situation, stating, 'they could have had a nice time with him up until that point'. The nurse believes families resist comfort care because 'sometimes people think they're choosing life versus death, whereas instead they're choosing the style of how things will go during dying'. This statement resonates with when the nurse expressed that families often think the patient will retain their current state of health, not understanding the loss of dignity and the pain associated with frivolous treatment.

The nurse also spoke of needing to slow down when caring for palliative patients, which would take a conscious effort on her part: 'you have to walk in there and just kind of turn a switch, because you're taking care of patients who are cure-based, and then you walk into that room literally right next door, and it's totally different.' She found herself feeling more relaxed when she 'flipped the switch' and took the time to listen to the family. It set the tone for the rest of her shift, and she seems to have found this very powerful.

The stories shared by this nurse were very emotional and moving. I am struck by the memories we carry with us as nurses. As humans, we fear death, and do all in our power to avoid it. To care for someone whose life is ending, to make them as comfortable as possible, to care for their spiritual side as well as the emotional needs of the family members is a very powerful, profound thing to do.

Themes: Caring for family, Slowing down, Caring spiritually for the patient, Receiving gratitude, Supporting each other.

The thinking that occurs at this point is part of the interpretive act to bring understanding to thinking. It is non-linear. Describing how the interpretation of data came into being is not an easy exercise, as Smythe and colleagues (2008: 1392) suggest: 'working with the data is an experience of thinking.' It is a difficult task to unravel how the thinking happened in the above example. The study required the discipline of writing, reading, re-writing and re-reading until a text materialised, yet, through the process of re-reading both the data and the philosophy relevant to the experience, other interpretations emerged (Smythe et al., 2008). However, this was not a linear process but one of going backwards and forwards until a text surfaced. As van Manen (1990: 79) indicates:

> Making something of a text or of a lived experience by interpreting its meaning is more accurately a process of insightful invention, discovery or disclosure – grasping and formulating a thematic understanding is not a rule-bound process but a free act of 'seeing' meaning.

Returning to read the philosophy of Heidegger and Gadamer at this point can enrich thinking as to the possibilities of what something might mean. This type of thinking has a mood that draws one to sensing what matters – overlooking the taken-for-granted and being open to thoughts that call attention to it. We notice what matters to us that resonates with our thinking. The interpretation goes back and forth to ensure that it reflects the voice of the participants' experience of the phenomenon.

Exemplar Case

When trying to understand the reluctance of patients with a cancer diagnosis to talk about their mortality, Dickerson returned to Heidegger's work on *being-towards-death*. He states that to be authentic we must live as 'being towards death'; however, in our society 'The they' believe that yes, people die, but not me, and not now. Societies and health care providers' reluctance to discuss end-of-life and palliative care as a therapeutic option, versus the hope of a cure, demonstrates our fascination with the cure and with a focus on the corporeal body versus living with the potential for death.

Dwelling with the data

In a Heideggerian sense, we 'dwell' (sit, take time) with the data. Heidegger explains that dwelling is not an attitude of idleness:

> When we speak of dwelling we usually think of an activity that man performs alongside many other activities. We work here and dwell there. We do not merely dwell – that would be virtual inactivity – we practice a profession, we do business, we travel and find shelter on the way, now here, now there. (Heidegger, 1993: 349)

Dwelling with the data is not a passive activity. You are doing business with it, practising a profession, travelling with the data, but also finding shelter in the voices, staying put in parts and moving along in other areas. In the end-of-life study, my (Dickerson's) thinking activities were taking us places, even though we physically dwelled in one spot, namely the study. In other words, while we are dwelling with the material, our mind is moving from one part to the next, making links through and between the voices of participants. While we are dwelling, we are building the meaning and understanding that are contained within the material, thus leading us to an interpretation of the data. Through returning to particular shelters, themes emerge that enable us to adequately describe and interpret the data.

Dwelling with the data is pondering, wondering and asking questions of meaning that resonate with us with each story. Reading along with philosophical texts may uncover meaning that creates an interpretive leap that then reveals meaning between the lines, offering an understanding of what matters most.

Exemplar Case

In conversing with patients with a lung cancer diagnosis regarding their sleep disturbances, the participants were not concerned with sleep difficulties and never mentioned their mortality. Sleep was not a priority in their lives and sleep disturbances were tolerated. At diagnosis, they said it was a lifelong experience: 'I always had sleep trouble.' During their cancer treatment, participants expected that sleep difficulties would be part of that treatment: 'I am tired, but the tumors are shrinking.' The treatment they sought and agreed to, bought them more time to avoid thinking about death. Reflecting on Heidegger's thoughts about being-towards-death, 'the they', the voice of our society, when confronted with death, think that death is something that happens to others and not them; similarly, the participants did not think about death – it happened to others, not them. They were unable to live authentically as being-towards-death. This interpretive leap uncovered the silences regarding end-of-life decisions that were being avoided.

At this point, some newer researchers can be overwhelmed by the volume of the data and the journey of thinking (Smythe, 2011). A reminder to seek the hermeneutic stance is helpful to meditatively question, think and write about the experiences. The dwelling meditation can occur when you have a moment of openness or unrelated activity, such as trying to fall asleep, upon awakening in early morning, taking a walk, doing a habitual behaviour such as showering or driving (although we warn students that it can be distracting and they may not see the stop sign; we recommend driving carefully). The interpretation is a pondering, thinking and writing about what the story is saying, weaving in philosophical notions and other texts to promote thinking, i.e. walking along with the philosophy.

Exemplar Case

Many stories have so many details and nuances that we recommend that students go back to the original research question and focus on unpacking the interpretations related specifically to that. For example, one of Dickerson's students was studying the communication of potential genetic risk for family members who found out a loved one had a genetic mutation for breast cancer, which significantly increased their own risk for that same cancer. The experience was profound and life-changing, which made it difficult to focus just on the communication of the risk, but she had to focus on the question and leave the life-changing stories for another analysis. We recommend that all students include secondary analysis in the consent form; that way they can use the de-identified transcripts for additional analysis.

Bubbling up

Dwelling with the data can be overwhelming to the novice researcher. As the data continues to be collected and each interview is interpreted, a back-and-forth from the parts to the whole collection of interviews occurs. To manage this part of the interpretation and the synthesis of meaning, one metaphor that reflects this action is *bubbling up* (Figure 7.4). In a hermeneutic stance, the researcher re-reads all of the original data and lets it sit in their mind like stew on the stove in a thick metal pot, slowly simmering – not boiling too fast and creating too many ideas – like a gentle meditation, allowing ideas and thoughts to bubble up, questioning and revealing what is concealed. As in the above exemplar, in the agency of care amongst participants with cancer, no consideration was given to end-of-life planning. What bubbled up was the insight that emerged, surfacing and coming to light the taken-for-granted view that became discernible. In this way, central concerns emerge, themes reflect connections between meanings across stories, and patterns connect themes.

Figure 7.4   The 'bubbling up' of meaning that arises from meditative thinking

Hermeneutic circle and converging conversations

The hermeneutic phenomenological approach to analysis is a continuous circular and reflexive process where themes emerge and the researcher returns to the data and starts to re-read it. The hermeneutic circle begins the moment you choose your topic of study (Sorrell Dinkins, 2005). In other words, what has gone before and what comes after are both crucial parts of the circle. We were in the hermeneutic circle without initially realising it. Ironside (2005) suggests that we cannot step in and out of the circle but must remain within it throughout the process, though we can go back and forth. As we think about the data, both the parts and the whole, we are also reading along with the philosophical and non-traditional literature to dialogue with the data, creating converging conversations between existing knowledge and understanding, and that newly revealed from the research data. Converging conversations (Diekelmann and Diekelmann, 2009) also emerge as the researcher explores critical feminist and post-modern texts that extend, support or overcome the identified themes. Cycles of understanding, interpretation and critique hold the interpretation open and problematic as insights are developed and realised. Each reading is a rethinking that may enhance, affirm or change the interpretation. Rewriting occurs with each new interpretation that provokes thinking and pondering of future possibilities (Figure 7.5).

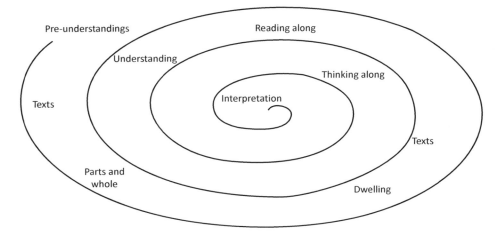

Figure 7.5 The hermeneutic circle

These converging conversations are a process of engagement with others (literature and researchers) that brings us to the fusion of horizons or a rendering of the shared interpretation of meaning to be presented. As Smythe (2005: 228) states: 'Within the experience of thinking there are no subheadings to categorize or arrange thinking. Thinking lives in rich, multidimensional ebb and flow, circling and recircling. Nevertheless, the written account demands a breaking down, and an order.'

Fusion of horizons

In the interpretations, there is a fusion of horizons (Gadamer, 2003) whereby the researcher and participants fuse their horizon of understanding and meaning to present a warranted interpretation of common meanings and shared practices. Navigating that complexity requires a *willingness* to use the skills of science, along with philosophical hermeneutic understandings and self-reflection (being reflexive), in order to render a meaningful result (Figure 7.6).

Producing an output

While there is belief that interpretations are never finished (Crist and Tanner, 2003) and the horizons of understanding are ever expanding, there is a time where a rendering of a product, manuscript and/or dissertation must be completed and disseminated

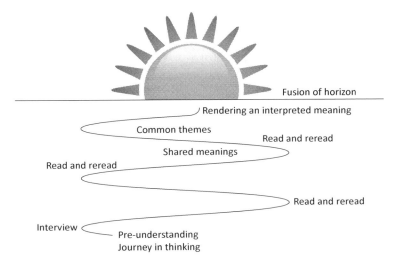

Fusion of horizon

Rendering an interpreted meaning

Common themes

Read and reread

Shared meanings

Read and reread

Read and reread

Read and reread

Interview

Pre-understanding

Journey in thinking

Figure 7.6 The researcher's journey towards the fusion of horizons (new understanding)

(see also Chapter 9: Writing and Dissemination). Creating a report is again an iterative process that creates an interpretation to give insight to meaning and understanding of the phenomenon. The report provides an interpretation so the reader can recognise the common meanings and shared practice with verbatim quotes to allow them to engage in an interpretation. It is a rigorous process of analysis that provides a text with sufficient excerpts from the data to present a credible account of the phenomenon, which makes sense to and resonates with the reader. Crucially, it must be understood that there are no attempts to claim any interpretation as 'right' or 'the truth': it is, instead, a representation of the fusion of horizons between particular participants and a particular researcher, at that moment in time and about that phenomenon. The final account is essentially dependent on these unique factors, informed as it is by the pre-understanding, culture and social context of the researcher and participants. The task of the researcher is not to present a definitive answer of what an experience 'is' for everyone, but a plausible, contextualised and credible account of what the experience means for a particular set of participants. The reader makes their own meaning, when the knowledge and experience they bring fuses with the new text, and it is for the reader to decide how applicable and transferable the new meanings are.

Alternative Approaches to Analysis

Analytical teams of Diekelmann and Ironside

Diekelmann and Ironside (2011) view analysis as an interpretation of historical consciousness and temporal situatedness. In this perspective, Heidegger's fore-structure of understanding is used, whereby all interpretations are based on background practices that provide a practical familiarity with the phenomenon, inform our perspectives and allow an anticipation of what is to be revealed in a circle of understanding. These understandings are formed from an engagement and openness to concerns of being that may be taken for granted.

Key to their approach is use of *analytical teams* to provide the balance and dialogic *sway* needed to increase the likelihood that the results of the inquiry reflect the phenomenon *as it shows itself*. The teams are comprised of methodology experts, content experts and those with experience of the phenomenon. Each team member reads the text and creates their own interpretive summary; these are shared in team meetings and provide a starting point for team analysis through discussion. Continuous dialogue with mentors and team members is an important part of the iterative analytical process unique to hermeneutic inquiry. As each new text is analysed, refining, expanding or challenging themes, any discrepancies are clarified by returning to the text and coming to a consensus. Continuous examination of the parts and whole ensure interpretations are warranted and reflected in the texts. The team also reads across texts, debates, brainstorms and discusses the interpretation to add insight and depth. As the themes are identified from the texts, they are held open and problematic until the team critique to extend, support or overcome. A pattern can also be identified that is present in all of the interviews and links them together. The team members review the entire analysis for plausibility, coherence and comprehensiveness. The product is a wide range of explicated texts so that the reader can recognise the common practices and shared experiences and find resonance with the insight and understanding. Team analysis is also helpful for managing prejudices which threaten the openness to possibilities of alternative meanings.

Exemplar Case

In a recent study, a team led by Dibley was exploring experiences of stigma amongst people with inflammatory bowel disease. The phenomenon was kinship stigma – stigma expressed towards individuals by members of their own family (Dibley, Williams and Young, 2019). For Dibley, who had an uneasy relationship with her own mother, it seemed 'obvious' that the impact on participants was much greater when the mother was the stigmatiser. By raising this with the team, the aspect of maternal stigma was explored in more detail and contextualised with the literature on expectations of parenting and the differences between expectations of children and society on mothers and fathers. The team analysis and attention to this topic mitigated against the potential negative bias of Dibley's prejudice, and created a pointing towards this 'thing which needed to be thought about'.

Patricia Benner's interpretive phenomenology

Patricia Benner began her research tradition initially referring to Heideggerian hermeneutic phenomenology and subsequently referred to interpretive phenomenology to give language to nursing practice. Benner had focused on explicating nursing practice in her seminal book, *From Novice to Expert: Excellence and power in clinical nursing practice* (1984), and further investigated the method in an edited book, *Interpretive Phenomenology: Embodiment, caring and ethics in health and illness* (Benner, 1994). Benner used observations and narrative interviews in a situation-based dialogue with nurses in individual and small group interview approaches to understand what the storyteller notices and the sense of salience about the situation. These are socially situated meanings, habits, practices and skills in the life world. The storyteller relies on socially shared, common, taken-for-granted background meanings that disclose social spaces or 'clearings' where we share social practices embodied in intentionality, habits, rituals, practices and everyday life. The approach usually uses participant observations, interviews to access participant experiences, and stories in everyday language. The interpretation involves independent and then consensual interpretations discussed within the team, offering multiple perspectives and insights. Interpretive leaps occur when examining an example that stands out from the other examples in a group of interviews. This is where the paradigm case emerges as a strong indicator of the particular patterns of concern. This offers a narrative account of the possibilities of understanding in a new way, and practical knowledge, engagement and reasoning in practice. The product involves identifying paradigm cases, exemplars and thematic analysis in a research team approach. This approach is valuable for those individuals who wish to explore the practice phenomenon.

Elizabeth Smythe's crafting stories

In her chapter on how to do hermeneutic interpretive phenomenology, Smythe (2011) explicated the idea of crafting stories as a way to work with the data to construct or craft a story from each interview and draw these together in an evocative telling of the story. These 'crafted stories' were shared with the participants as a gift. Crowther, Ironside, Spence and Smythe (2016: 827) further explain that: 'Stories thus act as a medium for researchers to invite readers into acquiring deeper insights and awareness about shared phenomenon ... a story brings multi-perspectival wholeness and possibility.' Crafting stories can be an activity during analysis to help move the researcher's thinking forwards, or these stories may be the end result of analysis.

Chapter Summary

Various hermeneutic scholars have provided suggested activities that comprise herme-neutic analysis. The construction of such models is paradoxical to the philosophical ideas that ground this approach to inquiry, yet researchers need examples to start their work. We have provided, in this chapter, several examples of analytical methods used by others, while also cautioning readers to approach their data with the unique and open perspec-tive that characterises this work. Thus, researchers are offered exemplar methods that provide a way, *e-methodos*, to get started in their own interpretive processes. The work of Diekelmann and Ironside, Benner, Vandermause and Smythe were discussed. Readers are provided with a variety of suggested processes by which they may construct a plan to interpret data and present findings.

Further Resources

These resources will help the reader recognise the approach to analysis and relevant hermeneutic stance, along with guides to nurture the appropriate skills, techniques and required meditative thinking.

Core readings

- Cohen, M., Kahn, D. and Steeves, R. (2000) *Hermeneutic Phenomenological Research: A practical guide for nurse researchers*. Thousand Oaks, CA: Sage.
- Crist, J. D. and Tanner, C. A. (2003) 'Interpretation/analysis methods in hermeneutic interpretive phenomenology', *Nursing Research*, 52(3), 202–205. doi: 10.1097/00006199-200305000-00011.
- Smythe, E. (2011) 'From beginning to end: How to do hermeneutic interpretive phenomenology', in Thomson, G., Dykes, F. and Downe, S. (eds) *Qualitative Research in Midwifery and Childbirth: Phenomenological approaches*. Abingdon, Oxon: Routledge, pp. 35–53
- Smythe, E. A., Ironside, P. M., Sims, S. L., Swenson, M. M. and Spence, D. G. (2008) 'Doing Heideggerian hermeneutic research: A discussion paper', *International Journal of Nursing Studies*, 45(9), 1389–1397. doi: https://doi.org/10.1016/j.ijnurstu.2007.09.005.

Further readings

- Benner, P. (1994) 'The tradition and skill of interpretive phenomenology in studying health, illness and caring practices', in *Interpretive Phenomenology: Embodiment, caring and ethics in health and illness*. Thousand Oaks, CA: Sage, pp. 99–127.

- Benner, P. E. (1984) *From Novice to Expert: Excellence and power in clinical nursing practice*. Frenchs Forest, NSW: Pearson.
- Crowther, S., Ironside, P., Spence, D. and Smythe, L. (2016) 'Crafting stories in hermeneutic phenomenology research: a methodological device', *Qualitative Health Research*, 27(6), 826–835. doi: 10.1177/1049732316656161.
- Diekelmann, N. and Ironside, P. (2011) 'Hermeneutics', in Fitzpatrick, J. and Wallace-Kazer, M. (eds) *Encyclopaedia of Nursing Research*, 3rd edn. New York: Springer, pp. 220–222.
- Ironside P. (2019) 'Hermeneutics', in Fitzpatrick, J. and Wallace-Kazer, M. (eds) *Encyclopaedia of Nursing Research*, 4th edn. New York: Springer, pp. 319–322.
- MacKey, S. (2005) 'Phenomenological nursing research: Methodological insights derived from Heidegger's interpretive phenomenology', *International Journal of Nursing Studies*, 42(2), 179–186. doi: 10.1016/j.ijnurstu.2004.06.011.

8

Reflexivity and Rigour

In this chapter, we address the risks to rigour that can arise in hermeneutic study, and the role of reflexivity and other techniques, including co-constitution during data collection (Chapter 6) and data analysis (Chapter 7), which enhance rigour, thus increasing the credibility, reliability and trustworthiness of the findings. Unlike post-positivistic/quantitative research, and descriptive phenomenology where the influence of the researcher is designed out of the study, the hermeneutic researcher is an integral part of study design and essential to its success, whilst also risking exerting an unwanted influence. Gadamer's concepts of pre-understanding (or prejudice) that are present in the researcher's horizon of understanding and which fuse with the participants' experiences, help explicate this concept. With reference to exemplars from hermeneutic scholars, we discuss the continuous thread of reflexivity which runs through any hermeneutic study, from conception to conclusion, and how the researcher, research team and/or supervisory panel ensure the researcher brings benefit (positive bias) to the study, whilst minimising risk (negative bias). The work of de Witt and Ploeg, and other notable scholars, will be used to illustrate the processes and evidencing of rigour within hermeneutic research.

Historically, qualitative research has been much criticised for not being able to meet the expectations and exact definitions of quality expected within the scientific community which traditionally was governed by what are now termed 'positivistic principles', based on Cartesian dualism.

Explanatory Box 8.1

Cartesian Dualism

René Descartes was a 17th-century philosopher who laid claim to and maintained the theory that the human mind and body were distinct entities which did not interact with each other. This 'separateness' between the physical and the cognitive has influenced the expectation that science is an abstract cognitive endeavour and one which the physical body should be excluded from. Mehta (2011) offers a useful critique of Cartesian dualism as applied to medicine.

If a study had not followed established quantitative rules, had not separated the researcher from the researched, did not have a large sample size, did not give a definitive answer to a question or hypothesis, and was not generalisable, then it was generally considered to be of poor quality and unable to add anything to scientific knowledge. Qualitative, and particularly post-positivistic, researchers reject Cartesian duality by acknowledging the interrelationship between mind and body, thus avoiding independence between researcher, subject and study participants. Instead, we have built research principles and methods around the value that is to be gained from a relationship between these components.

The core of this position is that, as post-positivists, we are not attempting to understand the world in a reductionist way, explaining something in isolation from any influences which may bear upon it. What positivists call 'confounders' – things external to the study which can affect the issue under investigation, post-positivists call 'context' – factors within a person's world which add meaning to their understanding of the experience being explored. Judging the quality of one with the rules of another, is never going to work out well – it's like complaining that a two-seater sports car cannot carry as many people or as much luggage as a 12-seater minibus; of course, it cannot – it isn't meant to – it's meant to be a sports car. And, equally, the 12-seater minibus that is not as agile, quick or manoeuvrable as the two-seater sports car is not meant to be a sports car – it's meant to be a minibus. Used appropriately for the right purpose, each is perfect. And so it is in research – when the aim of the researcher should be to use whichever approach is best suited to addressing the question, and demonstrating quality.

Yet research does need rules which ensure quality throughout the research process; in positivistic research, the landscape is awash with case report forms, internal and external audits, compliance agreements and so on, whilst post-positivists have slowly, over the years, developed ever-more robust methods of demonstrating that their methods are rigorous, and their research findings can be trusted. Quality in hermeneutic research is based on the philosophically-specific component of prejudice and the broad, post-positivistic principles of rigour and reflexivity, applied at every stage of the research endeavour.

Prejudice

A tour of any dictionary or thesaurus will produce evidence that prejudice is typically considered as negative. In law, prejudice is understood to lead to harm or injury, and in general use, it is a position which claims, presents or exerts an often negative or discriminatory influence of one person or group on another. Prejudice is reported daily whenever an individual or group makes assumptions about, or discriminates against, other individuals or groups. For example, the UK Police's 'stop-and-search policy' was considered prejudicial because the statistical evidence of its application demonstrated that the vast majority of individuals apprehended under this policy were young black men. Prejudice or 'pre-judging' means having a pre-formed negative or derogatory opinion about something or someone – and commonly without evidence to support that opinion.

In hermeneutic phenomenology, Gadamer (1960, 1975, 2003) invites us to think about prejudice in a different way. He uses the term to refer to our connectedness with the world; for Gadamer, 'prejudice' – a word which acknowledges that any connectedness we have naturally brings with it what Heidegger calls 'pre-understanding' – is an existing perspective of our own on our topic, experience or situation of research interest. This is the core of hermeneutics – our situatedness and relationship with the world, our status as 'always-already' interacting with, interpreting and gaining new knowledge about the world around us. Bhattacharya and Kim (2018: 1) explain that:

> Gadamer (1975/2006) ... argues for a new understanding of prejudice, claiming that prejudice, in fact, is a positive, enabling condition with a pervasive power in the phenomenon of understanding ... prejudice is an integral part of who we are, and therefore, we cannot ignore our own prejudice when we understand the Other. Unlike Cartesian thinkers, Gadamer posits that incorporating our prejudice into understanding, rather than avoiding it, is necessary as it represents the primary condition for a hermeneutical situation.

Prejudice from the Gadamerian, hermeneutic perspective is therefore not necessarily negative, but a means of acknowledging and opening ourselves up to the detail of our connectedness and our pre-understanding. As soon as we begin to think about our research topic, and what our question might be, to search the literature, to recruit participants, collect and analyse data, and present findings, then our Gadamerian prejudice and our Heideggerian pre-understanding are at play.

Exemplar Case

My PhD explored stigma in inflammatory bowel disease, but I (Dibley) was thrown towards that topic because of my own experiences of feeling stigmatised as a young gay woman growing up in Britain in the 1970s and '80s. Naturally, my perception of what it meant to be and feel stigmatised both informed and challenged my position throughout the study, so like every other hermeneutic scholar, I needed to manage these prejudices in a rigorous way. The aim of the hermeneutic researcher is to acknowledge their pre-informed (prejudiced) position and manage this so that the beneficial aspects enhance the study, whilst the potential impact of detrimental aspects is minimised. Spence (2017: 837) advises that:

> All human beings (including one's participants, supervisors, examiners, and self) have prejudices (Taylor, 1985b). These should be explored for how they enable and limit understanding rather than being denied and/or identified and bracketed from the interpretation.

As supervisors, all four of us engage our fresh-faced, eager new hermeneutic scholars in a conversation to explore their own prejudices. We invite them to focus on what it is that brings them to this topic, and why they want to explore it from this philosophical perspective. We lay out our own world view. The intention is for each of us – supervisor and student – to acknowledge our prejudices and understand which are potentially enabling and which are limiting, and even to appreciate that the same prejudice can be both an asset and a risk. For example, Dibley has had an experience of stigma which opens her up to the possibility of recognising and understanding it in others, but which, at the same time, risks closing her to the possibility that others may experience stigma in ways which differ from her own. Our early conversations with students invite them and us as supervisors to open ourselves up to possibilities of thinking about the things we think we already know, in new ways:

> Coming to understand one's prejudices, presuppositions, or preunderstandings and the ways in which these and those of others influence the research journey is a difficult and ongoing challenge. Undertaking 'presuppositions interviews' of students during their research projects assists to surface prior and evolving understandings in relation to the topic, literature, data, and emerging findings. (Spence, 2017: 838)

Surfacing these understandings enables the adoption of the phenomenological attitude in which 'the researcher strives to be open to the "other" and to attempt to see the world freshly, in a different way' (Finlay, 2009: 12). The initial conversation between student and supervisor, whilst essential for understanding the potential implications of prejudice, also introduces the student to a way of being phenomenological and developing this attitude which will facilitate the study and contribute to its quality.

Methodologically, the Gadamerian prejudice of hermeneutic research aligns with general qualitative challenges of subjectivity and insider status – each of which acknowledge that, in some way, the researcher has a welcome connection with the research they intend to do. The core technique for management of this prejudiced relationship is reflexivity and, done well, it enhances the rigour of the study.

Reflexivity Throughout the Research Process

Since the late 1990s/early 2000s, the proactive use of reflexivity has emerged as a way of managing the relationship between researcher and research:

> Researchers, especially within the qualitative tradition, who are keen to acknowledge the situated nature of their research and to demonstrate the trustworthiness of their findings, are seeking new tools. Using reflexivity, they find that subjectivity in research can be transformed from problem to opportunity. (Finlay and Gough, 2003: ix)

Reflection and reflexivity are different; reflection involves thinking retrospectively about a previous event in order to learn from it (Mezirow and Associates, 1990), while reflexivity is an active process of dynamic self-awareness which takes place as an event is happening (Dowling, 2006). The reflexive researcher constantly adjusts their influence, minimising negative and enhancing positive aspects of self to benefit the study, throughout the research process (O'Connor, 2011). From identification of the research topic and formulation of the question, to delivery of the project through the familiar framework of the research process, the reflexive hermeneutic researcher is constantly asking themselves: *What is it about me that helps or hinders the project, and what, if anything, do I need to do about it?*

The research idea

As discussed in Chapter 3, the idea for a research project never arises out of thin air. There is always some connection between the researcher and the issues they are interested in exploring, and it is important for the hermeneutic researcher to be reflexive about this. When the research idea first emerges and starts to take shape, the reflexive researcher should ask themselves, *Why am I interested in this topic? Who will it benefit? Is there another way of investigating it?* The purpose is not to deter the researcher from doing the project, but to adopt a phenomenological attitude so that they recognise exactly what their own influence is on the research idea. For example, Duffy and Dibley have both been drawn towards research that explores experiences amongst marginalised groups, informed undoubtedly by their own experiences of being marginalised. Both recognise that their experiences 'open a door', or provide an opportunity, to give voice to other marginalised groups, precisely because they are in a professional position to do so. They are able to say, *This has been our experience and it is an experience which informs, but does not rule, the work that we do.*

The literature search and the research question

As hermeneutic researchers acknowledging our Gadamerian prejudice and Heideggerian pre-understanding, we embark on our literature search and the development of our research question with our own preconceived ideas on the topic. In hermeneutics, this becomes problematic only if we fail to recognise that there may be – and most likely are – alternatives. Holding ourselves open then to the possibility of 'other' – other experiences, other perspectives, other explanations, other evidence – we must acknowledge that our starting position is just that – it is our point of departure for beginning our exploration of the literature and the development of our question. Throughout our literature search and review, we respond reflexively to the evidence appearing before us: *Does this research article help my question? Am I only choosing it because it supports my original view? Am I holding myself open to the possibility of the Other and considering alternatives?* Notice that we use the word 'considering' here – not accepting. Being aware of one's prejudices, holding open in the phenomenological attitude and being reflexive do not automatically require us to abandon our original view and accept alternatives, but they do require that we examine and critically consider alternatives and then adopt the most appropriate evidence to support our research plans. This cannot be done reflexively without being aware of one's starting position.

Recruiting study participants

We know from Chapter 4 that participant selection in hermeneutic phenomenological research is always purposive – it is essential that those invited to share their experiences, have had the experience of interest. Yet recruitment is not just about inclusion and exclusion criteria and an eligibility to participate – it is also about encouraging potential participants who might want to be involved, and it may be their perception of the researcher that will finalise their decision. Implicit bias is at play here too, and may encourage or discourage participation, so the hermeneutic researcher needs to ask themselves: *What is it about me that will likely encourage people to participate, and what will likely discourage them?*

Exemplar Case

I (Dibley) came to my PhD work (stigma in inflammatory bowel disease) as a nurse, an academic with prior experience of inflammatory bowel disease research, a member of society subject to the same broad social rules about hygiene and containment of body fluids and excrement, and an individual with a stigmatised identity. My cultural background instilled in me social rules about bodily functions and associated hygiene, yet my personal perspectives were and are influenced by professional clinical experience: I appreciate that illness or disability can affect control of body functions and the ability to maintain social rules, and I am less offended or disgusted by bodily functions and products than someone without my professional experience might be. I was also the owner of a discreditable (lesbian) identity (Goffman, 1963), and well recall, in my youth, the fear of being discovered to be anything other than the heterosexual single woman I appeared to be. Being reflexive whilst designing my PhD study required me to decide which of these attributes would be helpful, and which would not, in encouraging participation.

Dibley chose to foreground her professional and research persona, and not reveal her stigmatised identity even though, by then (2010), she did not feel stigmatised by it. Participants needed to feel confident that she had the professional skills to conduct the research, and there was no good methodological reason to reveal her personal identity – but it could have deterred potential participants with a particular heteronormative view. Dibley therefore promoted her professional identity as a nurse researcher with robust experience of talking to people with IBD about their disease and any related incontinence, but withheld her personal identity.

In contrast, we saw in Chapter 5 that Duffy did reveal her identity to participants, because given the cultural and social environment in Ireland at the time and the inherent risks of revealing oneself as gay, it was seen as a hook which would encourage participants into the study; if they were going to talk to anyone, it would be to her.

The decision about which aspects of the self to use are therefore guided by appropriateness, relevance to the topic and the need to enhance participation. Personal and professional aspects may well be appropriate – for example, Serrant-Green (2002) exploited her racial identity to enable research with minority ethnic communities, and Chesney (2000) used her role as a midwife to facilitate research with other midwives. Reflexivity during the decision-making process ensures that the enabling and limiting aspects of these prejudices are appropriately managed.

Data collection

In hermeneutic phenomenology, data collection is an art. Until this point in the research study, the researcher has had the luxury of time, dwelling in the academic environment and discussing with peers and their supervisor(s), to consider their prejudices and the potential impact of these on different study processes. Now, they find themselves 'in the thick of it', managing all the complex skills of the open or unstructured interview. There is a need to simultaneously listen, understand, assess, be alert to contradictions, decide on what to follow up and what to leave, and to take note of hesitations, descriptions, emotions and non-verbal signals (Mason, 2002; Legard, Keegan and Ward, 2003). Reflexivity is woven in as the researcher manages these tasks, whilst also practising reflexively to manage the prejudices they bring to the data collection event.

Active listening is well recognised as a core skill that enhances the quality of data produced during interviews or hermeneutic 'conversations' (Weger, Castle Bell, Minei and Robinson, 2014) and it requires reflexivity – a constant, open self-awareness that enables the researcher to bring the best out of the participant for the benefit of the study, whilst dampening down their own personal perceptions and limiting prejudices. The reflexive hermeneutic researcher should be asking themselves: *What am I hearing from this participant and is it coloured by my pre-conceived ideas? How do I re-phrase this issue to the participant without negatively prejudicing it* (introducing bias)? *Have I adopted the phenomenological attitude which keeps me open to the possibility of the other?*

The purpose is not to automatically rule out or ignore one's own prejudices, but to recognise where these sit in relation to the experience of the Other. It is the difference between asking the participant '*And is that because …?*' (driven by one's own perspective of what an experience means) and asking them '*Can you explain why it is that you feel like that?*' (driven by a suspicion of what the core of an issue might be); the latter enables the meaning to be offered up by the participant rather than extracted by the researcher. As we will see later, this technique is also an indicator of robustness, demonstrating that data were offered freely by participants.

The use of field notes during data collection is recommended to facilitate reflexivity; the practice enables the hermeneutic researcher to 'park' particular issues – be they methodological or theoretical, or ideas about the phenomenon of interest that are developing as a result of each interview – and to revisit these later to consider the relationship of these issues to their own prejudices.

Explanatory Box 8.2

The Value of Field Notes

One extract from the field notes during data collection for my PhD (Dibley et al., 2018) reveals my frustration at a particularly short interview I had just completed. I had travelled over 400 miles to interview this participant and was in her home for all of 10 minutes. Due to also interviewing others living in the vicinity, I wrote in my field notes:

> All this way for 10 minutes! What am I missing? How come I got such little data? What did I do wrong? Maybe there is some meaning in this that I cannot see. They said at that study day that there's always something of value in interview data, even if we can't immediately see it. I'm just going to have to sit with it and trust that something will show itself.

Something did show itself; the participant – who regularly experienced bowel incontinence because of her IBD – had talked about being raised by blind parents with an attitude towards disability and bodily imperfection which instilled in her the view that these need not be limiting or stigmatising. As the interviews proceeded, I realised that those brief 10 minutes had opened my thinking to a new possibility – that childhood experiences and childhood socialisation were each a central influence in participants' adult perception of their disease as being stigmatising or not.

Keeping field notes is a particularly useful technique if interviews are being conducted in quick succession or if travel between interviews is needed; field notes enable the safe placing of ideas that the student can return to, enabling them to free their mind, ready for whatever it is that they need to focus on immediately.

Data analysis

At analysis, reflexivity involves combining one's own knowledge and experience with what is discovered in the data to *aid* understanding, whilst avoiding the assumption that personal knowledge *is* understanding. Even though an experience might be shared, it cannot be assumed that all those sharing that experience have the same understanding of it (Platzer and James, 1997). Developing a showing/revealing of others' experiences involves the researcher in a 'complex and intense process, inextricably linked to the acts of interpretation and reflexivity' (Holloway and Freshwater, 2007). Crist and Tanner (2003: 203) remind us that:

> The interpretive team acknowledges (as much as possible) any assumptions that could both influence the investigator's conduct of interviews and observations as well as the whole team's interpretations.

An interpretive team is not compulsory in hermeneutic research but adds considerably to the rigour of the study because the involvement of others in the analysis process encourages the supportive yet robust challenge of the lead researcher or student's prejudices and preconceptions. The team is itself hermeneutic as the interplay between the range of knowledge and experience amongst team members, combined with the raw data and extant literature, come together to co-create a new understanding. The scholarly questioning by the team of assumptions which may be made during analysis enhances the reflexivity of the data collector, encouraging them to acknowledge places where presuppositions and prejudices may play out. We saw this evidenced in the example from the kinship stigma study, presented previously (Chapter 7: p. 130). Addressing presuppositions and prejudices as a team, consulting relevant literature, debating and discussing, lead the team to a shared understanding of the phenomenon, whilst avoiding the risk of making an unsubstantiated claim about an aspect which may only be hinted at in the data.

The challenge for the lone hermeneutic doctoral student, who must necessarily demonstrate that the work is their own, is to respond reflexively during data analysis when there is (at least in the UK or in Ireland) no core team to assist with analysis. During analysis, the lone researcher should ask themselves: *Am I seeing what I want to see here? Am I seeing what I expect to see here? Am I keeping myself open to the possibilities of alternative meanings and explanations within this data?* To achieve this, the student needs to have a very clear understanding of their own pre-understanding, which will have expanded during data collection as exposure to participants' stories prompts new thinking and ideas. A reflexive diary, noting these preconceptions, assumptions and ideas, can help focus the mind (Nadin and Cassell, 2006; Ortlipp, 2008). Again, the aim is not to automatically dismiss any of this preliminary thinking, but to reflexively consider it and be able to be as certain as we can be that the ideas taken forward are supported by the data.

Reflexivity is not something that a researcher 'does' at specific points during a study. It is a constant process, a hermeneutic cycle in itself, in which the researcher is *always-already* critically analysing their own position, insight and understanding in the light of ongoing research events, and coming to a new horizon of understanding about themselves and their research (Laverty, 2003). Being reflexive is demanding. It can be difficult to step back from our own pre-understanding and see the world as others might, whilst controlling the influence of self and being acutely self-aware (Clancy, 2013). Reflexivity requires an honesty and emotional vulnerability which can be personally challenging (Sampson, Bloor and Fincham, 2008); old emotional wounds may be re-opened and formerly reliable self-preservation strategies may be tested. A strong and supportive relationship with supervisors provides both emotional counterbalance and the necessary challenges to personal thinking which can propose alternative interpretations and facilitate the thread of reflexivity throughout a hermeneutic study.

Co-Constitution

In hermeneutic research, co-constitution is used in data collection, and in the analysis and presentation of findings. It is a core technique for managing the influence of self in the research, and for demonstrating rigour.

Co-constitution refers to an inseparable bond between the person and their world, with each being constructed by and constructing the other – they are what they are because of the world they live in, and their world is what it is because of the way it is interpreted and understood (Koch, 1995). Co-constitution also refers to an inseparable bond of interpretation between people: humans understand an experience due to an unavoidable combination of the background and pre-understanding of each person with the other in the same event. This stance led Heidegger to reject Husserl's notion of the phenomenological epoché (bracketing), arguing that background and pre-understanding are essential parts of how humans interpret and make sense of

their experience in the world, so everyone – including the researcher – must participate in the interpretation of the event:

> an interpretation of human existence cannot be neutral, dispassionate, theoretical
> contemplation, but must take into account the involvement of the enquirer him- or
> herself in the undertaking. Human beings are involved with their existence in such
> a way that hermeneutics must be able to accomplish this movement backwards and
> forwards between the existence to be examined and the nature of the examining
> enquirer. (Moran, 2000: 197)

Co-constitution in data collection

For the Heideggerian hermeneutic researcher, how a participant understands an
experience and the context in which it occurred, helps create their interpretation
of what the experience is. What is shown to the researcher at interview is understood as the participant's reality. The preconceptions that the researcher brings to
interviews and analysis are essential to the interpretive/hermeneutic process, and
any attempts to stand outside of one's own pre-understanding is considered 'absurd'
(Laverty, 2003).

One technique that qualitative researchers may use to verify the 'accuracy' of the
data is to send transcripts or analyses back to participants and invite them to confirm that the printed words are a 'truthful' representation of their experience (Guba
and Lincoln, 2017). The procedure has fallen under a more critical gaze in recent
years, with various criticisms levied at it, including concerns about the time delay
between data collection and verification – particularly if the research topic was
sensitive – and the erroneous notion that what is told at interview is an absolute
'truth' (Cho and Trent, 2006) and the failure to acknowledge that having told their
story at interview, the participant will likely have developed their own understanding of their experience and may now have a different insight into it. Birt, Scott, Cavers, Campbell and Walter (2016) explain that this member checking is a technique
to confirm validity, particularly to overcome the bias inherent when the qualitative
data collector is also the data analyst, though hermeneutic phenomenologists are
moving away from this technique (McConnell-Henry, Chapman and Francis, 2011).
We argue that it undermines the philosophical underpinnings of the research which
acknowledges and embraces the interrelationship between knowledge, the world
and the players in it, and that it fails to acknowledge that the purpose of hermeneutic phenomenological research is not to demonstrate absoluteness or truth, but
to reveal an understanding, given and created uniquely at that moment in time,
between the players in the interaction.

In the absence of member checking, confidence in the representation of participants' meaning is strengthened by the use of co-constitution at interview, so that the fusion of horizons (see Chapter 7: Data Analysis) is partially created during the interview event. Recapping phrases such as *'So are you telling me that …?'* secures confirmation from interviewees about an aspect of their story.

Exemplar Case

In this interview extract, Carl ('C', a pseudonym), a 54-year-old with Crohn's disease, is trying to explain how his disease makes him feel. Interested in his persistent expressions of embarrassment, I (Dibley) probe further ('I'). Italicised comments below each probe explain what I am doing to achieve co-constitution:

C: In our house we only had one toilet and I was in the toilet a lot, for hours in the morning and it was a fight to get in the toilet. So that was embarrassing yes, and eventually I just couldn't go to work and I was in the house all day. The tiredness was a lot to do with it as well, just through the disease. Um, but I was a builder by trade and I gave my job up at building and I'd done taxis years ago, so I tried to do that again. But I was getting caught in the car, got caught short in the car. So I remember a couple of times I had to run into a fast food restaurant and that and so trying to clean yourself in these places is really embarrassing. There's no bins in there to put anything in. You know, (chuckles), to leave stuff in. So it's really embarrassing. It's embarrassing to your friends, you know, it's not the nicest thing to talk about. So it has been embarrassing for the years I had before the stoma, a lot of times.

I: Right, and is that … do you know why it is that you feel so embarrassed?

[I correct my approach to avoid making an assumption of why he is embarrassed]

C: Just because of the way I was brought up, I was always clean and my mum was, you know, I was, I had to be clean and just from the smell or something – if you've had an accident you just feel really embarrassed and it's not the way to be, you know...

I: No, so for you it was because it's dirty?

[The 'No' indicates agreement with him about this not being the way to be, and the question about being dirty both follows up and confirms his reference to being clean]

C: It's dirty, yes. I never looked at poo before (laughs). You know, you never look in the toilet pan, you just do it and walk away.

I: Yes.

[Agreement]

C: Um, so this all became a new thing, you know, you were seeing it all the time, sort of thing and running, it's in your pants or whatever if you've had an accident, it's just disgusting to me, it was. Not natural, not natural, just not meant to do it. You don't even think of it if you don't have these problems.

I: No.

[Agreement]

C: So um that's really, it's embarrassing.

The extract demonstrates the way in which interaction between myself (Dibley) and Carl creates the shared understanding and agreement about why he feels so embarrassed – because the disease is unclean. I had suspected this, but the data is more powerful because the confirmation comes from him. With similar comments arising in other interviews, I could now confidently report concerns about dirt challenging the individual's expectation of cleanliness, and legitimately explore society's views and expectations of cleanliness and hygiene as they relate to having a bowel disease.

Co-constitution in analysis

In Chapter 7, we described the way that analysis occurs – either as a solo researcher conducting analysis alone, or as a team conducting analysis together. In both situations, the analyst(s) consult(s) the study data and the extant literature, and, mindful of their own preconceptions and prejudices, blends their own background and pre-understanding with those of the participant so that the eventual representation of the experience is a co-constitution of the understanding and experience of both parties, underpinned by relevant literature. The Heideggerian researcher presents this interpretation to a critical audience not as a 'truthful' explanation of what the phenomenon is universally understood to be, but as a representation, a showing/revealing of what the phenomenon can mean to those experiencing it. Hermeneutic phenomenologists

> put aside any claim that our research will produce objective, simplified, scientific concepts of truth ... our quest is not to prove or disprove, not to provide irrefutable evidence but rather to provoke thinking towards the mystery of what [a phenomenon] "is" (Smythe et al., 2008: 1391).

In terms of rigour, co-constitution in analysis reduces the risk that the researcher's prejudice and pre-understanding will exert a negative bias on the process and on the eventual reported findings; the researcher's influence is mitigated by consultation with others, and with literature which helps evidence meaning. Reflexivity and co-constitution are core techniques, threaded throughout the hermeneutic study, which not only reflect the principles of the underpinning philosophy, but also contribute to the quality of the research endeavour.

The Role of Rigour

Rigour is the means by which we further demonstrate the quality of our research – how we show that we have done our work well, to exacting standards, so that the reader can trust in our efforts. In post-positivistic research, rigour refers to the trustworthiness, credibility and dependability of a study, and to the transferability of the findings (Lincoln and Guba, 1982, 1985). The ways in which we achieve these requirements in hermeneutic research is best understood by drawing comparison with positivistic and general qualitative measures of rigour.

Validity, reliability and generalisability

In positivistic or quantitative research, the purpose is to produce a definitive answer to a precise question and/or prove or disprove one or more hypotheses. The quality or rigour of this type of research is judged on validity, reliability and generalisability (Shantikumar, 2018). Validity refers to the likelihood that a study, designed in a particular way, would produce specific data and answer the research question – in other words, that it does what it intends to do. Reliability refers to the likelihood that the study could be repeated using the same design – including profile and number of participants, data collection and analysis methods – and produce the same results; reliability is an indicator of consistency. Generalisability refers to the ability to extrapolate the findings from the study and apply these with confidence to any other members of the general population who match the characteristics of the study participants. Crucial to the concept of generalisability is that the study has included many participants whose demographic profile is representative of the target population. These concepts can be understood by thinking about a clock; a clock has validity as a clock because it does what is intended – it measures and demonstrates time. A clock has reliability because it measures time repeatedly and reliably – a minute is always the same length of time, an hour is always 60 times longer than a minute, and so on. Finally, a clock is generalisable, because wherever it is used on the earth (where time is always the same), it functions in the same manner.

Trustworthiness, credibility, dependability, confirmability and transferability

In post-positivistic or qualitative research, the purpose is to reveal insights into and understanding of human experiences; in hermeneutic phenomenological research, we aim to take this further and open ourselves and our readers up to the meaning of those experiences for our participants. We are not trying to say 'this experience means the same thing for all who endure/enjoy it'; instead, we are trying to say 'this experience, told to us in this way at this moment in time, appears to mean this for these participants, and we invite you into that understanding'. The quality of this type of research needs to be assessed in different ways because experience is not measurable (remember the two-seater sports car versus the 12-seater minibus). In qualitative research, the rigorousness of the study is demonstrated by the trustworthiness (credibility, dependability, confirmability and transferability) of the study (Lincoln and Guba, 1982: 3):

> All four of the 'trustworthiness' criteria that have been posed traditionally for inquiry can be met by naturalistic inquiry as well, albeit in somewhat redefined form – a form consistent with assumptions of the naturalistic paradigm. Thus, we have argued that the concept of internal validity should be replaced by that of credibility, external validity by transferability, reliability by dependability, and objectivity by confirmability.

Cypress (2017) presents a useful exploration of these concepts, using examples from a phenomenological study, but argues the case for using the terms validity and reliability whilst employing the concepts proposed by Lincoln and Guba.

The overall principle of trustworthiness

Trustworthiness refers to the degree of confidence that the reader may have in the way the study was conducted and its findings. Trustworthiness is enhanced through transparency – being clear and explicit about study design and delivery, acknowledging the situatedness/prejudice of the researcher and the bias this potentially creates, and evidencing the use of methods such as reflexivity and co-constitution. It is not enough to simply state that these tools were employed; the researcher should provide evidence of how or when and explain the significance to the reader. For example, Dibley and colleagues (2018) provide a distinct section within their publication, demonstrating exactly how issues of rigour were addressed within the study.

Credibility

Credibility refers to the integrity of the study processes and invites the reader to ask whether the study, designed and delivered using the described methods, would be likely to produce the findings that are reported (Shenton, 2004; Houghton, Casey, Shaw and Murphy, 2013). Techniques for achieving credibility include the transparent description of data collection and analysis processes, the use of verbatim quotes from participants to support the findings being presented, and the demonstration of shared as well as varied experience amongst participants. Maintaining an audit trail, for example of supervision, analysis meetings and decision-making processes, enables the researcher to demonstrate, if asked, the quality processes of their study which enhance its credibility (Koch, 2006).

Explanatory Box 8.3

Demonstrating Theme Development

One of the 'tasks' facing the hermeneutic phenomenologist is to convince the reader that the methods employed in analysis have been robust. To do this, some description of how the researcher moved from pages of raw data to the final themes/patterns, is necessary and, whilst for a final academic publication, such description will by necessity be brief, the Masters or doctoral student should be prepared to describe the analysis process in detail in their thesis. This may be aided by the use of diagrams to evidence the move from initial emerging ideas, through early multiple themes, to the final synthesised themes and/or patterns (Figure 8.1).

Dependability

Dependability broadly reflects the notion of reliability, which refers to the extent to which a study is repeatable. In quantitative research, it also refers to the replicability of findings, because it relies on the fact that not only is the study design the same, but also that the demographics of the study participants match those of previous iterations of the same study. Clearly, qualitative research cannot reproduce the same findings, and it is not trying to – in this situation, dependability refers to the ability of a study designed in a particular way, with different participants who have had the same experience as those in the original study, to produce findings which resonate with the existing qualitative knowledge about that experience. Koch (2006) explains that dependability refers to the ability of the reader to determine how findings were reached. Shenton (2004) proposes that dependability is one of the hardest quality components to demonstrate in qualitative research, and suggests that 'researchers should at least strive to enable a future investigator to repeat the study', although a clear audit trail evidencing the decision-making and rationale for any amendments to the study procedures, and the provision of samples of raw data, are useful techniques.

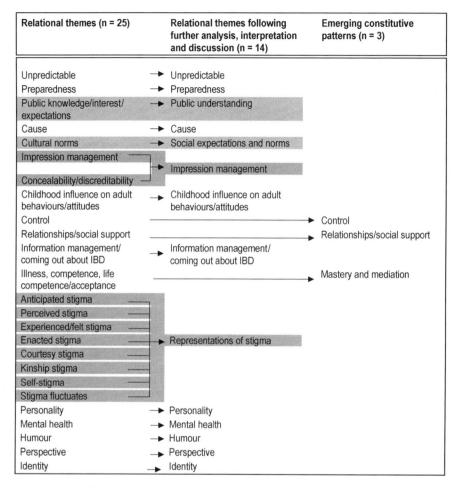

Relational themes (n = 25)	Relational themes following further analysis, interpretation and discussion (n = 14)	Emerging constitutive patterns (n = 3)
Unpredictable	→ Unpredictable	
Preparedness	→ Preparedness	
Public knowledge/interest/ expectations	→ Public understanding	
Cause	→ Cause	
Cultural norms	→ Social expectations and norms	
Impression management	→ Impression management	
Concealability/discreditability		
Childhood influence on adult behaviours/attitudes	→ Childhood influence on adult behaviours/attitudes	
Control		→ Control
Relationships/social support		→ Relationships/social support
Information management/ coming out about IBD	→ Information management/ coming out about IBD	
Illness, competence, life competence/acceptance		→ Mastery and mediation
Anticipated stigma		
Perceived stigma		
Experienced/felt stigma		
Enacted stigma	→ Representations of stigma	
Courtesy stigma		
Kinship stigma		
Self-stigma		
Stigma fluctuates		
Personality	→ Personality	
Mental health	→ Mental health	
Humour	→ Humour	
Perspective	→ Perspective	
Identity	→ Identity	

Figure 8.1   Example of development and synthesis of themes/patterns, from one of the authors' PhD studies: first review of relational themes from 25 down to 14, and emerging constitutive patterns

Note: Dark grey highlighting indicates the combining of two or more themes into one; light grey highlighting indicates a change of theme name

Confirmability

To achieve confirmability, researchers must be able to demonstrate that findings emerge from the data and not purely from their own presuppositions. Robust description of data analysis procedures, acknowledgement of any bias or prejudice, and verbatim extracts from the raw data, which enable the reader to see evidence of the interpretation, all serve to demonstrate the confirmability of findings. Specifically, verbatim quotes confirm the written interpretation and the notion of the phenomenological 'nod'. Tobin and Begley (2004) also propose that confirmability includes the notion of completeness, or thoroughness; this can be demonstrated through a detailed and precise description of processes, and evidence from audit trails and reflexive journals.

Transferability

The notion of transferability refers to the ability of the reader to take the findings of a qualitative study, and, having assessed the similarities between the components of the research and the setting they plan to transfer findings to, make the judgement that the outcomes of the reported study are relevant to and applicable in their own setting (Thomas and Magilvy, 2011). The decision about transferability lies with the reader, but it can be aided by a robust, transparent description of research setting, participants, data collection and analysis procedures, 'rich, thick description' (Grbich, 2007) and a demonstration of the relationship of the findings to the wider literature.

Rigour in hermeneutic phenomenological research

The principles relating to trustworthiness in qualitative research that we have already addressed go some way towards enabling us to demonstrate that our work is good, but may fall short when it comes to evidencing the quality (and therefore the robustness) of hermeneutic phenomenology with its specific principles of prejudice and pre-understanding, reflexivity and co-constitution. De Witt and Ploeg (2006) provide specific guidance for hermeneutic phenomenological research, recommending that we pay attention to balanced integration, openness, concreteness, resonance and actualisation. They are also clear that these components are 'expressions of rigour' rather than criteria of rigour (de Witt and Ploeg, 2006: 223). The reader is therefore invited to assess the expression of these components in a study, rather than assign some measure of quality.

Balanced integration refers to 'the articulation of the general philosophical theme … the intertwining of philosophical concepts in the study methods and findings, and a balance between the voices of study participants and the philosophical explanation' (de Witt and Ploeg, 2006: 224). The new understandings which are presented are a co-constitution between past knowledge and new experience of the researcher and the participant. As we discuss further in Chapter 9, this balanced integration is demonstrated most clearly when the core philosophical thinking is incorporated in the report of our findings.

Openness is the 'systematic, explicit process of accounting for the multiple decisions made throughout the study process' (de Witt and Ploeg, 2006), and it reflects the philosophical requirement of the researcher to open themselves up to the possibility of the other, to adopt the phenomenological attitude. In expressing the rigour in our research, we open ourselves up to the scrutiny of the Other by providing explicit accounts of what we have done and why. In other words, we provide an audit trail.

Concreteness reflects the relationship between findings and the real world so that the reader appreciates the situatedness of the phenomenon and understands the application of that phenomenon within the participant's world (de Witt and Ploeg, 2006; van Manen, 2016), and within the everydayness of life. One example from Dibley's PhD is the experience of having to 'jump the queue' to use a public toilet; every reader has the experience of queuing to use a public toilet, of expecting themselves and others to take their turn, and this aids understanding of the social dilemmas facing those who, because of the urgency associated with IBD, need to push to the front of the queue.

Resonance refers to the impact that findings have on the reader, and the extent to which the findings are recognised and make sense. Goffman's seminal 1963 text resonated with me (Dibley) when first I read it, because I felt it – in his observations about how others stigmatise, and how stigmatising 'others' the person of difference, I felt he was writing about a world I lived in daily, and understood. Resonance is what Frank (2004: 431) describes, in a metaphorical acknowledgement of the murder-mystery novel, as 'allowing the reader to discover the body, and then keeping them interested in it'. It is also what van Manen (1990), acknowledging the German philosopher Otto Bollnow (1903–91), refers to as 'the phenomenological nod' – the movement of the head that we make when we have seen, read or understood something which we recognise intuitively as being meaningful.

Actualisation refers to the future impact that findings will have, and is an expression, perhaps, of potential. Interpretation does not end at the conclusion of a study – findings continue to be re-interpreted and co-constituted with other evidence and other researchers' prejudice and pre-understanding, leading to new insights and consequences. Writing in 2006, de Witt and Ploeg were remarkably reticent about there being 'no formal mechanism … within the research community for recording actualisation' (p. 226). We propose that actualisation is the 'so what?' of our research – the point at which we define the relevance and impact our work does or can have in understanding experience, informing ongoing study, changing practice and influencing policy. Naturally, the evidence to determine actualisation may not emerge until some time after study completion. Research quality assessment exercises such as the Research Excellence Framework in the UK may provide one formal mechanism for demonstrating actualisation.

Lincoln and Guba (1982, 1985) and de Witt and Ploeg (2006) offer us guidance on how to assess rigour and its expressions in qualitative research generally, and hermeneutic phenomenology specifically; their frameworks also help us in the planning, designing and delivery of our research to ensure we design in these requirements, not only to enhance the quality of the study as we are doing it, but also to enable us to readily evidence that quality when we report it. Tobin and Begley (2004) evidence the debate between constructive and evaluative procedures, the former attending to quality during the research process, and the latter addressing the issue after the event. Overlooking quality issues during the process of research runs the risk of failing to see serious errors until it is too late, and these cannot then be corrected (Morse, Barrett, Mayan, Olson and Spiers, 2002). Ongoing reviews of these aspects during any hermeneutic phenomenological study help maintain a high standard of trustworthiness.

Chapter Summary

No study is perfect. There are always weaknesses and biases which influence outcomes and these should be openly acknowledged, but the researcher should demonstrate that they have made the best effort possible to manage these aspects to increase the reader's trust in the findings. Addressing prejudice and engaging in reflexivity and co-constitutive practices throughout the study, enhance rigour in ways which are philosophically relevant to hermeneutic phenomenology, enabling phenomenological researchers to counter criticism about the quality of the work they do.

Further Resources

These resources will help the reader broaden their understanding of the development and application of techniques to enhance rigour in qualitative (particularly hermeneutic phenomenological) research. In particular, Spence (2017) explores the philosophical stance required to address personal pre-understanding and prejudice.

Core readings

- Armour, M., Rivaux, S. L. and Bell, H. (2009) 'Using context to build rigor application to two hermeneutic phenomenological studies', *Qualitative Social Work*, 8(1), 101–122. doi: 10.1177/1473325008100424.
- De Witt, L. and Ploeg, J. (2006) 'Critical appraisal of rigour in interpretive phenomenological nursing research', *Journal of Advanced Nursing*, 55(2), 215–229. doi: 10.1111/j.1365-2648.2006.03898.x.

- Finlay, L. and Gough, B. (eds) (2003) *Reflexivity: A practical guide for researchers in health and social sciences*. Oxford: Blackwell Science.
- Spence, D. G. (2017) 'Supervising for robust hermeneutic phenomenology: Reflexive engagement within horizons of understanding', *Qualitative Health Research*, 27(6), 836–842. doi: 10.1177/1049732316637824.

Further readings

- Koch, T. (2006) 'Establishing rigour in qualitative research: The decision trail', *Journal of Advanced Nursing*, 53(1), 91–100. doi: 10.1111/j.1365-2648.2006.03681.x.
- Underwood, M., Satterthwait, L. and Bartlett, H. (2011) 'Reflexivity and minimization of the impact of age-cohort differences between researcher and research participants', *Qualitative Health Research*, 20(11), 1585–1595.

9
Writing and Dissemination

Chapter Overview

In this chapter, we discuss the ways in which hermeneutic projects may be written and presented, and disseminated in scientific and lay venues. The methodological approach differs from that of traditional science and is not universally understood, so reviewers are variously informed about how to critique manuscripts and offer guidance. We believe it is incumbent upon hermeneutic researchers to clarify their approaches and results for others. We will address the challenges and opportunities of the enterprise of dissemination by discussing various audit mechanisms, techniques of language and rhetorical practices that have been successful for hermeneutic scholars in the presentation of their work. Practical examples of how to write results, respond to reviewers and present or defend modifications will be provided. Critiques of the methodology and the disseminated products will provide readers with real-world solutions for anticipated challenges and suggestions for spreading important new findings from their hermeneutic work.

The value of hermeneutic work lies in the way it is received by others, the way in which the interpretation changes the audience. New understanding of often-overlooked ideas is expected and a new hermeneutic question often emerges from the interpretive results. As such, there are no particular rules for the ways in which results are rendered, but there are important signifiers that characterise the dissemination of hermeneutic work. The illumination and interpretation of experience is amorphous, yet the reader must have something familiar to grasp. Therefore, the wording of patterns and themes, accompanied by exemplars, requires an ability to craft a tangible result that resonates in a community of science or a group of stakeholders associated with the phenomenon of interest.

The receptivity of the scientific community toward ontological research such as this is growing. There has been a history of dissonance between 'qualitative' and 'quantitative' researchers that is diminishing in this post-structuralist period as questions related to health care proliferate. Hermeneutic phenomenology has been described as "the black hole of methods" by some, partly because research processes cannot be appropriated consensually. This requires increased attention to language and rhetorical argument that connects with a variety of perspectives. To be acceptable in scientific venues such as peer-reviewed journals and conferences, researchers must adapt to the needs of their audiences to accomplish their dissemination goals. The following are some suggestions for presenting hermeneutic findings and seeking dissemination venues.

Writing as Process and Product

The presentation of findings is, ultimately, the goal of the research and the reason for writing. Findings are the answer to the research question(s). There are various ways to present findings, some of which will be described below. The steps in the research process, including design, recruitment, data collection and data analysis, culminate in the large task of writing up the findings. There are, however, other important writing tasks – those that constitute the implementation of the study as a whole.

Writing is a form of language expression – the use of words to convey an idea. But the words themselves are a way to something more. Through language, however clear or ambiguous, meaning is revealed: 'To hermeneutically understand language is precisely to pierce through the façade of uttered language in order to bring attention to the things which our words attempt to share, but without fully succeeding, hence their indigence or "secondary"' (Grondin, 1995).

Grondin here reflects Heidegger's conversation about the way of language, about the use of words as a way of understanding beyond grammar and syntax. Our use of writing serves similarly, as we write poetry or narrative interpretations of transcribed interviews. The practice of writing itself is an interpretive activity. As such, field notes, interpretations and conversations between analysts are all a part of the exercise of negotiating common understanding. Therefore, all writing activity contributes to the dialogue that moves us toward the understanding we seek.

Thinking takes time and a ruminating effort to uncover new and familiar ideas. Keeping written notes that document decision points in the interpretive process helps propel the cadence of thinking as ideas emerge over the course of a project. Consulting a thesaurus stimulates recognition of meaning and helps authors find just the right word or phrase to convey the essence of an experience or describe common experiences across a cohort. Richardson and St Pierre (2018) describe using writing to think, using styles of writing that convey socio-political directions, and questioning the assertion of meaning through language. They advocate for writing practices and exercises, including creative writing, so that thinking can flourish.

Presenting hermeneutic findings

The development of an interpretation of common patterns, themes or ideas that represents the phenomenon in question follows the systematic and focused analysis described in Chapter 7. These patterns signal understandings of phenomena that are experiences, events or overlapping ideas that carry meaning. They need to be rendered in language that conveys an understanding that can be grasped by the reader or audience. Therefore, naming patterns is an art and part of the analysis and dissemination process.

Sometimes an analysis reveals an overarching constitutive pattern (Benner, 1994), which is a 'showing' of meaning that appears in all transcribed data, and across all of the patterns (which may be called sub-patterns or relational themes) (Diekelmann, 2001). At other times, meaning reveals itself as a way of being human, or an activity.

There may be two or three overall constitutive patterns that subsume two or three sub-patterns or relational themes. There is no one framework by which we identify patterns and themes. These 'showings' or areas of meaning reveal themselves in the course of the analysis as the phenomena 'show themselves', and researchers move into deeper understanding throughout the analytical discussion. It is the role of the researcher to name these areas of meaning and describe them in a way that resonates with the audience, that answers the research question with the use of words that signify the intended meaning. The pattern names can be chosen to signify activity or a state of being, identifying experience rather than a concept or fact or thing. This is in keeping with the relational and fluid nature of being, which is the focus of concern in hermeneutic studies. The patterns and relational themes create a language that answers the research question and can quickly be grasped.

The naming of patterns and themes in hermeneutic phenomenology differs from more positivistic methodological approaches, like content analysis, where concepts or categories are sought. For example, in a study describing and interpreting the experiences of adolescent girls in chemical dependency treatment (Vandermause, Fougere, Liu and Odom-Maryon, 2018), a content analysis and a hermeneutic analysis revealed different patterns/themes. The content analysis revealed five themes that were relevant to the girls: (a) *romantic partners*, (b) *moms*, (c) *siblings*, (d) *friends*, and (e) *future*. These were the areas in which participants focused their comments. A collection of comments and summary description of these areas answered the research question of 'what is it like…?' from a content-oriented perspective. However, the hermeneutic patterns were named differently; they included: (a) *Getting along: Negotiating Self and Others*, and (b) *Getting Better: Sensing a Future*. Each pattern subsumed themes that included *Belonging*, *Being loved/being betrayed* and *Being myself* in the first pattern, and *Helping others*, *Willing a change* and *Looking ahead* in the second pattern. Note that the hermeneutic patterns and themes relate to ontological experiences instead of categorical ideas.

It is important to tell the story of a phenomenon through a choice of words that signals an ontological orientation and creates understanding by hinting at ideas that the reader must take in and think about. The presentation of such findings is done differently than in traditional scientific method as it proffers new thinking, even as it relays the findings as an interpretation. The interpretation is, itself, a result. It is the product and purpose of the study. Therefore, the interpretation, written in the form of patterns or constitutive patterns and relational themes, is written in ways that might resemble a discussion in other methodological paradigms. It is often a re-telling of the narrative derived from the interview transcripts, using exemplars from the interview text and interpretive commentary that clarify the meaning that is discussed.

Exemplar Case

Humour is an effective antidote to tension and stress which shields people against negative effects of a situation by enabling a positive re-appraisal of a challenging event (Abel, 2002). As a coping mechanism, humour seems to improve people's social quality of life (Nezlek and Derks, 2001), but there is a difference between laughing **with** and laughing **at** someone. Glenn (2003) explains laughing **at** as hostile laughter, designed to ridicule and demean, and laughing **with** as affiliative, giving a sense of support and shared understanding. Tina [a pseudonym], whose efforts to retain stool by clenching buttocks and holding the anal sphincter in a tight squeeze, whilst trying to reach the toilet, cause her to perform 'funny walks'. She explains:

> The family tend to take the Mickey out of me [tease me] because they know when it's my colitis that makes me go to the toilet, because they'll, when I come out they'll go, 'Oh that was a new walk mum!' (Laughs). And they'll start parading up and down the living room showing me my latest walk to the toilet! [Tina, 45, ulcerative colitis, experienced incontinence, no stigma]

Tina's family laugh **with** her about the physically amusing aspects of her disease, and, in doing so, show their understanding and support.

The use of gerund forms of words (words ending in -ing) in the naming of the patterns allows for a representation that implies activity and change, and presents an image or idea that is memorable to the reader. Thus, a new story is told, one that gathers a gestalt and conveys a collective understanding for the reader to see in a glimpse – see and remember. The way this is written for the reader matters. It is the rhetorical element that is intended to persuade or show for the reader an uncovering, a new understanding about the phenomenon of concern.

A discussion section can follow the rendering of patterns and the associated interpretation or the 'discussion' can be laced into the interpretation. It is customary to pull from additional literature related to the newly found patterns, or to revisit earlier literature reviews to comment on how extant literature relates to the new findings. The inclusion of newly sought or extant literature is a way to link findings to what is known or currently accepted. It can demonstrate the relevance and transferability of our work to the wider academic community.

There are other ways to present findings that are consistent with the philosophical foundation of hermeneutics. One mechanism is the generation of a composite narrative or story that relates common ideas from all interviewees in a study. This technique, described by Crowther et al. (2016), presents the 'crafted stories' as findings.

As such, the reader is taken into the account experientially through the story, which conveys the experience like a transcript. This methodological technique may be controversial because the text that is presented appears to be fictional. It is, in fact, a story derived from the careful analysis of multiple texts and substantiated by a team of analysts committed to the integrity of the story.

Another mechanism is to return to the philosophies of Heidegger and Gadamer and to bring these into discussion to point the reader towards an understanding of the findings in the light of core philosophical thinking. For instance, in the earlier example of Gale's exploration of transition to parenting amongst couples with an IVF-assisted pregnancy (see Chapter 3, p. 45), the student drew on Heidegger's writings about technology (in relation to the IVF) and ready-at-hand/unready-at-hand (in relation to infertility) to enrich and reveal meaning in the experience of the participants. Techniques such as these help demonstrate the balanced integration described in Chapter 8 (p. 153), which enhances the quality of the study by demonstrating the golden thread which links together the components of any hermeneutic phenomenological study.

In all cases, it is the researcher's responsibility to bring the reader in, to help the reader see the phenomenon clearly and listen to the interpretive suggestion that is conveyed convincingly by a well-written commentary.

Presenting the experience of others

The nature of hermeneutic findings is often personal and involves the intimate lives of others. The researcher enters a sacred trust, of sorts, and is called upon to present a co-constructed finding, consisting of the understanding of the researcher themselves and the research participant. This understanding, though derived from genuine dialogue and intense analytical focus during analysis, remains a construction of the researcher. In some cases, researchers may return to participants to share their understanding and interpretation, but not in the way of member checking, a process by which researchers ask participants or members of the population of study to verify facts of the account. Rather, a return to participants may be done to reveal flaws in understanding of the phenomenon as a whole – a kind of continued dialogic interview to refine understanding (Birt et al., 2016). The 'accurate' and repeated expression of an event or experience is not sought. In hermeneutics, it is understood that an interpretation continues to evolve, that it is an expression of an idea that is genuine and meaningful and that reveals human experience, but the details of the occurrence or experience are contributory to understanding the essential being of the phenomenon in question, not verifiable points to be confirmed. In this way of understanding meaning, it is possible that specific individual accounts may be obscured and participants' subjective experiences may be subsumed by the overall interpretive summary.

It is important that participants understand the part they play in the co-construction of the interpretive result, and that they are comfortable that their contribution has been sufficiently included in the summary of results. At the same time, participants may not recognise themselves in the final analysis literally. That is, the researcher has incorporated the stories of their participants and presented findings in ways that keep the identities of these participants secure. Exemplars are chosen that will not reveal identities. For example, in a study by Kaufman (Kaufman, 2020) of the health care experiences of persons with large portions of their bodies tattooed, much of the meaning participants conveyed relative to their body art was described, not in the eloquent words of the participants describing the body art itself, but in a narrative explanation that would not identify individuals. The way in which the story is retold, therefore, requires an artful use of language that is close to the phenomenon but not the thing itself. The word choices become a work of art, a revealing that creates an image and '[lets] something be seen' (Heidegger, 1959, 1971: 226). This is a form of poetry and expression to engender understanding.

It is also important to consider the way in which participants are named in the presentation of findings. Often, pseudonyms are used to protect confidentiality, but the choice of representative names requires its own thoughtfulness. Do we choose names that reveal gender or racial identities – matched to the participant or not? Do we allow participants to choose their own pseudonyms as we quote their words? Do we use a bank of names from a list of persons representing the population of interest? All of these techniques have been used to present the words of study participants and each technique can be analysed for how well it represents the cohort of interest. These are interpretive acts and require the same degree of planning and consultation that pattern names require.

Sometimes participants are clear that they are willing to be represented as themselves, that their real names be used. This is also a matter requiring thoughtfulness and caution. The evocative interview style that leads to the transcripts can be surprising to participants. They may reveal experiences they had forgotten or that they had not prepared to disclose. We say they can rescind their permission at any time in the data collection process, but often participants are unclear following an interview and do not recognise the extent of their sharing immediately. It is incumbent upon an ethical researcher to think ahead and protect participants as much as possible. The revelation of actual identities should be very carefully decided; in most cases, pseudonyms that are representative of the population and confidential are recommended.

Explanatory Box 9.1

Thesis Writing

The technique required for writing a thesis is very different from writing for publication in a peer-reviewed journal. In the former, there may be a word limit of up to 120,000 (excluding references), whilst the most generous peer-reviewed journal may give a maximum word limit of 'only' 7000. In a thesis, the student is required to provide a depth of detail and explanation that is sufficient to convince the examiners that the work is their own, and that they demonstrate a doctoral level of scholarliness. The prospect of trimming one's life work down to a mere fraction of that seems impossible at first – but guidance from supervisors, being precise and focused, and presenting the fundamental essence of the thesis, are key.

Seeking dissemination venues

Dissemination is the ultimate purpose for this research, which is intended to uncover previously overlooked phenomena that are questioned for a particular purpose – to understand meaning, to change everyday behaviour or practice, to lead to new knowledge, or to question the unknown. Sharing the developing understanding is part of the process. In the academic environment, local, regional or national/international conferences are excellent venues to share pilot or final results. Poster presentations can be very useful, even during a study, because preliminary or formative findings can be discussed with others who have an interest in the phenomenon of concern. Conference participants can add insights and their own knowledge and experience to a discussion about the phenomenon. Such discussions may even be considered contributory to an ongoing analysis.

Other venues for presentation are local gatherings, podcasts and even multi-media representations that address lay audiences and convey findings that resonate with the everyday lives of those with a stake in the phenomenon of concern. The object of the study is to raise awareness and understanding of issues of concern and to participate in the everydayness of situations. Returning to communities to share findings is consistent with the participatory approach that characterises hermeneutic work. Acknowledging funders is common, but it is also important to acknowledge participants and community stakeholders for the roles they have played in the implementation of the project. Hermeneutic research is relational, from the first thought to the dissemination of findings.

Working with reviewers

Qualitative research has taken its place as a necessary contribution to the state of the science of health care today. Many reputable journals publish in a variety of research genres, including hermeneutic phenomenological studies. The field of experienced hermeneutic researchers is small, however, and reviewers may not be experienced in evaluating hermeneutic phenomenology. Even those reviewers that are comfortable with qualitative methodologies may lack the nuanced understandings of philosophical hermeneutics and the way in which philosophy guides the research endeavour. Reviewers may be comfortable with content analysis, descriptive forms of phenomenology or grounded theory as qualitative foundations, but these methodological directions differ significantly from hermeneutics, despite some resemblances. For example, reviewers may ask about member checking or whether the same questions were asked of each participant. They may want a more detailed description of the sampling strategy or the analytical process. Sometimes reviewers insist on an analytical description that is consistent with more positivistic qualitative forms and, in this case, the author must engage the reviewer, explaining the methodological detail, either in or outside the manuscript. Thus, authors of hermeneutic phenomenology need to be prepared for dialogue regarding their rendering of results. Ultimately, it is the author's responsibility to make themselves understood.

The variety of qualitative genres challenges scholars, even today. This was clear in a study of qualitative researcher experiences that included accounts from a majority of funded researchers out of the first funding cycle of the Patient-Centered Outcomes Research Institute (PCORI) (Vandermause, Barg, Ismail, Edmundson, Girard and Perfetti, 2017). The first PCORI-funded projects were primarily qualitative or included strong qualitative components and were written by researchers interested in the voice of the patient or citizen stakeholder. The hermeneutic interviews with these researchers revealed the joy and meaning the researchers ascribed to the qualitative methodologies they used, but they also highlighted the difficulties in publishing that many of them still faced. Hermeneutic phenomenology, a genre that is often even more mysterious to reviewers, caught some critique by some of the researchers using more commonly understood methodologies, such as content analysis. Despite common methods used across qualitative methodologies, criticism sometimes comes from other qualitative researchers.

Some journals require reviewers to use checklists for reporting qualitative research such as the consolidated criteria for reporting qualitative research (COREQ) (Tong, Sainsbury and Craig, 2007), which purports to provide criteria for qualitative research related to in-depth interviews and focus groups. While the criteria are grouped in relevant domains: research and reflexivity, study design and data analysis reporting, the items do not always match hermeneutic phenomenological studies – for example, methodological orientation of interpretive phenomenology, participant checking, description of coding tree, derivation of themes, and data saturation. The researcher should be aware that these criteria may be used to evaluate their manuscript and should address each question appropriately. For instance, when the COREQ criteria states: 'Were transcripts returned to participants for comment and/or correction?' the hermeneutic researcher should explain the philosophical reasons why this approach is unsuitable, and what has been done instead to provide equivalent assurances of veracity.

Table 9.1 Example of presenting responses to reviewer comments

Reviewer query	Author response	Changes to manuscript
How could you pre-set sample size in this qualitative study? Generally, researchers sample until they find saturation of data so please explain this decision.	In the methodology used, the number 15 was expected to be appropriate to provide rich data sufficient to answer the research question, which was the case. This was based on author experiences and corroborated by literature on sample size.	Fifteen of these patients, a number typically suitable for providing descriptive experiences likely to answer the research questions (Creswell, 2013), also participated in in-depth recorded interviews, upon enrolment and again upon study completion.
I would like to see how you have helped assure the rigour of the data.	The analysis of these data was conducted using a rigorous enactment of hermeneutic phenomenological analysis techniques. Several scholarly resources are cited in the text and these can be expanded to delineate steps in analysis if this would be useful. We have tried to maintain a concise paper and accurately reflect the traditions used.	In keeping with phenomenological traditions, the interpretive results were discussed alongside audit trails, analytical team member challenges.
Was an interview guide used to ensure consistency across interviews?	The interview guides provided open-ended questions to encourage narrative story telling. This guides the dialogue with additional probes used to expand understanding and focus on the phenomenon of the study.	Added table two – the interview guide with potential probes to situate the participant in the experience of the phenomenon.
How were the interview questions developed? Were the interview questions derived from another instrument or investigator developed?	Interview questions were based on open-ended questions to obtain each participant's experience with good and bad sleep in the context of their life stories. The investigator developed the questions based on methods and study goals.	Added discussion of the development of the interview questions by the research team.
For the analysis, when differences existed among analysts, was there a threshold for mutual agreement established before conduct of the study?	Analysis described in detail related to interpretive phenomenology – team analysis consists of discussion and comparison of themes, returning to text for further analysis and consensus building during the process of analysis, not in advance of it.	More detail added to the analysis section on consensus building.
Culture in the USA is not monolithic; thus, using a sampling frame that assumes all subjects have a common sleep culture may be premature. In order to justify the sampling decision, please provide evidence/explanation as to why all members of this population should be considered as coming from a culture of common meanings and shared practices. For this reason, purposive sampling may have been more appropriate.	The sampling resulted in rich narratives that provided data for an interpretive analysis. The texts are most important. The goal was to understand the meaning of good and bad sleep in a healthy population sample, not a specific culture. This study is an analysis of the narratives from the sample. There are no claims that this is generalisable to the USA. Goal is to understand what a sample of healthy people understand about their sleep. Everyone sleeps, thus it is purposive from that perspective.	

The use of clear and descriptive techniques is, therefore, important, as is a concise way to render results while allowing the storied meaning of experience to be known. This is a skill of language and dialogue, tools the hermeneutic phenomenologist must hone. The results are often offered as a conversation with the reader, a way of showing the meaning of the phenomenon of interest in an understandable way. This is also true for responding to reviewers.

Reviewers may raise astute questions that the authors had not considered. Thinking through and responding to such questions can make a manuscript much better. (In our work, we sometimes acknowledge reviewers, particularly if the critique extended the interpretation and deepened the understanding.) Sometimes, however, a reviewer's requests may take the writing away from a hermeneutic stance and the author must respond by explaining more in the manuscript or answering to the issue with the reviewer. A simple three-column table is useful in such responses, whereby the first column consists of reviewer comments; the second, the author's response to the reviewer ('thank you, changes will be made'; or an explanation of why changes will not be made); and the third, what was changed in the manuscript, if anything (Table 9.1). Such a 'conversation with reviewers' is often beneficial and leads to a better manuscript and a better educated reviewer on hermeneutic phenomenology. In the final analysis, it is a way to language that the hermeneutic researcher must foster, remaining open to the dialogue and debate regarding methodology, curious about the receptivity of others to hermeneutics, and responsible to interpret – to translate to scientific and lay communities the experiences of those the researcher questions in ways others understand:

Dear reviewers,

Thank you for your careful review of this manuscript. The reviewers provided specific questions and comments, which we believe we have addressed and which improve the article. The manuscript has been revised to answer to specific reviewer suggestions, including some reorganization and the addition of clarifying information regarding methods. We hope you are pleased with this revised version.

Chapter Summary

Writing is personal and public, and there are ways to disseminate it that speak broadly to the thinking that is common in hermeneutic phenomenology, a use of language and structure that is congruent with the philosophy that underlies the approach. The purpose for our study, however, is the generation of new knowledge, a conveyance of understanding and meaning that is something different from our thinking when we started. Particular directions or steps for writing contradict the open purpose of the research. Yet there are ways that we interpret and translate our findings that unlock the lines of thinking that took us into the research and open up a stream of understanding that we hope the reader or audience will engage with. We want our findings to resonate with those interested in our phenomenon of concern, to make a difference to those for whom our topics matter, to enlighten. Thus, we continue our conversations and our questions in a dialogue that continues to evolve.

Further Resources

For guidance on core practices and processes relevant to writing and publication:

- Higgs, J. G., Horsfall, D. and Grace, S. (eds) (2009) *Writing Qualitative Research on Practice*. Rotterdam: Sense Publishers.
- Richardson, L. and St Pierre, E. (2018) 'Writing: A method of inquiry', in *The Sage Handbook of Qualitative Research*. Thousand Oaks, CA: Sage, pp. 818–838.
- The Writing Centre, University of Wisconsin – Madison: https://writing.wisc.edu/handbook/assignments/planresearchpaper
- Wallace, M. and Wray, A. (2016) *Critical Reading and Writing for Postgraduates*, 3rd edn. London: Sage.

For advice about ways of disseminating phenomenological research:

- Galvin, K. T. and Todres, L. (2011) 'Research based empathic knowledge for nursing: A translational strategy for disseminating phenomenological research findings to provide evidence for caring practice', *International Journal of Nursing Studies*, 48(4), 522–530. doi: 10.1016/j.ijnurstu.2010.08.009.
- Keen, S. and Todres, L. (2007) 'Strategies for disseminating qualitative research findings: Three exemplars', *Forum Qualitative Sozialforschung*, 8(3), Art. 17. Available at: www.qualitative-research.net/fqs (accessed 11 January 2020).

Part III Summary

In this part, we have addressed the thinking and doing of data collection and analysis, guiding the reader through the philosophical and practical aspects of these most exciting components of the study which, if the design is robust, enable us to collect rich, contextual data and grasp us in the absorbing work of analysis. Examples from our own work have been used to illustrate and explain, so that the reader is shown the ways in which data is gathered and explored. We continue to incorporate the golden thread of Heidegger's and Gadamer's philosophy, explaining their influence through to the end of the study.

Part IV
Personal Entrées into Hermeneutic Phenomenology

Introduction

Heidegger stated that 'there is no one phenomenology' reflecting his philosophical stance of the uniqueness we all bring to our experience and understanding of the world we inhabit. Just as our experiences differ, so do our journeys into and through hermeneutic phenomenology.

The routes we have taken into hermeneutic phenomenological research are diverse; we offer our stories here as means of demonstrating that there are many paths, and no 'right way' in either duration or direction of engaging with this philosophy and methodology. What matters is that you find your own path into thinking so that you open yourself up to the possibilities of your own being-in-the-world, as a way to understanding and appreciating the experiences of others.

Coming to Thinking

Dr Lesley Dibley

First encounters with phenomenology

I think I have always been a phenomenologist, but not realised it – looking back to the beginning of my nursing career and the decisions I made which led me purposefully away from my childhood home and into this future, everything I did and understood and knew about my world was influenced by the knowledge and experiences I had accrued along the way. A defining moment came early in my career, when, in the second of my three years of nurse training, I completed a placement on the children's ward. I cared for a baby only a few weeks old, who had been diagnosed with Hirschsprung's disease. This condition is characterised by a lack of ganglionic cells in the smooth muscle of the intestine, usually the colon and rectum, resulting in disruption to peristalsis – the wave-like action which moves contents through the gastrointestinal tract. The effect of the disruption is to cause a blockage in the intestine, which can only be resolved by removing the affected portion of the gut surgically. Consequently, and depending on how much of the colon is affected, there is lifelong impact on gut function. I remember looking at this tiny scrap, after she had been operated on, and wondering what her life would be like, out there, in the world. It was the start of an interest that endures for me to this day – a recognition that, in the lives of people with chronic conditions, the hospital is a very small part of their experience of that condition, and the much larger part is how they live with it in their everyday world.

Initially, I understood this view of the world simply as qualitative, but later began to realise that my experiences not only steered me towards things of interest in my professional life – people living with chronic conditions – but also contributed to the way I understood and interacted with others in my everyday world. I was, without realising it, 'being' phenomenological. At the time, the world of health research was primarily positivistic – if it couldn't be counted or measured, then it didn't count as evidence. Qualitative research was seeking out its own language, arguing its borders and influences, but was still – in the late 1980s – governed and measured by quantitative principles. This, to me, seemed illogical – like using the wrong tool for a job and then complaining that it isn't effective. In the early 1990s, as the scholarly debate around qualitative philosophies and language raged around me, my reading and relationship with interpretive phenomenology began as I completed the research component of my first degree. In the early days, a key influence was Tina Koch's (1995) paper, 'Interpretive approaches in nursing research: The influence of Husserl and Heidegger'. This was where I started to grapple with the core differences and the complex language it entailed, finding enlightenment in the clarity of structure and presentation of information about these two branches of phenomenology. It is a paper I returned to often, and still recommend to students, as a means of grasping the fundamental concepts of phenomenology.

Engaging with the thinking of hermeneutic phenomenology

To begin with, my reading was, I suppose, functional. I would have a methodological question for which I needed an answer and would look for the text which would tell me, 'This is what it is'. As such, I was not really thinking – just accessing information superficially and not stopping to ponder the complexities and depth of what I was reading. Over time, this has grown – perhaps for me, being certain of the core principles provided the necessary framework upon which my complex thinking and understanding have been built. Via MPhil and PhD studies (Dibley, 2009; Dibley et al., 2018), I started finding the work of Pam Ironside, Liz Smythe and Deb Spence, and began to appreciate the complex interplay between the philosophy of Heidegger (and later, Gadamer), the methodology of hermeneutic phenomenological research, and the methods employed to deliver it. I attended the Institute for Heideggerian Hermeneutics for the first time in 2014; the event took place over two weeks – the first focused on methodology, whilst the second explored the underpinning philosophy. Having flown across from the UK, I stayed for both weeks, and it was the start of the second week that opened my eyes to a community of hermeneutic scholars that I had not known existed. The Monday morning was like a reunion event for long-lost friends, and I listened in amazement as people introduced themselves and recounted how many years they had been coming back to what Sherrie Sims called 'brain camp'. *Why*? I asked myself, *Do people keep coming back*? I soon understood. Thinking along with other hermeneutic scholars, engaging in debate and learning from them, is sustaining and encouraging. I was already reading Heidegger's (1927, 1962) *Being and Time*, and Moran's (2000) *Introduction to Phenomenology*, trying not to force my understanding but to let readings sit with me, insight blooming slowly like a long-awaited flower. In the company of other hermeneutic scholars, and encouraged by mentors like Pam Ironside and Sherrie Sims, I learnt to allow myself to linger in those readings, and trust that understanding would come.

In a deeply hermeneutic phenomenological loop, I came, through thinking, to allow myself not to understand at the first, second or perhaps third reading, but to trust that as other influences moulded and grew my knowledge, the aha! moment would eventually emerge. And it did, and it still does. In the reading of hermeneutic phenomenological literature, as in the analysis of data, the 'dwelling in' gives space for thinking – a calm amidst the storm of responsibilities in my daily and working life. It is a headspace I have learnt to be able to take myself to more readily, and I find calmness and creativity within its nebulous boundaries.

Methods papers also informed my thinking: Diekelmann et al. (1989) and Crist and Tanner's (2003) guidance on analysis techniques, and Alqaissi and Dickerson's (2010) paper, which provided a lovely example of how to present findings at the very point I was grappling with that in my PhD. Another key turning point was a discussion paper by Smythe et al. (2008), through which I finally began to crystallise my understanding of the complex relationship between me as-researcher and the philosophy, methodology and methods of hermeneutic phenomenological research. Writings on language – *Poetry, Language, Thought* (Heidegger, 2001), *On the Way to Language* (Heidegger, 1971) and *Truth and Method* (Gadamer, 2003) – helped me refine my understanding of the role of language as the means by which humans express experience, and how, in phenomenological research, language informs and is informed by human experiences of 'being'.

Of the hermeneutic phenomenological studies I have done so far, two in particular have provided an opportunity to put my advancing knowledge into practice. My PhD studies explored the experience of stigma in people with inflammatory bowel disease (IBD) and brought together social interactionism through the lens of stigma theory and hermeneutic phenomenology. The PhD provided the opportunity to really develop my understanding of the relationship between philosophy, research methodology and method, and to indulge in the deeply absorbing experience of hermeneutic data analysis. Through careful moving back and forth across and between transcripts, the experiences of my study participants emerged, revealing the complex interplay between them and their world, and the influences which predisposed or protected them from feeling stigmatised (Dibley et al., 2018).

I had also uncovered the hint of a new description of stigma – one which originated from family members and was directed towards people with IBD. I called this 'kinship stigma' – and set about a follow-up phenomenological study to explore this concept in more detail. Necessarily, the PhD had been a solo enterprise, and I really wanted to experience the team analysis which is so beneficial in hermeneutic phenomenology. I built an international team, including renowned phenomenologists, and together we delivered the study. I collected all data in the UK, and team analysis of the anonymised transcripts was conducted by Skype©. It was an amazing experience – working with other scholars, each bringing their own knowledge, understanding and insight to the interpretive process to reveal meaning. We consulted other literature during analysis to help reveal themes, patterns and meaning – rather than turning to it afterwards to explain our findings, as is common in other qualitative approaches. We found kinship stigma to be a deeply troubling experience for participants, with a subtly different, more distressing impact than stigmatising attitudes coming from non-family. Participants simply wanted their illness experience to be acknowledged and expected that family would be supportive. They were disappointed and dismayed when, alongside a lack of acknowledgement and support, close family members behaved in ways which were experienced as stigmatising. The study has enabled us to raise the awareness across all sociological and health-related professions that professionals cannot assume that the individual they are caring for, has the support of their family (Dibley et al., 2019).

Key hermeneutic thinking for me

Understanding Heidegger's philosophy, and the research methodology and methods developed from it, are just the starting points. I could pick out certain concepts of Heidegger's which particularly appeal – such as *'throwness'*, *'our past being before (ahead of) us'*, or his concerns about the influence of technology. I could identify certain aspects of research design which are considered the 'right way' to be doing this type of research – such as the specific technique for interviewing, the reflexivity, and the benefits of team analysis. Yet the key hermeneutic thinking for me is that these three components – philosophy, methodology and methods – are not only inherently linked in their own hermeneutic circle as each informs the other, but are also inextricably linked to who I am, as person, as individual, as-researcher.

My post-positivistic ontological and epistemological view of the world gives me a perspective on the nature of reality and knowledge which necessarily influences the way I do research. Ontologically, I place more value and meaning on understanding and appreciating that the reality of human existence and what it means to 'be' (to live in the world) are what they appear to be for each of us, and may not necessarily be the same as another's reality. Epistemologically, I recognise that there is factual knowledge, but am drawn towards the personal, experiential knowledge which we, as humans, use to interpret and make sense of our world. My composite view of the world, which I bring with me into my research, blends these two positions together in an overall personal philosophy of 'being-in-the-world'. Consider the 9/11 attacks in New York; the events happened and can be reported factually in terms of the numbers of people confirmed to have died or be missing presumed dead. Yet, for each of us, our ontological and epistemological view creates an understanding of that event based on personal experiences and perceptions – I watched, in horror, from thousands of miles away in the UK, and felt an overwhelming sense of helplessness at realising that, if someone could decide to carry out such an horrific attack here at home, there would be nothing at all I could do to protect my loved ones. My children were, at the time, very small – my experiential knowledge of being a parent was primarily about their protection and care, and that necessarily informed my understanding of the event.

In many ways, ontology and epistemology are hermeneutic – a back-and-forth blending of positivist and post-positivist standpoints – neither entirely one thing nor the other. My position within this philosophical melee aligns me with hermeneutic thinking – the philosophy, methodology and methods 'make sense' to me because they reflect my post-positivist ontological and epistemological stance. In my academic work, as I coach, encourage and guide students on their own research journey, my starting point is always to ask them to reflect on their own ontological and epistemological position. In doing so, they come to understand whether their world views align with the philosophy of hermeneutic phenomenology or not, and we then discuss whether the philosophical approach is right for them. If it is, there is potential for them to come to understand the complex hermeneutic relationship between philosophy, methodology and method. If it isn't, we start discussing other alternatives.

Bibliography

Dibley, L. B. (2009) 'Experiences of lesbian parents in the UK: Interactions with midwives', *Evidence Based Midwifery*, 7(3), 94–100.

Dibley, L., Norton, C. and Whitehead, E. (2018) 'The experience of stigma in inflammatory bowel disease: An interpretive (hermeneutic) phenomenological study', *Journal of Advanced Nursing*, 74, 838–851. doi: 10.1111/jan.13492.

Dibley, L., Williams, E. and Young, P. (2019) 'When family don't acknowledge: A hermeneutic study of the experience of kinship stigma in community-dwelling people with inflammatory bowel disease', *Qualitative Health Research*, 1–16. doi: 10.1177/1049732319831795.

Professor Suzanne Dickerson

In the late 1980s, I was completing my masters in adult health nursing cardio respiratory focus. Due to my family's personal experiences during my father's multiple heart attacks, I was inspired to know more about how families cope with having a loved one experience a cardiac event. The literature never explored this phenomenon, thus my research question required a qualitative approach. I initially sought the mentoring of the only qualitative researcher on my programme who utilised grounded theory, which is based on the philosophy of Husserl and grounded in sociology. At the time, I was in the minority of nurse researchers who used the method and recognised the need for mentoring. I presented my finding at the first Qualitative Health Research conference in Alberta, Canada, where I met Guba and Lincoln, van Manen and Morse, among others. I found my place among these enthusiastic researchers who challenged the positivist paradigm.

Encountering hermeneutic phenomenology as a research methodology

Throughout my doctoral studies, I came to understand the differences among qualitative approaches and shifted toward hermeneutic phenomenology, which focused on the meaning of the phenomenon versus social processes of grounded theory. In the late 1990s, I also joined the Heideggerian Methodology Institute, started by Nancy Diekelmann in Madison, Wisconsin. This community of scholars supports the hermeneutic phenomenological approach that we write about in this book. Since 1998, I have attended the Advanced Institute for Hermeneutical Studies yearly, where we continue to read philosophers and engage in deep thinking and converging conversations with philosophers such as Palmer, Polkinghorne, Maly, Mitchell, Aho, in deep discussions of the philosophy of Heidegger, Gadamer and Merleau-Ponty. For example, we read Heideggers' *Being and Time*, *Contributions*, *On the Way to Language* and *Zollikon Seminars*; and Gadamer's *Truth and Method*.

Engaging in the thinking

During my career as an academic and a scholar, my research and teaching have centred on integrating the philosophical works of Heidegger and Gadamer into my approach of understanding the world. Heidegger's reflections on technology are particularly relevant to my inquiry into the use of technology in health care settings. As Heidegger so aptly explains: 'Everywhere we remain unfree and chained to technology ... we are delivered over to it in the worst possible way when we regard it as something neutral; for this conception of it makes us utterly blind to the essence of technology' (Heidegger, 1977: 4).

This statement underpins the necessity of studying the meanings of technology for users. My scholarship has uncovered the meaning of technologies for patients that can have both positive and negative effects for those who use it. If we remain cognisant of the effects of technology on patients, then we can make reasonable decisions to support the desired effect for those who choose to embrace it. We are only beginning to understand the full potential of technology in our world and we must remain open to the possibilities and potentialities in the future.

As a senior member of the Hermeneutic Phenomenology Institute, I have participated in this worldwide community of scholars for over 20 years and have met regularly to discuss philosophy and mentor others in the methods. My discussions with the group have more recently focused on the use of interpretive findings in developing therapeutic approaches to clinical problems that meet the varied and individual needs of the individuals working to accommodate new treatments into their lives. Technology can be used to assist others by creating a bridge between patients and providers. As Heidegger wrote: 'The bridge swings over the stream ... not just connecting the banks that are already there, but emerge as banks only as the bridge crosses the stream ... the bridge gathers around, leads in many ways' (Heidegger, 1971/2001: 152).

Thus, technologies such as the internet can provide a gathering place for teaching, learning and sharing stories that assist in interpreting and integrating change into our lives.

My studies

The focus of my research initially was to study help-seeking in individuals and families coping with chronic illness. Subsequently, my research plan focused on gaining an understanding of technology–patient interactions that assist in the self-care management of chronic illness. This work is especially important to understand the effects of technology in changing provider–patient relationships to one of a partnership in care management. This is timely research given the health care industry's movements to encourage self-care, and the struggles of providers (nurses) in accommodating to the changes. By understanding the meaning of the experiences of these individuals seeking help when living with their condition, it became apparent that patients considered the technology to be a critical component to promoting health and humanness. The technology of assistive devices (implantable cardioverter defibrillators (ICD), continuous positive airway pressure (CPAP), and the internet) share similar features and purposes. The devices extend humanness by helping the individuals deal with the uncertainty of illness. The devices also have some sort of trade-off cost or disadvantage, ultimately affecting the ability and/or the course of action one takes to self-manage their illness, while achieving their life goals. For example, for a patient with an ICD, who experiences 'death as a symptom', the uncertainty surrounding device firings can cause acute anxiety (Dickerson, 2002). Insight into this experience can alert a practitioner to provide help such as organising a support group (Dickerson, Posluzney and Kennedy, 2000) and/or online support (Dickerson, Flaig and Kennedy, 2000). When patients share their experiences with others, they learn how to gain a healthy context for living with an ICD from others with similar experiences (Dickerson, 2005). As advanced practice nurses, the clinical nurse specialist (CNS) appropriately facilitates a support group, which also provides support especially to newly implanted recipients to improve quality of life and manage anxiety (Dickerson, Wu and Kennedy, 2006). Use of the internet by patients for health information seeking can also change provider–patient relationships (Dickerson and Brennan, 2002); however, frequent internet users also have their own story to tell, with subtle gender differences and digital-divide implications (Dickerson, 2003; Dickerson, Reinhart, et al., 2004). On the other hand, cancer patients have found that the internet is a valuable tool for obtaining information and support during the cancer trajectory to maintain their hope (Dickerson, Boehmke, Ogle and Brown, 2006) and solve problems (Dickerson, Reinhart, Boehmke and Akju-Zahea, 2011). Internet-savvy patients have learned to filter the good information from the uncertain to meet their individual needs. From this research, it is evident that provider–patient relationships have shifted to focus on patient preferences: where providers are information consultants, clinic visits become consultations for decision-making and active partnerships are formed (Dickerson, Boehmke, Ogle and Brown, 2006). The goal then is to empower patients and democratise care.

I am also participating as the qualitative partner in mixed methods studies where the pragmatic integration of multiple approaches is used to best answer research questions such as understanding sleep/wake disturbances in patients with advanced lung cancer over time (funded by the Oncology Nursing Foundation).

Using hermeneutic phenomenology to gain insight into patient–technology interactions can also be the basis for developing meaning-based interventions. For the CPAP technology, known for poor adherence, by understanding the contextual issues around adhering to CPAP, one grasps that the treatment requires considerable accommodations being made to changing one's routine (Dickerson, Wu and Kennedy, 2006; Dickerson and Akhu-Zaheya, 2007). After gaining this insight and looking at the evidence-based literature, I used this unique approach to develop a multimodal complex intervention that provides an armament of practical advice, information, trouble-shooting tips, and self-monitoring tools for patients to self-tailor and manage their care. Qualitative approaches were instrumental in understanding the cultural, environmental and contextual barriers to using CPAP. The use of expert-patient stories to motivate and role-model for the new user is also an essential component for peer modelling behaviour change. Using qualitative approaches facilitates knowledge translation into practice. The resulting intervention is complex, multifaceted, meaning-based and contextual. This approach to improving clinical practice is innovative, being sensitive to patient preference.

Key hermeneutic thinking for me

In using hermeneutic phenomenology as a method, foremost in my view is the understanding that language speaks us, so that as self-interpreting beings, language provides a dialogue with participants' stories reflecting the background meanings to enable us to understand their experience. Second, understanding that our backgrounds are constituted by experience, history and culture provides a horizon of understanding with which to interpret the stories. A fusion of horizons occurs when interpreter and participant gain an understanding and the interpreter acknowledges their pre-understanding to avoid inserting their own biases into the interpretation. This way, the participants' stories or voices can be heard. Through interpretations, common meanings and shared practices are interpreted to understand the meaning of experiences. These meanings can inform and facilitate the development of interventions that use the phronesis or practical wisdom of experienced participants' background meanings. In an intervention, phronesis or reflective understanding guides and addresses the need to make practical decisions involving monitoring and adjusting practical actions that become part of our background. This is opposed to a technical-rational approach of scientific knowledge that does not address individual uniqueness (Polkinghorne, 2004).

Bibliography

Dickerson, S. S. (2002) 'Redefining life while forestalling death: The experience of living with sudden cardiac death through technology', *Qualitative Health Research*, 12(3), 360–372.

Dickerson, S. S. (2003) 'Gender differences in stories of everyday internet use', *Health Care Women International*, 24(5), 434–451.

Dickerson, S. S. (2005) 'Patient–technology interactions: Internet use for gaining a healthy context for living with an implantable cardioverter defibrillator ICD', *Heart & Lung*, 34(3), 157–168.

Dickerson, S. S. and Akhu-Zaheya, L. (2007) 'Life changes in individuals diagnosed with sleep apnea while accommodating to continuous positive airway pressure (CPAP) devices', *Rehabilitation Nursing*, 32(6), 241–250.

Dickerson, S. S. and Brennan, P. (2002) 'The Internet as a catalyst for shifting power in provider–patient relationships', *Nursing Outlook*, 50(5), 195–203.

Dickerson, S. S. and Feitshans, L. (2003) 'Internet users becoming immersed in the virtual world: Implications for nurses', *CIN Computers Informatics and Nursing*, 21(6), 300–308.

Dickerson, S. S., Flaig, D. and Kennedy, M. C. (2000) 'Therapeutic connection: Help seeking on the internet for persons with implantable cardioverter defibrillators', *Heart & Lung*, 29(4), 248–255.

Dickerson, S. S., Kingman, K. and Jungquist, C. (2016) 'Common meanings of good and bad sleep in a healthy population sample', *Sleep Health*, 2, 253–259. http://dx.doi.org/10.1016/j.sleh.2016.06.004.

Dickerson, S. S., Posluzney, M. and Kennedy, M. (2000) 'Help seeking in a support group for recipients of implantable cardioverter defibrillators (ICD) and their support persons', *Heart & Lung*, 29(2), 87–96.

Dickerson, S. S., Wu, Y. B. and Kennedy, M. (2006) 'A CNS-facilitated ICD support group: A clinical project and evaluation', *Clinical Nurse Specialist*, 20(3), 146–153.

Dickerson, S. S., Boehmke, M., Ogle, C. and Brown, J. K. (2006) 'Seeking and managing hope: Patients' experiences using the internet for cancer care', *Oncology Nursing Forum*, 33(1), E8–17.

Dickerson, S. S., Reinhart, A., Boehmke, M. and Akhu-Zaheya, L. (2011) 'Cancer as a problem to be solved: Internet use and provider communication by men with cancer', *Computers Informatics Nursing*, 29(7), 388–395.

Dickerson, S. S., Abu Sabbah, E., Zeigler, P., Chen, H., Steinbrenner, L. and Dean, G. (2012) 'Sleep is not a priority when living my life after a diagnosis of lung cancer', *Oncology Nursing Forum*, 39(5), 492–499.

Dickerson, S. S., Abbu Sabbah, E., Gothard, S., Zeigler, P., Chen, H., Steinbrenner, L. and Dean, G. (2015) 'Experiences of patients with advanced lung cancer: Being resigned to sleep–wake disturbances while maintaining hope for optimal treatment outcomes', *Cancer Nursing*, 38(5), 358–365. doi: 10.1097/NCC.00000000000206.

Heidegger, M. (1971/2001) *Poetry, Language, Thought* (trans. A. Hofstader). New York: Harper & Row.

Heidegger, M. (1977) *The Question Concerning Technology and other Essays* (trans. W. Lovitt). New York: Harper & Row.

Polkinghorne, D. (2004) 'Techne and phronesis', in D. Polkinghorne (eds.) *Practice and Human Sciences: The case for a judgement-based practice of care*. Albany, NY: SUNY Press, pp. 97–104.

Dr Mel Duffy

Research projects require the researcher to think about how the research will be carried out. It will be necessary to place it within the epistemological (theories of knowing) and methodological (theories of doing). Questions will be raised about the substantial research question(s) and how it/they will be answered. If the research pertains to the experience of everyday life, then decisions have to be made about which methodology fits with the question(s). In all of this, the 'how' of doing must be accompanied by 'the way of thinking' about 'the how of doing'. Heidegger informs us that there is an intimate connection between thinking and questioning (Gray, 2004: xiii). So is he saying that those who question, think or those who think, question? To think is to be human and, in a Heideggerian sense, thinking defines the nature of being human (Gray, 2004: xii).

A small child has a rich vein of questioning everything. They are adept with the how, why and wherefore of all that surrounds them, with their favourite 'but' in relation to the answer that may be offered. In other words, a child pushes their thought unbeknown to themselves further through 'but': 'but how', 'but why'. A child will keep going until their questioning is exhausted or they lose interest. The child's loss of interest could be interpreted as reaching a conclusion for now, perhaps with further questioning later as they sit/rest in the place they are. I would postulate that we all derive from this rich oasis of our childhood, yet we may be taken aback by the nature of thinking that a research project requires. Indeed, within the supervisor–research student relationship, asking 'What is your question?' may lead to much torturous rumination. The research student may ask: 'What do you mean?' It is the thinking that goes into the question(s) that leads to questions of the thinking. This piece will attempt to unravel why hermeneutic phenomenology sits well with my way of being.

While I was that child who incessantly could not accept the first answer but always went seeking further answers, the question arises: 'What was it about my way of questioning that has led to where I am today?'. On first glance, one could say this is the way I have always been, but the reality is I have evolved to become the thinker I am today and will hopefully evolve further as I age. It took time for me to find my path in thinking. As an undergraduate student, I was lucky to study both Sociology and Philosophy. In a way, they are twin subjects as all thinking comes out of Philosophy, with branches diverging into different disciplines. As my thinking grew in those early days, I discovered I was interested in people and how a phenomenon was for them. So my question began with, 'What is it like for you?'

Initial toe dipping

Over time, I noticed I was beginning to gain an interest in groups that were marginalised in society. My first port of call for an undergraduate dissertation in 1988 was the subject of rape. What I was interested in was the societal structures that resulted in cases not making it to court. This may appear as far away from hermeneutic phenomenology as you could get, but I was interested in how the structures of society prevent engagement. This was at the end of the 1980s in Ireland and another societal engagement that was being negated was HIV/AIDS. The silence that surrounded the emerging HIV/AIDS epidemic was deafening, which led me to undertake a Masters by research on the topic of 'Living with HIV/AIDS'. Back in the 1980s, Ireland's silence embraced difference of any kind, whether that be sexuality, sexual practices and/or sexual orientation. There was only one way of being and that was heterosexual: if you did not fit, you either stayed silent, passed as heterosexual or left your place of origin, heading for the cities or simply emigrating. In 1987, Ireland's national TV flagship programme *The Late Late Show*, which had a soap box segment on a multiplicity of subjects, broadcast a piece about HIV/AIDS. The discussion after the presentation dissolved into angry interactions on anal sex. Apparently, gay men engage in no other form of desire or outcome/sexual practice than that. What engaged my interest during the show was the lack of humanity and the inability of others to hear about a lived experience being a reality for others. Rather, people were more engaged in putting their abhorrence of the Other and its perceived sexual practices into the public realm. Instead, it absorbed my need to explore the experience of people and their families around the phenomenon of HIV/AIDS. I embarked on exploring this and began engaging with Dublin AIDS Alliance. I was intrigued by members of the medical profession who would arrive at a meeting almost by apparition and leave in a similar manner, without in some cases naming themselves. While I had encountered stigma, this was the epitome of what contagion by association not only looked like but also of how it played out in public spaces. In that dissertation, I was sitting theoretically in the sociological field of symbolic interactionism. While it was not until I embarked on my PhD that I embraced hermeneutic phenomenology, my Masters dissertation was a stepping stone towards embracing the lived experience, and towards grasping the meaning and understanding that people give to their lives and to social events. The ways of thinking I am interested in, are rooted in the philosophy of Heidegger and Sartre. In the PhD, I was concerned with how lesbian women maintain a sense of self as lesbian women in Irish health care, either as health care providers or recipients of health care. Heidegger (1962) was concerned with being-in-the-world and offered a theoretical framework whereby lesbian women could be seen as active participants in the world, creating understanding and giving meaning to their existence. Sartre (1969), on the other hand, offered me a lens through which I could examine how lesbian women experience the self, in the world of health care.

Finding my tribe

During my PhD journey, I attended my first Heideggerian Methodology Institute and Advanced Institute for Hermeneutical Studies in 2006. This experience enabled me to first test out how I was thinking about and doing hermeneutic phenomenology. It gave me the freedom to think out loud with people who listened and gently turned me towards what I needed to read or the road to travel down. It also offered me a group of thinkers and scholars who did not think 'I was odd' – at least I did not feel odd in this space. Over time, the Institute has become the food and water of my soul, my thinking, and the participants sustain my being. Hermeneutic phenomenology recognises that we are all active in the world, we are not passively going through life; we are engaged, we make decisions, whether those decisions have good or bad outcomes; and we find both meaning and understanding in every decision and/ or action we undertake. Meaning and understanding may not be readily available to us as we engage in action; rather, they may come to us later as we reflect on an action. We are reflective human beings whereby we examine what we think and why we do what we do. Many of us often ask the question: why did I do that? It is this questioning that enables us to move forward to do things differently the next time. This is what I am interested in when I undertake a piece of research. I am interested in how an individual(s) experience(s) a particular phenomenon under investigation. The other attractive element of this approach is that the individual who is engaged in the phenomenon that I am interested in – and I as individual and as-researcher – are both active in the world. In other words, the understanding that researchers have is not divorced from the real world but rather engaged in it, an engagement that is central to this way of undertaking research.

Studies undertaken

Since completing my PhD, I have undertaken a number of studies utilising hermeneutic phenomenology. Four commissioned reports have been completed. The first was on the professional and family experience of childhood interventions with a Marte Meo framework. Within this study, we were interested in how families experience the therapeutic intervention that is Marte Meo, and in the experience of practitioners of Marte Meo. Marteo Meo is utilised with families that have children with learning disabilities. It enables families to see the child beyond the labelling and brings the child back to their parents. The second study examined the culture of diversity in An Garda Síochána (the Irish police force). We were particularly interested in the experiences of lesbian, gay and bisexual officers. The reality of LGB police officers was that being out and openly gay is not fully acceptable, evidenced by the fact that participants remained closeted, or, if open, were fearful of a lack of career progression. As such, there appears to be a 'glass ceiling' in relation to LGB persons serving in An Garda Síochána, and, if anyone is different, they should keep their head under the radar, thus remaining invisible. Within this project, we uncovered the processes of hiding the self and of passing as those who are the same as the norm of the group. The third completed study explored the experiences of families of those in end-of-life care in private nursing homes. Here we uncovered the unknown aspect of families in the nursing home. While nursing homes tend to come at the end of the journey of life, relatives' experience of the end of life can begin years previously at the moment they realise that there is something not quite right within the world of their relative. The fourth was a study on Relationship and Sexuality Education (RSE) at Irish second-level school. This study had four cohorts of principals, teachers, students and parents/legal guardians. It sought to uncover the meaning and understanding that each group gave to RSE in Irish second-level schools.

Some studies are close to our hearts and we undertake them regardless of funding – one such study explored the lived experience of older lesbian women in Ireland. This was exciting as it drew on the stories of bravery that older lesbian women told of living their lives. Powerful institutions of society were able to construct lesbianism from: a medical perspective as mentally ill; the religious perspective as immoral; the criminal justice system as a crime or deviance; and the consumerist paradigm that today views lesbianism as a lifestyle. Older lesbian women gave insightful stories of how they experienced these constructs of their existence and negotiated their life, knowing that there were consequences for being 'found out'.

For me, hermeneutic phenomenology has enabled me to enter the lives of others and seek an understanding of the meaning that they give to their lives in relation to the phenomenon being investigated. It has been both a privilege and an honour to be invited into their lives and to listen to their stories. People have been both gracious and giving in the unravelling of their lives, and it is our duty to treat them within an ethical code whereby we recount their world to others to gain a greater understanding of life in the world we inhabit.

Bibliography

Alhashimi, E. and Duffy, M. (2018) 'Parents and/or young males' beliefs, attitudes and opinions regarding male HPV vaccine: A systematic review', *World Journal of Pharmaceutical Research*, 7(2), 62–73. doi: 10.20959/wjpr20182-10525.

Cithambaram, K., Duffy, M. and Courtney, E. (2018) 'End-of-life care research on people with intellectual disabilities: Challenges for proactive inclusion in an Irish context', *British Journal of Learning Disabilities*, pp. 1–7. https://doi.org/10.1111/bld.12260.

Duffy, M. (1993) *Positive Proof! The emergence of HIV/AIDS and the Irish response*. Cork: Sociological Association of Ireland.

Duffy, M. (2010) 'Diversity in the Irish workplace: Lesbian women's experiences as nurses', *The International Journal of Diversity in Organisations, Communities and Nations*, 10(3), 231–241.

Duffy, M. (2011) *Voices from the Hinterland: Lesbian women's experience of Irish health care*. Saarbrücken: Lambert Academic Publishing.

Duffy, M. (2011) 'Lesbian women's experiences of being different in Irish health care', in Thomson, G., Dykes, F. and Downes, S. (eds) *Qualitative Research in Midwifery and Childbirth: Phenomenological approaches*. London: Routledge, pp. 79–95.

Duffy, M. (2011) 'Lesbian women's experience of coming out in an Irish hospital setting: A hermeneutic phenomenological approach', *Sexuality Research and Social Policy*, 8(4), 335–347. doi: 10.1007/s13178-011-0065-y.

Duffy, M. (2018) 'Emerging, submerging lesbians in Ireland', in Maillot, A. and Bruen, J. (eds) *Non-violent Resistance: Counter-discourse in Irish culture*. Oxford: Peter Lang, pp. 175–191.

Duffy, M. and Courtney, E. (2015) 'Coming to terms with the limitations of the self: Families choosing a nursing home for a loved one', *Ageing & Society*, 5(3), 39–47.

Heidegger, M. (1962) *Being and Time* (trans. J. Macquarrie and E. Robinson). New York: Harper & Row.

Professor Roxanne Vandermause

My love of nursing practice and desire to change health care prompted my return to academia after years of practice in various settings. I was moving through an advanced practice educational programme, eager to gain my specialty education and credentials to practise as a gerontological advanced practice nurse. I was making my way through courses in research and theory and found myself in Nancy Diekelmann's graduate course on Qualitative Research. We learned about various qualitative methodologies, all of which introduced new ways to think about the practice questions I had wondered about in the course of my career. We got to the modules on hermeneutic phenomenology and engaged in exercises that applied a way of thinking that was new to me. In Nancy Diekelmann's class, we sat in a circle, engaged in open conversation, wrote reflective pieces and read them aloud. We graded ourselves. This was indeed an avant-garde approach to teaching and learning that excited my intellectual curiosity.

Hermeneutic phenomenology was a mouthful. Sometimes it was called *Heideggerian hermeneutic phenomenology* and its mystique was as appealing as the narrative work we did in class. I became mesmerised by the possibilities for the expression of stories, the study of philosophy and the debate of ideas available to this methodological approach. I wanted more and, when Trish Young, Diekelmann's PhD student, pointed out in class that I might want to be involved in working with Diekelmann and her students in the summer Heideggerian Hermeneutic Institute, a two-week intensive that drew scholars from around the country and the world, I thought I had gone to heaven. I was completely hooked and turned to study Heidegger and the hermeneutic phenomenological approach to inquiry FULL-heartedly.

Diekelmann accepted me as a PhD student and I joined Pam Ironside, Trish Young and others in studying hermeneutic phenomenology, night and day. We students hosted the Institute in subsequent years and also travelled to and put on local conferences that Diekelmann arranged, learning from philosophers and scholars who put thinking at the centre of scholarship and practice. I learned that experience itself can be examined and analysed. I read essays by Heidegger and learned, from Heideggerian philosophers (Dreyfuss, Sheehan and Maly), ways of interpreting Heidegger's work and applying it to thinking about what it means to be in any situation. I learned how to think about ontology in the practice of living and recognised this line of thinking as something completely synergistic with the practice of nursing, a practice grounded in everyday living and holistic activity.

My dissertation work in the area of women's addiction was a hermeneutical phenomenological study of the experiences of nurses assessing women for alcohol dependency (Vandermause, 2007). There were screening tools available but also many indications that advanced practice nurses (APNs) were not adequately diagnosing alcohol dependency. Talking to APNs during in-depth hermeneutic interviews and analysing the texts of those conversations with a team astute in the approaches of hermeneutic analysis (Elizabeth Rice and Jolanda Sallman) revealed a much deeper understanding of the process of diagnosis and produced unexpected and contradictory understandings, such as the notion that 'hesitating to diagnose' might be an effective strategy. New ways to think about interacting with addiction were uncovered and we were suddenly able to open up another avenue of thinking about the ways in which women with addictions interact with health practitioners. This work led to a number of studies and publications that changed the way we think about addiction.

One of the most rewarding experiences of hermeneutic phenomenological work is the response of others to presented and published interpretations. Narrative interpretations provide credible data that support interpretations of text from thoughtfully conducted interviews. New questions are generated from otherwise overlooked understandings that are illuminated and well described. I remember a presentation I gave, years ago, that highlighted the experience of women with an addiction who seek health care for any physical problem. One of the presentation attendees contacted me the next day to say he would never again see women with an addiction who visit his emergency room the same way. This study revealed the suffering of many of these women (Vandermause, 2009), and presenting the work to nurses who see such patients made an immediate impact. Hermeneutic work can change practice immediately.

Moving forward in my career, I was able to study many phenomena using hermeneutic approaches. I have attended our summer institutes with various scholars of Continental philosophy and hermeneutics, and learned the many ways we can think about what it means to be in complex health care situations. I have conducted hundreds of interviews and led or participated in hundreds of analytical sessions. I have learned along with my students, opening to their particular interests, publishing with them and guiding them to develop their own important work. Engaging in a hermeneutic analysis session with others, who are focused and open to a way of thinking that may be surprising and unusual, is a most fulfilling experience, leading to new language and, hopefully, to the transformation of health care delivery through new understanding. There is a joy in the work that is deep and authentic, meaningful and relational, worth teaching and extending to address the challenges of tomorrow.

Bibliography

Altman, M., Kantrowicz-Gordon, I. and Vandermause, R. (2014) 'Synergy among multiple methodologies: Investigating parents' distress after preterm birth',

International Journal of Qualitative Methodologies, 13, 335–346. doi: https://doi.org/10.1177/160940691401300116.

Fleming, S. and Vandermause, R. (2012) 'The phenomenon of embodiment and the birthing experience', *International Journal of Qualitative Methods*, 11(5), 783–784.

Fleming, S., Vandermause, R., Shaw, M. and Severtsen, B. (2017) 'Grand multiparous mothers' embodied experiences of natural and technological altered births', *The Journal of Perinatal Education*, 26(2), 85–95. http://dx.doi.org/10.1891/1058-1243.26.2.1.

Fleming, S., Boyd, A., Ballejos, M., Kynast-Gales, S., Malemute, C., Armstrong, Shultz, J. and Vandermause, R. (2013) 'Goal setting with type 2 diabetes: A hermeneutic analysis of the experiences of diabetes educators', *The Diabetes Educator*, 39(6). doi:10.1177/0145721713504471.

Fritz, R. and Vandermause, R. (2017) 'Data collection via in-depth email interviewing: Lessons from the field', *Qualitative Health Research*. doi: 10.1177/10497323 16689067.

Girard, S., Vandermause, R., Eddy, L. and Hoeksel, R. (2017) 'Experiences of registered nurses who voluntarily withdraw from their RNBSN program', *Journal of Nursing Education*. doi: http://dx.doi.org/10.3928/01484834-20170421-02.

Kantrowitz-Gordon, I. and Vandermause, R. (2013) 'Photo-elicitation enhances a discourse analysis of parents' distress', *International Journal of Qualitative Methods*, 12, 782–783.

Kantrowitz-Gordon, I. and Vandermause, R. (2015) 'Metaphors of distress: Photo-elicitation enhances a discourse analysis of parents' accounts', *Qualitative Health Research*, 1–13. doi: 10.1177/1049732315575729.

Kantrowitz-Gordon, I., Altman, M. and Vandermause, R. (2016) 'Prolonged distress of parents after pre-term birth', *Journal of Obstetric, Gynecological and Neonatal Nursing*, 45(2), 196–209. doi: 10.1016/j.jogn.2015.12.004.

Sameshima, P. and Vandermause, R. (2009) 'Parallaxic praxis: An artful interdisciplinary collaborative research methodology', in Prendergast, M., Leggo, C. and Sameshima, P. (eds) *Poetic Inquiry: Vibrant voices in the social sciences*. Rotterdam: Sense, pp. 275–285.

Sameshima, P., Vandermause, R., Chalmers, S. and 'Gabriel' (2009) *Climbing the Ladder with Gabriel: Poetic inquiry with a methamphetamine addict in recovery*. Rotterdam: Sense.

Smith, C. L., Vandermause, R., Severtsen, B., Wilson, M., Barbosa-Leiker, C. and Roll, J. (2018) 'Seeking chronic pain relief: A hermeneutic exploration', *Pain Management Nursing*. doi: 10.1016/j.pmn.2018.05.001.

Vandermause, R. K. (2008) 'The poiesis of the question in philosophical hermeneutics: Questioning assessment practices for alcohol use disorders', *International Journal of Qualitative Studies on Health and Well-Being*, 3(2), 68–76. doi: https://doi.org/10.1080/17482620801939584.

Vandermause, R. K. (2012) 'Being wholesome: The paradox of methamphetamine addiction and recovery – A hermeneutical phenomenological interpretation within an interdisciplinary, transmethodological study', *Qualitative Social Work*, 11(3), 299–318. doi: https://doi.org/10.1177/1473325011401470.

Vandermause, R. and Fleming, S. (2011) 'Philosophical hermeneutic interviewing', *International Journal of Qualitative Methods*, 10(4), 367–377. doi: https://doi.org/10.1177/160940691101000405.

Vandermause, R. and Townsend, R. (2010) 'Teaching thoughtful practice: Narrative pedagogy in addictions education', *Nurse Education Today*, 30, 428–434. doi: https://doi.org/10.1016/j.nedt.2009.09.017.

Vandermause, R. and Wood, M. (2009) 'See my suffering: Women with alcohol use disorders and their primary care experiences', *Issues in Mental Health Nursing*, 30(12), 728–735. doi: http://dx.doi.org/10.3109/01612840903230081.

Vandermause, R., Barbosa-Leiker, C. and Fritz, R. (2014) 'Innovations in research education: Findings from a study of teaching/learning research using multiple analytical perspectives', *Journal of Nursing Education*, 53(12), 673–677. doi: http://dx.doi.org/10.3928/01484834-20141120-02.

Vandermause, R., Roberts, M. and Odom-Maryon, T. (2018) 'Relational health in transitions: Adolescents in chemical dependency treatment', *Substance Use and Misuse*. doi: 10.1080/10826084.2017.1408655.

Vandermause, R., Fougere, M., Liu, Y. H. and Odom-Maryon, T. (2018) 'Relational health and recovery: Adolescent girls in chemical dependency treatment', *Journal of Addictions Nursing*, 29(1), 4–12. doi: 10.1097/JAN.0000000000000207.

Part IV Summary

In this final part, we hope to have inspired and encouraged the reader along their own journey into and through Heidegger's philosophy, the methodological approach of hermeneutic phenomenology, and the many areas of exploration that present as a possibility for the thoughtful researcher. Our final message would be to encourage you to take time to read, think and learn, and, as we have all been advised by our own hermeneutic mentors over the years, to trust yourself that understanding will come.

References

Abel, M. (2002). 'Humor, stress, and coping strategies', *Humor*, 15(4), 365–381.

Alqaissi, N. and Dickerson, S. S. (2010) 'Exploring common meanings of social support as experienced by Jordanian women with breast cancer', *Cancer Nursing*, 33(5), 353–361. doi: 10.1097/NCC.0b013e3181d55d33

Baker, C., Norton, S., Young, P. and Ward, S. (1998) 'An exploration of methodological pluralism in nursing research', *Research in Nursing & Health*, 21(6), 545–555. doi: 10.1002/(SICI)1098-240X(199812)21:6<545::AID-NUR8>3.0.CO;2-8.

Baker, S. and Edwards, R. (2012) 'How many qualitative interviews is enough?', *NCRM EPrints Repository*. Available at: http://eprints.ncrm.ac.uk/2273 (accessed 1 January 2020).

Benner, P. (1994) 'The tradition and skill of interpretive phenomenology in studying health, illness and caring practices', in Patricia, B. (ed) *Interpretive Phenomenology: Embodiment, caring and ethics in health and illness*. Thousand Oaks, CA: Sage, pp. 99–127.

Benner, P. E. (1984) *From Novice to Expert: Excellence and power in clinical nursing practice*. Frenchs Forest, NSW: Pearson.

Bergum, V. (1989) *Woman to Mother: A transformation*. Grandby, MA: Bergin & Garvey.

Bhattacharya, K. and Kim, J.-H. (2018) 'Reworking prejudice in qualitative inquiry with Gadamer and de/colonizing onto-epistemologies', *Qualitative Inquiry*, online, doi: 10.1177/1077800418767201.

Birt, L., Scott, S., Cavers, D., Campbell, C. and Walter, F. (2016) 'Member checking: A tool to enhance trustworthiness or merely a nod to validation?', *Qualitative Health Research*, 26(13), 1802–1811. doi: 10.1177/1049732316654870.

Boden, Z. and Eatough, V. (2014) 'Understanding more fully: A multimodal hermeneutic-phenomenological approach', *Qualitative Research in Psychology*, 11(2), 160–177. doi: 10.1080/14780887.2013.853854.

Breatnach, C. R., Nolke, L. and McMahon, C. J. (2019) 'Retroaortic innominate vein in a patient with transposition of the great arteries: The surgical implications', *Cardiology in the Young*, 29(6), 840–841. doi: 10.1017/S1047951119000763.

Byrne, A. (2000) 'Researching one an-other', in Byrne, A. and Lentin, R. (eds) *(Re)searching Women: Feminist research methodologies in the social sciences in Ireland*. Dublin: Institute of Public Administration, pp. 140–166.

Caelli, K. (2000) 'The changing face of phenomenological research: Traditional and American phenomenology in nursing', *Qualitative Health Research*, 10(3), 366–377. doi: 10.1177/104973200129118507.

Chenail, R. J. (2009) 'Communicating your qualitative research better', *Family Business Review*, 22(2), 105–108. doi: 10.1177/0894486509334795.

Chesney, M. (2000) 'Interaction and understanding: "Me" in the research', *Nurse Researcher*, 7(3), 58–69. doi: 10.7748/nr2000.04.7.3.58.c6121.

Chevrier, R., Foufi, V., Gaudet-Blavignac, C., Robert, A. and Lovis, C. (2019) 'Use and understanding of anonymization and de-identification in the biomedical literature: Scoping review', *Journal of Medical Internet Research*, 21(5), e13484. doi: 10.2196/13484.

Cho, J. and Trent, A. (2006) 'Validity in qualitative research revisited', *Qualitative Research*, 6(3), 319–340. doi: 10.1177/1468794106065006.

Claassen, C. (2005) *Whistling Women: A study of the lives of older lesbians*. Binghampton, NY: The Haworth Press.

Clancy, M. (2013) 'Is reflexivity the key to minimising problems of interpretation in phenomenological research?', *Nurse Researcher*, 20, 12–16. doi: 10.7748/nr2013.07.20.6.12.e1209.

Clunis, D. M., Garner, J. D., Freeman, P. A., Nystrom, N. M. and Fredriksen-Goldsen, K. I. (2005) *Lives of Lesbian Elders: Looking back, looking forward*. Binghampton, NY: The Haworth Press.

Cohen, M. and Omery, A. (1994) 'Schools of phenomenology: Implications for research', in Morse, J. (ed.) *Critical Issues in Qualitative Research Methods*. Thousand Oaks, CA: Sage, pp. 136–156.

Cohen, M., Kahn, D. and Steeves, R. (2000) *Hermeneutic Phenomenological Research: A practical guide for nurse researchers*. Thousand Oaks, CA: Sage.

Connelly, L. M. (2014) 'Ethical considerations in research studies', *Medical Surgical Nursing*, 23(1), 54–55.

Cooke, A., Smith, D. and Booth, A. (2012) 'Beyond PICO: the SPIDER tool for qualitative evidence synthesis', *Qualitative Health Research*, 22(10), 1435–1443. doi: 10.1177/1049732312452938.

Cooper, J. M. (1977) 'Aristotle on the forms of friendship', *Review of Metaphysics*, 30(4), 619–648. doi: revmetaph197730450.

Creswell, J. (2007) *Qualitative Inquiry and Research Design*, 2nd edn. Thousand Oaks, CA: Sage.

Creswell, John W. (2013) *Qualitative Inquiry and Research Design: Choosing among five approaches* (3rd ed.). Thousand Oaks, CA: Sage.

Crist, J. D. and Tanner, C. A. (2003) 'Interpretation/analysis methods in hermeneutic interpretive phenomenology', *Nursing Research*, 52(3), 202–205. doi: 10.1097/00006199-200305000-00011.

Crotty, M. (1997) 'Tradition and culture in Heidegger's Being and Time', *Nursing Inquiry*, 4, 88–98.

Crotty, M. (2005) *The Foundations of Social Research: Meaning and perspective in the research process*. London: Sage.

Crowther, S., Ironside, P., Spence, D. and Smythe, L. (2016) 'Crafting stories in hermeneutic phenomenology research: A methodological device', *Qualitative Health Research*, 27(6), 826–835. doi: 10.1177/1049732316656161.

Cutcliffe, J. R., Joyce, A. and Cummins, M. (2004) 'Building a case for understanding the lived experiences of males who attempt suicide in Alberta, Canada', *Journal of Psychiatric and Mental Health Nursing*, 11(3), 305–312. doi: 10.1111/j.1365-2850.2003.00722.x.

Cypress, B. S. (2017) 'Rigor or reliability and validity in qualitative research: Perspectives, strategies, reconceptualization, and recommendations', *Dimensions of Critical Care Nursing*, 36(4), 253–263. doi: 10.1097/DCC.0000000000000253.

Dahlberg, H. and Dahlberg, K. (2003) 'To not make definite what is indefinite: A phenomenological analysis of perception and its epistemological consequences in human science research', *The Humanistic Psychologist*, 31(4), 34–50. doi: 10.1080/08873267.2003.9986933.

Darbyshire, P., Diekelmann, J. and Diekelmann, N. (1999) 'Reading Heidegger and interpretive phenomenology: A response to the work of Michael Crotty', *Nursing Inquiry*, 6(1), 17–25. doi: 10.1046/j.1440-1800.1999.00004.x.

De Witt, L. and Ploeg, J. (2006) 'Critical appraisal of rigour in interpretive phenomenological nursing research', *Journal of Advanced Nursing*, 55(2), 215–229. doi: 10.1111/j.1365-2648.2006.03898.x.

Denscombe, M. (2003) *The Good Research Guide: For small-scale social research projects*, 2nd edn. Buckingham: Open University Press.

Dibley, L. (2009) 'Experiences of lesbian parents in the UK: Interactions with midwives', *Evidence-based Midwifery*, 7, 94–100.

Dibley, L., Norton, C. and Whitehead, E. (2018) 'The experience of stigma in inflammatory bowel disease: An interpretive (hermeneutic) phenomenological study', *Journal of Advanced Nursing*, 74(4), 838–851. doi: 10.1111/jan.13492.

Dibley, L., Williams, E. and Young, P. (2019) 'When family don't acknowledge: A hermeneutic study of the experience of kinship stigma in community-dwelling people with inflammatory bowel disease', *Qualitative Health Research*, online, doi: 10.1177/1049732319831795.

Dibley, L., Norton, C., Schaub, J. and Bassett, P. (2014) 'Experiences of gay and lesbian patients with inflammatory bowel disease: A mixed methods study', *Gastrointestinal Nursing*, 12(6), 19–30. doi: 10.12968/gasn.2014.12.6.19.

Dickerson, S. S., Reinhart, A., C. H., Bidani, R., Rich, E., Garg, V. and Hershey C. O. (2004) 'Patient Internet use for health information at three urban primary care clinics', *The Journal of American Medical Informatics Association*, 11(6), 499–504.

Dickerson, S. S., Sabbah, E. A., Ziegler, P., Chen, H., Steinbrenner, L. M. and Dean, G. (2012) 'The experience of a diagnosis of advanced lung cancer: Sleep is not a priority when living my life', *Oncology Nursing Forum*, 39(5), 492–499. doi: 10.1188/12.ONF.492–499.

Dickerson, S. S., Sabbah, E. A., Gothard, S., Ziegler, P., Chen, H., Steinbrenner, L. M. and Dean, G. (2015) 'Experiences of patients with advanced lung cancer: Being resigned to sleep-wake disturbances while maintaining hope for optimal treatment outcomes', *Cancer Nursing*, 38(5), 358–365. doi: 10.1097/NCC.0000000000000206.

Diekelmann, J. and Diekelmann, N. (2009) *Schooling Learning Teaching: Toward narrative pedagogy*. Bloomington, IN: iUniverse.

Diekelmann, N. (2001) 'Narrative pedagogy: Heideggerian hermeneutical analyses of lived experiences of students, teachers, and clinicians', *ANS: Advances in Nursing Science*, 23(3), 53–71. doi: 10.1097/00012272-200103000-00006.

Diekelmann, N. and Ironside, P. (2011) 'Hermeneutics', in Fitzpatrick, J. and Wallace-Kazer, M. (eds) *Encyclopaedia of Nursing Research*, 3rd edn. New York: Springer, pp. 220–222.

Diekelmann, N. L., Allen, D., Tanner, C. A. and National League for Nursing (1989) *The NLN Criteria for Appraisal of Baccalaureate Programs: A critical hermeneutic analysis*. New York: National League for Nursing.

Dowling, M. (2006) 'Approaches to reflexivity in qualitative research', *Nurse Researcher*, 13(3), 7–21. doi: 10.7748/nr2006.04.13.3.7.c5975.

Draucker, C. B. (1999) 'The critique of Heideggerian hermeneutical nursing research', *Journal of Advanced Nursing*, 30(2), 360–373. doi: 10.1046/j.1365-2648.1999.01091.x.

Dreyfus, H. (1991) *Being-in-the-world: A commentary on Heidegger's Being and Time*, Division 1. Cambridge, MA: The MIT Press.

Duffy, M. (2008) Voices from the hinterland: Lesbian women's experience of Irish health care. Unpublished PhD thesis, Dublin City University.

Duffy, M. and Courtney, E. (2014) The journey through death and dying: Families' experiences of end-of-life care in private nursing homes. Paper, Dublin City University.

Duffy, M. and Sheridan, V. (2012) Cultures of diversity: Sexual orientation in An Garda Síochaná. Paper, Dublin City University.

Duffy, M., Corby, D., Corocoran, Y., Clinotn, G. and Pierce, M. (forthcoming) Professional and lay knowledge of the lived experience of Irish nursing homes: A study of young people with disabilities, their families and the decision makers. Paper, Dublin City University.

Dunwoody, D. R., Jungquist, C. R., Chang, Y.-P. and Dickerson, S. S. (2019) 'The common meanings and shared practices of sedation assessment in the context of managing patients with an opioid: A phenomenological study', *Journal of Clinical Nursing*, 28(1–2), 104–115. doi: 10.1111/jocn.14672.

Edwards, C. and Titchen, A. (2003) 'Research into patients' perspectives: Relevance and usefulness of phenomenological sociology', *Journal of Advanced Nursing*, 44(5), 450–460. doi: 10.1046/j.0309-2402.2003.02828.x.

Edwards, R. and Ribbens, J. (1998) 'Living on the edge: Public knowledge, private lives, personal experience', in Jane, R. and Rosalind, E. (eds) *Feminist Dilemmas in Qualitative Research: Public knowledge and private lives*. London: Sage, pp. 2–20.

Elden, S. (2003) 'Taking the measure of the Beiträge', *European Journal of Political Theory*, 2(1), 35–56. doi: 10.1177/1474885103002001278.

Erman, E. (2017) 'What is "critical" about critical theory?', *Philosophy and Social Criticism*, 43(3), 300–301. doi: 10.1177%2F0191453716671272.

Escudero, J. (2015) 'Heidegger's black notebooks and the question of anti-Semitism', *Gatherings: The Heidegger Circle Annual*, 5, 21–49.

European Commission (2018) *Ethics in Social Science and Humanities*. Available at: https://ec.europa.eu/research/participants/data/ref/h2020/other/hi/h2020_ethics-soc-science-humanities_en.pdf (accessed 9 April 2020).

Fernandez, A. (2016) 'Language, prejudice and the aims of hermeneutic phenomenology: Terminological reflections on "mania"', *Journal of Psychopathology*, 22, 21–29.

Finlay, L. (2009) 'Debating phenomenological research methods', *Phenomenology & Practice*, 3(1), 6–25. doi: 10.29173/pandpr19818.

Finlay, L. and Gough, B. (eds) (2003) *Reflexivity: A practical guide for researchers in health and social sciences*. Oxford: Blackwell Science.

Fowler, H., Fowler, F. and Thompson, D. (1995) *Concise Oxford Dictionary*. Oxford: Oxford University Press.

Frank, A. W. (2004) 'After methods, the story: From incongruity to truth in qualitative research', *Qualitative Health Research*, 14(3), 430–440. doi: 10.1177/1049732303261955.

Gadamer, H. (1960) *Truth and Method*. New York: Seabury Press.

Gadamer, H. (1975) *Truth and Method*. London: Sheed & Ward.

Gadamer, H. (2003) *Truth and Method* (trans. J. Weinsheimer and D. G. Marshall), 2nd edn. London: Continuum.

Gale, E. A. (2020) *Returning to the Path: A hermeneutic phenomenological study of parental expectations and the meaning of transition to early parenting in couples with a pregnancy conceived using in-vitro fertilization*. London: University of Greenwich.

Giorgi, A. (2005) 'The phenomenological movement and research in the human sciences', *Nursing Science Quarterly*, 18(1), 75–82. doi: 10.1177/089431840 4272112.

Glaser, B. and Strauss, A. (1967) *The Discovery of Grounded Theory*. Chicago, IL: Aldine Publishing.

Glenn, P. (2003) *Laughter in Interaction*. Cambridge: Cambridge University Press.

Glover, R. (2017) 'Leaping-in and leaping-ahead: A hermeneutic phenomenology study of being-responsible in psychotherapeutic supervision', *Counselling & Psychotherapy Research*, 17(3), 240–247.

Goble, E., Austin, W., Larsen, D., Kreitzer, L. and Brintnell, E. S. (2012) 'Habits of mind and the split-mind effect: When computer-assisted qualitative data analysis software is used in phenomenological research', *Forum: Qualitative Social Research*, 13(2), Article 2. Available at: www.qualitative-research.net/index.php/fqs/ article/view/1709/3340 (accessed 3 January 2020).

Goffman, E. (1963) *Stigma: Notes on the management of spoiled identity*. Englewood Cliffs, NJ: Prentice-Hall.

Gorner, P. (2002) 'Heidegger's phenomenology as transcendental philosophy', *International Journal of Philosophical Studies*, 10(1), 17–33.

Gray, J. (1976) 'Introduction', in Heidegger, M. (ed.) *What is Called Thinking?* (trans. J. G. Gray). New York: Harper Perennial, pp. vi–xvi.

Gray J. (2004) Introduction. In M. Heidegger (ed.) *What is called thinking?* New York: Harper Perennial.

Grbich, C. (1999) *Qualitative Research in Health: An introduction*. Thousand Oaks, CA: Sage.

Grbich, C. (2007) *Qualitative Data Analysis: An introduction*. Thousand Oaks, CA: Sage.

Greenfield, B. H. and Jensen, G. M. (2010) 'Understanding the lived experiences of patients: Application of a phenomenological approach to ethics', *Physical Therapy*, 90(8), 1185–1197. doi: 10.2522/ptj.20090348.

Grondin, J. (1995) *Sources of Hermeneutics*. Albany, NY: SUNY.

Guba, E. and Lincoln, Y. (2017) 'Paradigmatic controversies, contradictions and emerging confluences, revisited', in Denzin, N. and Lincoln, Y. (eds) *The Sage Handbook of Qualitative Research*, 5th edn. Thousand Oaks, CA: Sage, pp. 108–150.

Hansen-Ketchum, P. and Myrick, F. (2008) 'Photo methods for qualitative research in nursing: An ontological and epistemological perspective', *Nursing Philosophy*, 9(3), 205–213. doi: 10.1111/j.1466-769X.2008.00360.x.

Heap, J. L. and Roth, P. A. (1973) 'On phenomenological sociology', *American Sociological Review*, 38(3), 354–367. doi: 10.2307/2094358.

Heidegger, M. (1927) *Sein und Zeit*. Halle: M. Niemeyer.

Heidegger, M. (1959) *On the Way to Language* (trans. P. D. Hertz). New York: Harper & Row.

Heidegger, M. (1962) *Being and Time* (trans. J. Macquarrie and E. Robinson). New York: Harper & Row.

Heidegger, M. (1966a) 'Conversation on a country path about thinking', in *Discourse on Thinking* (trans. J. M. Anderson and E. H. Freund). New York: Harper & Row, pp. 58–90.

Heidegger, M. (1966b) 'Memorial address', in *Discourse on Thinking* (trans. J. M. Anderson and E. H. Freund). New York: Harper & Row, pp. 43–57.

Heidegger, M. (1971) *On the Way to Language* (trans. P. D. Hertz). New York: Harper & Row.

Heidegger, M. (1976) *What is Called Thinking?* (trans. J. Gray). New York: Perennial.

Heidegger, M. (1977) *The Question Concerning Technology and other Essays* (trans. W. Lovitt). New York: Harper & Row.

Heidegger, M. (1982) *The Question Concerning Technology* (trans. W. Lovitt). New York: HarperCollins.

Heidegger, M. (1993) 'Building dwelling thinking', in Krell, D. F. (ed.) *Basic Writings: Martin Heidegger*. London: Routledge, pp. 347–363.

Heidegger, M. (1999) *Contributions to Philosophy (Beiträge zur Philosophie)* (trans. P. Emad, K. Maly and D. Vallega-Neu). Bloomington, IN: Indiana University Press.

Heidegger, M. (1971/2001) *Poetry, Language, Thought* (trans. A. Hofstadter). New York: Perennial.

Holloway, I. and Freshwater, D. (2007) *Narrative Research in Nursing*. Oxford: Blackwell.

Houghton, C., Casey, D., Shaw, D. and Murphy, K. (2013) 'Rigour in qualitative case-study research', *Nurse Researcher*, 20(4), 12–17. doi: 10.7748/nr2013.03.20.4.12. e326.

Hyde, B. (2010) 'Godly play nourishing children's spirituality: A case study', *Religious Education*, 105(5), 504–518. doi: 10.1080/00344087.2010.516215.

Ironside, P. (2003) 'New pedagogies for teaching thinking: The lived experiences of students and teachers enacting narrative pedagogy', *Journal of Nursing Education*, 42(11), 509–516.

Ironside, P. (ed.) (2005) *Beyond Method: Philosophical conversations in healthcare research and scholarship*. Madison, WI: University of Wisconsin Press.

Johnson, P. (2000) *On Heidegger*. Wadsworth Philosophers Series. Belmont, CA: Wadsworth Thomas Learning.

Jones, P. (2003) *Introducing Social Theory*. Oxford: Polity Press.

Jones, S. R., Carley, S. and Harrison, M. (2003) 'An introduction to power and sample size estimation', *Emergency Medicine Journal* (EMJ), 20(5), 453–458. doi: 10.1136/emj.20.5.453.

Kantrowitz-Gordon, I. and Vandermause, R. (2016) 'Metaphors of distress: Photo-elicitation enhances a discourse analysis of parents' accounts', *Qualitative Health Research*, 26(8), 1031–1043. doi: 10.1177/1049732315575729.

Karnieli-Miller, O., Strier, R. and Pessach, L. (2009) 'Power relations in qualitative research', *Qualitative Health Research*, 19(2), 279–289. doi: 10.1177/1049732308329306.

Kaufman, L. (2020) *A Descriptive Phenomenological Study of Body Art Patients and their Health Care Experience*. Proquest.

Koch, T. (1995) 'Interpretive approaches in nursing research: The influence of Husserl and Heidegger', *Journal of Advanced Nursing*, 21(5), 827–836. doi: 10.1046/j.1365-2648.1995.21050827.x.

Koch, T. (1996) 'Implementation of a hermeneutic inquiry in nursing: Philosophy, rigour and representation', *Journal of Advanced Nursing*, 24(1), 174–184. doi: 10.1046/j.1365-2648.1996.17224.x.

Koch, T. (2006) 'Establishing rigour in qualitative research: The decision trail', *Journal of Advanced Nursing*, 53(1), 91–100. doi: 10.1111/j.1365-2648.2006.03681.x.

Lange, M. M., Rogers, W. and Dodds, S. (2013) 'Vulnerability in research ethics: A way forward', *Bioethics*, 27(6), 333–340. doi: 10.1111/bioe.12032.

Laverty, S. M. (2003) 'Hermeneutic phenomenology and phenomenology: A comparison of historical and methodological considerations', *International Journal of Qualitative Methods*, 2(3), 21–35. doi: 10.1177/160940690300200303.

Lee, R. M. (1993) *Doing Research on Sensitive Topics*. London: Sage.

Legard, R., Keegan, J. and Ward, K. (2003) 'In-depth interviewing', in Ritchie, J. and Lewis, J. (eds) *Qualitative Research Practice: A guide for social science students and researchers*. London: Sage, pp. 138–169.

LeVasseur, J. J. (2003) 'The problem of bracketing in phenomenology', *Qualitative Health Research*, 13(3), 408–420. doi: 10.1177/1049732302250337.

Lincoln, Y. S. and Guba, E. G. (1982) Establishing dependability and confirmability in naturalistic inquiry through an audit. Paper presented at the Annual Meeting of the American Educational Research Association (AERA). New York, March.

Lincoln, Y. S. and Guba, E. G. (1985) *Naturalistic Inquiry*. Thousand Oaks, CA: Sage.

Lindseth, A. and Norberg, A. (2004) 'A phenomenological hermeneutical method for researching lived experience', *Scandinavian Journal of Caring Sciences*, 18(2), 145–153. doi: 10.1111/j.1471-6712.2004.00258.x.

Malterud, K., Siersma, V. D. and Guassora, A. D. (2016) 'Sample size in qualitative interview studies: Guided by information power', *Qualitative Health Research*, 26(13), 1753–1760. doi: 10.1177/1049732315617444.

Mason, J. (2002) *Qualitative Researching*. London: Sage.

McConnell-Henry, T., Chapman, Y. and Francis, K. (2011) 'Member checking and Heideggerian phenomenology: A redundant component', *Nurse Researcher*, 18, 28–37. doi: 10.7748/nr2011.01.18.2.28.c8282.

McDermott, E. (2004) 'Telling lesbian stories: Interviewing and the class dynamics of "talk"', *Women's Studies International Forum*, 27(3), 177–187. doi: 10.1016/j. wsif.2004.04.001.

McDonald, P. W. and Dickerson, S. (2013) 'Engendering independence while living with purpose: Women's lives after leaving abusive intimate partners', *Journal of Nursing Scholarship*, 45(4), 388–396. doi: 10.1111/jnu.12044.

Mehta, N. (2011) 'Mind–body dualism: A critique from a health perspective', *Mens Sana Monographs*, pp. 202–209. doi: 10.4103/0973-1229.77436.

Mezirow, J. and Associates (1990) *Fostering Critical Reflection in Adulthood: A guide to transformative and emancipatory learning*. San Francisco, CA: Jossey-Bass.

Moher, D., Liberati, A., Tetzlaff, J., Altman, D. G. and PRISMA Group (2010) 'Preferred reporting items for systematic reviews and meta-analyses: The PRISMA statement', *International Journal of Surgery*, 8(5), 336–341. doi: 10.1016/j. ijsu.2010.02.007.

Moran, D. (2000) *Introduction to Phenomenology*. Abingdon, Oxon: Routledge.

Moran, D. (2002) 'Editor's introduction', in Moody, T. and Moran, D. (eds) *The Phenomenology Reader*. London: Routledge, pp. 1–26.

Morse, J. M., Barrett, M., Mayan, M., Olson, K. and Spiers, J. (2002) 'Verification strategies for establishing reliability and validity in qualitative research', *International Journal of Qualitative Methods*, 1(2), 13–22. doi: 10.1177/ 160940690200100202.

Mott, R. L. (2019) What is the meaning of livestock production for long-standing 4-H members? A hermeneutic phenomenological study. Unpublished PhD thesis, University of Missouri-Columbia.

Nadin, S. and Cassell, C. (2006) 'The use of a research diary as a tool for reflexive practice: Some reflections from management research', *Qualitative Research in Accounting & Management*, 3(3), 208–217. doi: 10.1108/11766090610705407.

Nezlek, J. and Derks, P. (2001) 'Use of humor as a coping mechanism, psychological adjustment, and social interaction', *Humor*, 14(4), 395–413.

O'Connor, S. (2011) 'Context is everything: The role of auto-ethnography, reflexivity and self-critique in establishing the credibility of qualitative research findings', *European Journal of Cancer Care*, 20(4), 421–423. doi: 10.1111/j.1365-2354.2011.01261.x.

Oakley, A. (2005) *The Ann Oakley Reader: Gender, women, and social science*. Bristol: Policy Press.

Ortlipp, M. (2008) 'Keeping and using reflective journals in the qualitative research process', *The Qualitative Report*, 13(4), 695–705.

Oxford Centre for Evidence-Based Medicine (OCEBM) Working Group (2011) *The Oxford 2011 Levels of Evidence*. Available at: www.cebm.net/index.aspx?o=5653.

Oxtoby, K. (2016) 'Is the Hippocratic oath still relevant to practising doctors today?' *BMJ*, p. i6629. doi: 10.1136/bmj.i6629.

Pain, H. (2012) 'A literature review to evaluate the choice and use of visual methods', *International Journal of Qualitative Methods*, 11(4), 303–319. doi: 10.1177/160940691201100401.

Paley, J. (1998) 'Misinterpretive phenomenology: Heidegger, ontology and nursing research', *Journal of Advanced Nursing*, 27(4), 817–824. doi: 10.1046/j.1365-2648.1998.00607.x.

Palmer, R. (1969) *Hermeneutics. Studies in Phenomenology and Existential Philosophy*. Chicago, IL: Northwestern University Press.

Pariseau-Legault, P., Holmes, D. and Murray, S. J. (2019) 'Understanding human enhancement technologies through critical phenomenology', *Nursing Philosophy*, 20(1), e12229. doi: 10.1111/nup.12229.

Platzer, H. and James, T. (1997) 'Methodological issues conducting sensitive research on lesbian and gay men's experience of nursing care', *Journal of Advanced Nursing*, 25(3), 626–633. doi: 10.1046/j.1365-2648.1997.t01-1-1997025626.x.

Ray, M. (1994) 'The richness of phenomenology: Philosophic, theoretic and methodologic concerns', in Janice, M, M. (ed) *Critical Issues in Qualitative Research Methods*. Thousand Oaks, CA: Sage, pp. 117–133.

Reinharz, S. (1992) *Feminist Methods in Social Research*. New York: Oxford University Press.

Richardson, L. and St Pierre, E. (2018) 'Writing: A method of inquiry', in Norman, K. D. and Yvonne, S. L. (eds) *The Sage Handbook of Qualitative Research*. Thousand Oaks, CA: Sage, pp. 818–838.

Richardson, W. S., Wilson, M. C., Nishikawa, J. and Hayward, R. S. A. (1995) 'The well-built clinical question: A key to evidence-based decisions', *ACP J Club*, 123(3), A12–13.

Robertson-Malt, S. (1999) 'Listening to them and reading me: A hermeneutic approach to understanding the experience of illness', *Journal of Advanced Nursing*, 29(2), 290–297. doi: 10.1046/j.1365-2648.1999.00830.x.

Roth, W. M., Masciotra, D. and Boyd, N. (1999) 'Becoming-in-the-classroom: A case study of teacher development through coteaching', *Teaching and Teacher Education*, 15(7), 771–784. doi: 10.1016/S0742-051X(99)00027-X.

Sameshima, P., Vandermause, R., Chalmers, S. and 'Gabriel' (2009) *Climbing the Ladder with Gabriel: Poetic inquiry of a meth addict in recovery*. Rotterdam: Sense.

Sampson, H., Bloor, M. and Fincham, B. (2008) 'A price worth paying?', *Sociology*, 42(5), 919–933. doi: 10.1177/0038038508094570.

Sartre J. P. (1969) *Being and Nothingness: An essay on phenomenological ontology*. Oxford: Routledge Classics.

Saunders, B., Sim, J., Kingstone, T., Baker, S., Waterfield, J., Bartlam, B., Burroughs, H. and Jinks, C. (2018) 'Saturation in qualitative research: Exploring its conceptualization and operationalization', *Quality and Quantity*, 52(4), 1893–1907. doi: 10.1007/s11135-017-0574-8.

Schleiermacher, F. (1998) *Hermeneutics and Criticism and Other Writings*. Cambridge: Cambridge University Press.

Serrant-Green, L. (2002) 'Black on black: Methodological issues for black researchers working in minority ethnic communities', *Nurse Researcher*, 9(4), 30–44. doi: 10.7748/nr2002.07.9.4.30.c6196.

Seo, J. Y., Kim, S. & Dickerson, S. S. (2014). 'Navigating the unfamiliar healthcare system: Korean immigrant women's lived experience of childbirth in the United States', *JOGYN*, 43, 305–317. DOI: 10.1111/1552-6909.12313

Shantikumar, S. (2018) *Validity, Reliability and Generalisability*. HealthKnowledge. Available at: www.healthknowledge.org.uk/content/validity-reliability-and-generalisability (accessed 7 January 2020).

Shenton, A. K. (2004) 'Strategies for ensuring trustworthiness in qualitative research projects', *Education for Information*, 22(2), 63–75. doi: 10.3233/EFI-2004-22201.

Shuster, E. (1997) 'Fifty years later: The significance of the Nuremberg Code', *New England Journal of Medicine*, 337(20), 1436–1440. doi: 10.1056/NEJM199711133372006.

Smith, J. A., Flowers, P. and Larkin, M. (2009) *Interpretive Phenomenological Analysis: Theory, method and research*. London: Sage.

Smythe, E. (2005) 'The thinking of research', in Ironside, P. M. (ed.) *Beyond Method: Philosophical conversations in healthcare research and scholarship*. Madison, WI: University of Wisconsin Press, pp. 223–258.

Smythe, E. (2011) 'From beginning to end: How to do hermeneutic interpretive phenomenology', in Thomson, G., Dykes, F. and Downe, S. (eds) *Qualitative Research in Midwifery and Childbirth: Phenomenological approaches*. Abingdon, Oxon: Routledge, pp. 35–54.

Smythe, E. and Spence, D. (2012) 'Re-viewing literature in hermeneutic research', *International Journal of Qualitative Methods*, 11(1), 12–25. doi: 10.1177/160940691201100102.

Smythe, E. and Spence, D. (2019) 'Reading Heidegger', *Nursing Philosophy*, online. doi: 10.1111/nup.12271.

Smythe, E. A., Ironside, P. M., Sims, S. L., Swenson, M. M. and Spence, D. G. (2008) 'Doing Heideggerian hermeneutic research: A discussion paper', *International Journal of Nursing Studies*, 45(9), 1389–1397. doi: https://doi.org/10.1016/j.ijnurstu. 2007.09.005.

Sokolowski, R. (2000) *Introduction to Phenomenology*. Cambridge: Cambridge University Press.

Sorrell, J. and Dinkins, C. (2005) 'Shared inquiry: Socratic-hermeneutic interpeviewing', in Pamela, M. I. (ed) *Beyond Method: Philosophical conversations in healthcare research and scholarship*. Madison, WI: University of Wisconsin Press, pp. 111–147.

Sorrell, J. and Dinkins, C. (2006) 'An ethics of diversity: Listening in thin places', in Christine, S. D. and Jeanne, M. S. (eds) *Listening to the Whispers: Re-thinking ethics in healthcare* (Volume V). Madison, WI: University of Wisconsin Press, pp. 310–314.

Spence, D. G. (2017) 'Supervising for robust hermeneutic phenomenology: Reflexive engagement within horizons of understanding', *Qualitative Health Research*, 27(6), 836–842. doi: 10.1177/1049732316637824.

Starman, A. (2013) 'The case study as a type of qualitative research', *Journal of Contemporary Educational Studies*, 1, 28–43.

Stebbins, R. (2001) *Exploratory Research in the Social Sciences*. Thousand Oaks, CA: Sage.

Stenstad, G. (2006) *Transformations: Thinking after Heidegger*. Madison, WI: University of Wisconsin Press.

Stewart, D. and Mickunas, A. (1990) *Exploring Phenomenology: A guide to the field and its literature*, 2nd edn. Athens, OH: Ohio University Press.

Thomas, E. and Magilvy, J. K. (2011) 'Qualitative rigor or research validity in qualitative research', *Journal for Specialists in Pediatric Nursing*, 16(2), 151–155. doi: 10.1111/j.1744-6155.2011.00283.x.

Tobin, G. A. and Begley, C. M. (2004) 'Methodological rigour within a qualitative framework', *Journal of Advanced Nursing*, 48(4), 388–396. doi: 10.1111/ j.1365-2648.2004.03207.x.

Tong, A., Sainsbury, P. and Craig, J. (2007) 'Consolidated criteria for reporting qualitative research (COREQ): A 32-item checklist for interviews and focus groups', *International Journal for Quality in Health Care*, 19(6), 349–357. doi: 10.1093/intqhc/mzm042.

Vandermause, R. (2007) 'Assessing for alcohol use disorders in women: Experiences of advanced practice nurses in primary care settings', *Journal of Addictions Nursing*, 18(4), 187–198. doi:10.1080/10884600701699347.

Vandermause, R. and Wood, M. (2009) 'See my suffering: Women with alcohol use disorders and their primary care experiences', *Issues in Mental Health Nursing*, 30(12), 728–735. doi: 10.3109/01612840903230081.

Vandermause, R., Sanner-Stiehr, E. and Smith, M. (Presentation April 15, 2018) *Generational influences in RN work patterns and turnover*. The Future of Nursing Research: Economic Realities and Creative Solutions. Cleveland, Ohio.

Vandermause, R., Fougere, M., Liu, Y. H. and Odom-Maryon, T. (2018) 'Relational health and recovery: Adolescent girls in chemical dependency treatment', *Journal of Addictions Nursing*, 29(1), 4–12. doi: 10.1097/JAN.0000000000000207.

Vandermause, R., Barg, F. K., Ismail, L., Edmundson, L., Girard, S. and Perfetti, A. R. (2017) 'Qualitative methods in patient-centered outcomes research', *Qualitative Health Research*, 27(3), 434–442. doi: 10.1177/1049732316668298.

Vandermause, R. K. and Fleming, S. E. (2011) 'Philosophical hermeneutic interviewing', *International Journal of Qualitative Methods*, 10(4), 367–377. doi: 10.1177/160940691101000405.

Van Manen, M. (1990) *Researching Lived Experience*. London, ON: University of Western Ontario.

Van Manen, M. (2016) *Researching Lived Experience: Human science for an action sensitive pedagogy*, 2nd edn. New York: Routledge.

Wang, C. and Burris, M. A. (1997) 'Photovoice: Concept, methodology, and use for participatory needs assessment', *Health Education and Behavior*, 24(3), 369–387. doi: 10.1177/109019819702400309.

Weger, H., Castle Bell, G., Minei, E. M. and Robinson, M. C. (2014) 'The relative effectiveness of active listening in initial interactions', *International Journal of Listening*, 28(1), 13–31. doi: 10.1080/10904018.2013.813234.

Weston, K. (2004) 'Fieldwork in lesbian and gay communities', in Hesse-Biber, S. and Leavy, P. (eds) *Approaches to Qualitative Research: A reader on theory and practice*. Oxford: Oxford University Press, pp. 177–184.

Williams, M. and May, T. (1996) *An Introduction to the Philosophy of Social Research*. Abingdon, Oxon: Routledge.

Willis, J. (2007) *Foundations of Qualitative Research: Interpretive and critical approaches*. Thousand Oaks, CA: Sage.

Wojciechowski, C. (1998) 'Issues in caring for older lesbians', *Journal of Gerontological Nursing*, 24(7), 28–33. doi: 10.3928/0098-9134-19980701-07.

Younge, L., Sufi, H. and Dibley, L. (2020) 'Regular clinical supervision to enhance wellbeing in inflammatory bowel disease specialist nurses: A small pilot study', *Gastrointestinal Nursing*, 18(3), 36–42.

Index

Page numbers in **bold** indicate tables and in *italic* indicate figures.

Made in the USA
Columbia, SC
09 June 2024

36909905R00128